CONSEQUENCES

The Criminal Case of David Parker Ray

By J. E. Sparks

Yellow Jacket Press
Roswell, New Mexico

CONSEQUENCES

The Criminal Case of David Parker Ray

For information contact publisher/editor at YellowJacketPress:
publisher@yellowjacketpress.com

Consequences: The Criminal Case of David Parker Ray is a non-fiction true crime book. The characters named herein are real people. The author tried to accurately portray them and events based upon extensive research, interviews, available information, court documents and trial transcripts.

This second edition has new information, obtained by the author after publication of the first edition, including from persons who had personally known David Parker Ray or were involved with the case.

Cover design by Jan Girand, publisher/editor of YellowJacketPress.
Interior design and layout by Dana McCausland.
Photos taken by author unless noted as "courtesy photo." Courtesy photos include those on front and back covers of the book.

YellowJacketPress
Roswell, New Mexico

Library of Congress Cataloging-in-Publication Data

Sparks, J. E.
Consequences: The Criminal Case of David Parker Ray by J. E. Sparks
ISBN 0-9787734-0-3
ISBN 0-9787734-0-3 (paper)

Dedication

This book is dedicated to Dan. Without him, my life would be like a holey parachute, without purpose, containing nothing.

This book honors the memory of my brother, Jerry Sparks, who died unexpectedly March 26, 2006. Even while concerned about the health of his wife, Betty, and involved in her battle with cancer, he was a dedicated manuscript proofreader. His highly valued critiques and encouragement are priceless. I miss him.

Introduction

David Parker Ray, a serial criminal sexual sadist, had helpers—mostly women. The one known to be his longest lasting assistant was never tried and is now not even under supervision.

Investigators knew who the perpetrators were and had them in custody from the beginning of the case. Then they discovered that the crime scene, alone, provided more than two thousand pieces of evidence, including journals, drawings and audio recordings made by David Ray that showed he had multiple victims. But the prosecution was only allowed to present a fraction of those pieces of evidence to the jury. The judge suppressed critical FBI information because it was not presented to the defense on schedule. The court did not allow the most critical piece of prosecutory evidence at the first trial, and it was heavily redacted when jurors of the second trial heard it. Few were called to testify from a long list of potential witnesses. Not surprisingly, the first trial ended without a conviction.

This case was beset with other problems and delays long before all of the trials ended. One of the three known surviving victims died. The judge died unexpectedly in his shower. The defense attorney suffered a terrible personal loss.

Ray was never tried for murder. He was accused of and tried for only the kidnapping and rape of his three known victims.

David Ray had many victims. His sadistic practices spanned forty-five years, and many investigators believe nearly one hundred women died in his captivity. But where were the bodies? Except for the remains of one man found in Elephant Butte Lake with circumstantial connections to Ray, none were found. Where were the many videos that investigators believe Ray had made, based upon evidence found at the scene? Only one useful video, identifying a victim, was found. Somewhere there must be many more.

This case had an unsatisfactory ending. Countless open cases throughout the Southwest and beyond remain unresolved.

The David Parker Ray case is now officially closed, but many aspects of it remain open, perhaps forever.

This second edition, published in October 2007, contains valuable new information gathered after *Consequences: The Criminal Case of David Parker Ray* was first published in December 2006.

This new added information includes:

- Childhood experiences that may have caused David Ray to become sexually sadistic.
- David Ray's young formative years.
- David Ray's teen years.
- David Ray's schoolmates knew him as a slight, shy, withdrawn boy when he was already practicing sadism.
- Multiple conflicting personas of David Parker Ray, as a teen and as an adult.
- Insightful characteristics of David Ray, his personality and behavior, even a surprising physical description, by people who knew and worked with him at Elephant Butte.
- A former wife or live-in companion he probably killed, probably a victim previously unknown to investigators.

Acknowledgments

This book could not have been written without assistance and information provided by: New Mexico Mounted Patrol (NMMP) Col. Dan Girand, consultant; Agent Lou Mallion, Department of Public Safety, Special Investigations Division, involved with investigation of this case; K. C.Rogers, now-retired New Mexico State Police (NMSP) sergeant and one of the case's lead investigators, who later founded and heads ASPEN—Alternative Sentencing Programs and Educational Network; NMSP Lt. John Briscoe, then case investigator; NMSP Sgt. Rich Libicer, then agent who managed the David Parker Ray case; James Jennings, retired NMSP deputy chief, later Regional Director of HIDA—High Intensity Drug Trafficking Area, now retired; "Lucy Schmidt," David Ray's neighbor; Jolene Starr, executive assistant to Sheriff Terry Byers; Sierra County Sheriff's Deputy Lawrence Gaston, who initially investigated the disappearance of Marie B. Parker; Rob Coon, Chaves County's then chief deputy sheriff, now sheriff; Pat O'Hanlon, T or C librarian and former Sierra County Sheriff's radio dispatcher; Brad Spencer, Sierra County Sheriff's Office records clerk, made a special deputy to assist with prisoner transports; Dannette Monnét, Department of Public Safety crime analyst supervisor; Kathy McClean, Clerk of the 7th Judicial District Court; Sgt. Mike Waring, commander of the NMSP Search and Recovery Dive Team; Sonny Hope, NMMP, State's Search and Recovery Dive Team member since 1988, now retired; Dr. Don Rossi, criminology psychologist, retired Michigan State Police; and Von Weddige, then-captain of the NMMP volunteer state agency, in charge of security of the David Ray crime scenes during the investigation.

New Mexico Mounted Patrol (NMMP) is a unique state agency, its history going back to 1936; it was authorized in 1941 by the State Legislature to assist any law enforcement agency in New Mexico asking for its assistance. At one time the state's second largest law enforcement agency, NMMP is comprised of trained volunteers.

I also appreciate the help provided by others herein unnamed.

Valued manuscript readers included DPS Agent Lou Mallion; Dr. Robert Sproull and his wife, Peg; Don Bullis, retired DPS criminal intelligence operational supervisor, columnist and author; Barbara Corn Patterson, author, and retired rancher and registered nurse; Gerald C. Sparks, retired government analyst; Wendy Lunsford, retired attorney.

I thank Lucinda Schroeder for her insight and encouragement, and Dana McCausland, for her patience and helping to prepare this book for the publisher.

Besides those named in credits above, many of whom were formally interviewed and taped, information and some photos in this book and on its cover came from additional sources including, but not limited to: court documents, audio trial transcripts and other trial records, published AP articles, and Sierra County newspapers—the *Herald* and the *Sentinel*.

For this second edition published in 2007, in addition to the above credits, I want to thank the following for valued new information or assistance provided: K. C. Rogers, again; Robert Smoot, NMSP Search and Recovery Dive Team member, currently employed by Federal Law Enforcement Training Center (FLETC) in Artesia, NM; Danny Kiper, a former NMSP sergeant, currently deputy U.S. Marshal; Susan Gray, FLETC; Howard Goetsch, fifty combined years of service with Wisconsin State Police and federal law enforcement, now retired; Dr. Robert and Peg Sproull, again; Ronald Hadley; Rusty Burgess, long-time volunteer at Elephant Butte Lake State Park; Rolf Hechler, southwest regional manager of New Mexico State Parks; Ray Kirkpatrick, FLETC; others who had known David Ray but asked to be unnamed, including a former high school mate of Ray's; and James S. "Scotty" Farris, retired law enforcement officer.

I also value the assistance of Dr. David Ikenberry, who proofread this second edition's manuscript.

I took some liberties with re-enactments, such as the detailed accounts of the three victims' kidnappings, but those were based upon known facts. With due diligence, I carefully researched the subject and consulted with experts on the case or in their related fields. Regardless, the responsibility for any errors within this book is mine.

CONSEQUENCES

The Criminal Case of David Parker Ray

By J. E. Sparks

Yellow Jacket Press

Elephant Butte, New Mexico

Map of Elephant Butte, New Mexico, area with emphasis on the State Park land near the lake on which residents leased land on Pike, Catfish, Trout, Bass and Ridge roads. To reach David Parker Ray's property on Bass Road, officers took State Road 195 into Elephant Butte, to Rock Canyon Road, to Springland Boulevard to Hot Springs Landing to Bass Road.

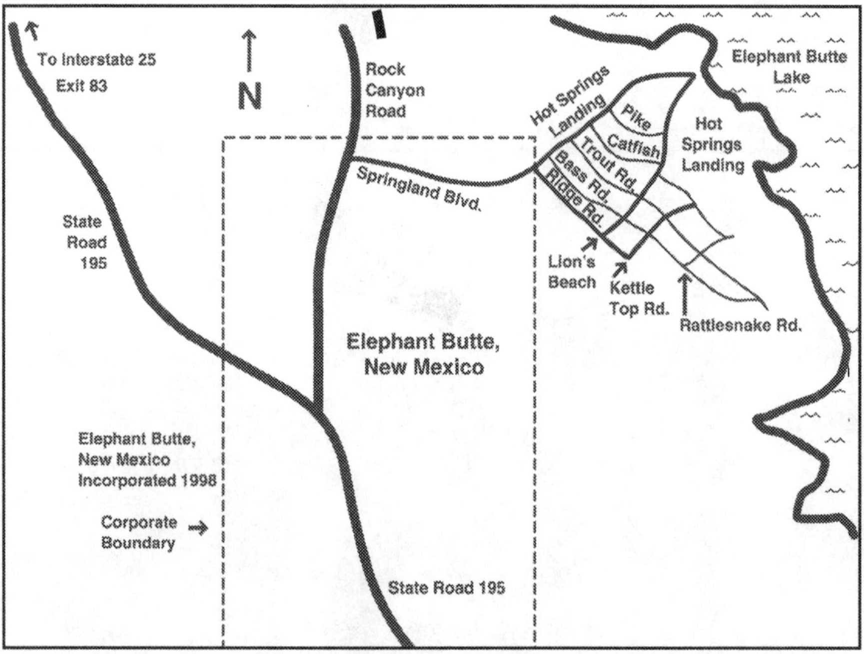

Table of Contents

Prologue

The girl rode her bicycle down I-25 near the small community of Hatch in southwestern New Mexico—famous for its green *chíle*. There she disappeared; her bike was the only evidence left behind. She was one of a hundred or more unexplained disappearances all over the southwestern United States, and perhaps even in Mexico, that investigators suspect might be linked to David Parker Ray. He was a kidnapper and murderer and, even worse, a rare entity known as a serial sexual sadist, one of only twenty-five known to investigators.

His diaries reveal that he committed his first crimes as a teenager, and continued for forty-five years. As he entered his forties and fifties, he began to take only the most tractable ones—the lonely females who hung around bars looking for one-night stands with anyone—including strangers, the druggies, the homosexuals on the prowl; the prostitutes who would go with anyone and do anything for a few bucks to support their drug habits; and young ones left to their own devices without parental supervision.

As he grew older, he started taking a stun-gun or some other disabling weapon on his hunting forays, just in case he needed a little help when he had the urge to grab someone. He was growing old.

"Grabbing a hooker is easier than grabbing a housewife," Ray said in 1993 on one of the recordings he played for his victims.

But always, he chose victims who were vulnerable in one form or another. Perhaps they traveled alone and had car trouble on a deserted highway. Perhaps they walked late at night after a quarrel with a parent or boyfriend. Perhaps they were simply gullible or too trusting of a stranger or a casual acquaintance.

"There are a hundred-thousand disappearances a year in the United States alone," said Agent Lou Mallion during an interview in a restaurant in late 2002. Mallion, a special investigations agent with New Mexico Department of Public Safety, was one of those assigned to investigate the David Parker Ray case in March 1999.

"Many of them are never seen again. If you disappeared, and your husband came to us with your name, your description, your social security number, we couldn't do much. Adults have a right to disappear if they want. We cannot infringe on your right to go and do whatever you choose. All that information your husband gave to the local police would do little good even if identifiable remains showed up in another town, another state. There's no central computer or repository of information for missing adults, so there'd be no way to connect the two pieces of intelligence without an awful lot of luck."

In addition, few women are fingerprinted, and the majority of the files and fingerprint records of common citizenry are of those who served in the military. The percentage of enlisted men and women dwindled considerably since the ending of the draft, further reducing the size of an accessible source of general public information.

A data bank of citizens' DNA would be even more useful for crime solving, but is unlikely because of legal implications.

On another occasion, in a different restaurant in late 2002, K. C. Rogers shared some of his insights. "See those girls sitting in the booth over there?" asked the retired State Police sergeant who had been the case's command center commander during the David Parker Ray investigation. "If David were here, if he was in the right mood, if he wanted them, they'd be his. There's no doubt about that.

"Everyone who worked the case now sees the world differently," he said. "Now every time we see a girl or young woman, we see her as a potential victim for David. The ones who became familiar with the case have had a changed view of normal life. Like David's victims, one day we woke up and were changed forever."

He added, "They may think they do, but no one wants to know everything. They start out asking for [case] details, but very soon they—even the tough guys who thought they'd seen and heard everything—ask you to stop. They don't want to hear any more; they can't handle it. Still," said K. C., "people need to know what David Parker Ray did."

"On a scale of one to one-hundred, this case is a ninety-nine," Darren White, then-Secretary of the New Mexico Department of Public Safety, told media in March 1999. He also said, "The nightmare is behind bars." Perhaps Ray was behind bars, but he had disciples and wasn't the only predator out there. The world has many more.

“If publicity about this case makes people aware and keeps even one girl or woman from getting hurt, it is worth it,” said Mallion.

“The story needs to be told, but told right,” said New Mexico State Police Sgt. Rich Libicer in Las Cruces on October 21, 2002. Libicer, one of the primaries on the case, was displeased with publications he had seen on the subject, written like tabloids and filled with errors.

The facts of this case are sensational enough; they need no embellishment.

This book is a study of the David Parker Ray case as it unfolded, from crime-scene discovery and investigations, through multiple trials to its unsatisfactory completion. Unsatisfactory because of countless missing person files left open.

It is also a tale of the towns and county it impacted.

Preface 1 – Kelli

They were kissing and messing around in the bedroom. Kelli thought it was fun until Patrick tried to get into her shorts.

"Stop it!"

"What the hell do you think I married you for? Just to look at you? I'm your husband, for Crissake! You can't tell me no!"

"Watch me!" she yelled. "Just because we're married doesn't mean you own me. You can't make me if I don't want to!" She was furious. It was the same old thing. She thought Patrick, her husband of nine days, was immature, selfish and insensitive.

All he cares about is sex, sex, sex! It's not my fault I can't let him. It hurts, dammit! Why can't he understand that? Why can't he love me without that?

Kelli knew Patrick's parents heard the words they yelled at each other that evening, like many other days and nights for more than a week. She also knew they didn't like her.

She jumped up from the bed, ran out of the room and the house.

She wore white shorts and a white t-shirt. She had sandals on her feet, but her long legs were bare except for the tattoos on her right leg—a heart tattoo that encircled her ankle and a large modernistic swan on her calf.

Earlier in the day, for the fun of it, Kelli's friend, Cassie, had braided her long blonde hair in tight tiny rows all over her head, like cornrow braids. The girls thought it was funny. Whoever heard of blonde dread-locks?

With Kelli's pretty face and expressive brown eyes, the hairdo actually looked good on her. Not bad at all, she had thought as she looked at herself in the mirror. She rather liked the result, especially when she thought Cassie was disappointed that it wasn't as unbecoming as she'd probably hoped. Kelli already knew that Cassie—who had the hots for Patrick—was jealous of her, but she didn't care because she was the one who landed him! Kelli silently taunted and mentally stuck out her tongue at Cassie.

After wandering around the neighborhood in the dark for a while, feeling sorry for herself, she returned and spent the rest of the night on the living room couch sulking. Early the next morning she left the house, telling Patrick's mother that she was going for a walk and would be back soon. She just needed to get away for a while, she told Judy Murphy. She hadn't yet bathed or changed her clothing from the night before, which was unlike her, but she was too depressed to care. Patrick usually complained that she showered or bathed too often.

After their impromptu marriage, Kelli had moved into the Murphy house on Wyona Street in Truth or Consequences with Patrick and his parents, Janet "Judy" and Steve Murphy.

Before that, Kelli had lived with friends or in small apartments in T or C or Elephant Butte beside the lake. Ever since she had moved to Sierra County, New Mexico, she often partied with Jesse Ray and her friends at bars and their homes. For Kelli's friends, partying usually meant drinking to excess and drugs; sometimes they got pretty wild. Kelli had already seen enough of what liquor and drugs did to others, how they caused lost control and bad behavior; she wanted none of that. She refused to take drugs, and she seldom drank. She only had a drink now and then with her friends when she was thirsty. She ran with this crowd because most of them were her own age, and she enjoyed the lively company, the music and noise. She was young and wanted to have fun. She hung with her friends at bars because that was where they were. She mostly just chatted, danced and played pool.

Kelli knew how Patrick's mother felt about her. Judy disapproved of her friends and her, especially after she and her son began seeing each other and then suddenly married. Kelli knew Judy assumed she was no different than the friends with whom she hung around. That's unfair, Kelli thought.

Patrick and Kelli had been aware of each other for more than a year, but while he was home on Navy furlough, they became better acquainted at local bars. Kelli was tall, blonde and pretty, and had an outgoing personality. Young Patrick—well-built from military training—cut a handsome and sexy figure in his form-fitting white uniform.

Physically attracted to each other, they were soon comparing tattoos. She had one on her breast that he particularly admired.

Within a few weeks, they were married.

It had begun as a lark because Cassie wouldn't leave Patrick alone. They planned to invite all their friends to their mock wedding—the mock part to be known only to themselves. However, they got carried away with their plans and actually were married at the county courthouse in Truth or Consequences, nothing mock about it.

Patrick was twenty years old, not yet old enough to legally drink, but that didn't matter in T or C and Elephant Butte bars. Kelli was twenty-five.

He did not have a place of his own, didn't need it. Since high school, he spent most of his time on a naval base in San Diego, or on shipboard. He lived with his parents during the little time he was on leave, at home in T or C.

The Murphys were displeased with their son's unexpected marriage to Kelli. It happened too fast and he didn't know much about her; they didn't like what they saw or heard. Gossip around their small community indicated she was not the young innocent they thought their son to be, and she ran with a rough crowd known to do drugs. And they thought she slept around. The Murphys believed the young couple was seriously mismatched, and the girl probably used her forward, feminine ways to entrap their inexperienced son, tempting him with sex.

Kelli knew how they felt about her; in their little house, she heard their talk often enough, just as they heard her and Patrick. There was no privacy.

When Kelli left the Murphy house that morning of July 25, 1996, she seethed with anger towards Patrick and his judgmental parents.

She wanted sympathy and moral support, not more criticism. She walked to a friend's house, and from there, together they went to other friends' houses and eventually to the usual bars where they hung out. She went to Rocky's and Raymond's, and she finally ended up early that evening at the Blue Waters Saloon in Elephant Butte, seven miles from home. Jesse Ray was among the crowd Kelli was with most of the afternoon and evening.

Jesse openly flaunted the fact that she was homosexual—Kelli had heard many, inside and outside their crowd, call Jesse "dyke on a bike," a catchy nickname that stuck. Kelli expected Jesse, unlike some of the other girls, to be sympathetic to her and not to Patrick about her sex problem. She was sure Jesse would understand since apparently she didn't like to mess around with guys anyway. But with the boisterous crowd, Kelli forgot to mention it to Jesse. She just had a good time and ignored her personal problems for awhile.

Earlier in the day, when everyone began drinking, Kelli was named the designated driver because they knew she didn't drink much. She finally had one beer that evening in Blue Waters. She was thirsty.

When she and her group had entered the windowless metal prefab Blue Waters building about 7 p.m., it took a few moments for her eyes to adjust to its darkness after coming in from the outdoors where the setting sun was blinding.

Jesse Ray—Glenda Jean Ray was her real name but she preferred Jesse with the male spelling—was a "dishwater" blonde and had facial features too small and plain to be pretty. Her small face did not match her unusually tall and lanky build; she was taller than many men.

As the evening grew later, most of the crowd drifted away, but Kelli and Jesse continued to hang together at the saloon while Jesse tipped quite a few beers. With her small glasses slipped down onto the end of her nose, she shot games of pool—something she did well—while Kelli and a few others watched and cheered her on. Jesse knew she was good with a pool stick. After successful shots into the corner pockets, she grinned and took deep bows, her loose-fitting glasses at risk of falling off her face.

Finally, about 11 p.m., after most of the patrons had left the saloon, Jesse offered Kelli the seven-mile ride back home to T or C. Jesse stumbled as they walked outside to the parking lot where her big black motorcycle was parked. She said she first had to go to her dad's on Bass Road, a mile away, so she could drink coffee to sober up.

Kelli asked her to take her to a friend's house instead, but Jesse insisted that she was going to her dad's.

Kelli had previously met Jesse's dad, David Parker Ray, who worked at the park and she had been at his house, outside of it anyway, with Jesse in the past.

Why not? Besides, she was in no hurry to go home to pawing Patrick.

She climbed onto the bike behind Jesse. She didn't like motorcycles; they were too powerful and she felt too exposed and vulnerable on them, especially as a passenger, hanging onto its rear-end. There was no place to put her feet, little with which to stabilize herself, nowhere to get a grip. It took a lot of balance, more than she thought she had, even after just one beer.

Kelli didn't want to tell the tough, fearless Jesse that she was scared.

She climbed on. Jesse hit the gas. The cycle reared for a moment with the front wheel lifting from the pavement like a horse going into a buck. They peeled out of the parking lot, throwing gravel. Kelli wrapped herself as tightly around Jesse as she could, hanging onto the lean body, clad in a slippery black leather jacket despite warm weather.

The evening was already exciting. Kelli expected to remember it long afterwards; that is, if she lived through this wild ride.

Being a married lady now, she figured she'd have fewer fun, uninhibited times from now on. She rehearsed how she'd tell Patrick about it, her anger towards him dissipating. She really did like her husband; he was a nice guy, really handsome, and turned women on. She knew she was lucky he was hers.

Kelli began to feel the heat from the manifold on her bare leg, remembering that was one of the reasons bikers wore leather pants.

They drove down the asphalt Springland Road; shortly after the blacktop abruptly ended and it became Hot Springs Landing, Jesse turned the bike onto the short, curving Bass Road, and drove a short distance to the doublewide gate leading to her father's property.

From the Blue Waters Saloon, the ride took perhaps fifteen minutes. The doublewide gate was partially ajar. Jesse whipped the cycle around, nearly throwing Kelli off, and drove through the narrow gateway opening into the expansive dirt-packed yard. In the carport near the front door, she stopped the bike as abruptly as she had begun the ride.

Kelli was thankful to safely reach the Ray home and be able to get off the machine. Her legs were wobbly and trembling when she walked inside with Jesse.

Jesse's dad seemed to be expecting them.

^^^^^^^

Three days later, on Sunday, David Parker Ray, dressed in his tan and green Elephant Butte Lake State Park uniform, delivered Kelli to the Murphy house in his white Ram Charger.

Bewildered and nearly doubled over in pain, Kelli had no memory of the past three days. She could only remember waking up a little while ago in David's vehicle. She had small confusing snatches of memory that made no sense but left her fearing him.

Judy was digging weeds in the yard when the young woman stumbled up onto the porch. David remained standing by his pickup, watching and listening intently.

Judy stood up, brushed the dirt off her knees and hurried to meet the girl on the porch, pointedly standing between her and the door. Judy called through the screen-door to Patrick and her husband to come outside, that Kelli was here.

"Where have you been?" asked Judy, hostility in her voice and manner. She looked Kelli up and down; her anger visibly increased.

Father and son stepped out onto the porch.

Kelli said she didn't know. She couldn't remember anything. She was sick and in pain, and she believed something bad had happened to her. She didn't know what.

The Murphys—Patrick, Judy and Steve—stood, an immovable block in front of the door, staring at her, clearly disbelieving and disgusted.

Kelli wore the same white shorts and t-shirt they had last seen her wearing more than three days earlier, but she was barefoot. The silver wedding ring Patrick had given her, and necklace and anklet, perhaps also earrings, were missing. Her braided hair was a mess, she was dirty and she smelled horridly. Her white shorts were soiled with blood. She appeared to be on drugs.

David Ray stepped to the edge of the porch to politely explain. He said he found Kelli wandering around on the beach below his house, as if she were lost, in a drugged and dehydrated state. He said he gave her a drink and brought her home to them where he knew she belonged.

To the Murphys, especially in his uniform, Ray appeared to be a responsible and concerned adult. They recognized him; he was Jesse's father and worked at the State Park. They looked at Kelli. They did not believe her; they believed their eyes and what David told them.

Kelli admitted that she remembered almost nothing, but she believed she was in trouble—that much her malfunctioning brain, memory and senses told her—and she was ill. She desperately needed help. She was about to vomit. She wanted to go into the house, bathe, change clothes, take painkillers and lie down. She was emotionally and physically exhausted.

Judy, standing firmly in front of the door with arms crossed, told her she could not enter.

Kelli was stunned. The Murphys were her family now; she expected them to believe her and help her. She couldn't understand why they wouldn't let her in the house.

Judy informed her that Patrick would soon be returning to duty in San Diego and intended to annul their marriage before he left. She told Kelli to meet him at the courthouse tomorrow and sign the annulment papers. Once that was done, they would briefly let her in the house to pick up her personal belongings if she promised to never come back.

Patrick asked her to leave their premises.

Kelli stood on the porch staring at them in disbelief.

"Well, what else would you expect from him when you left and were gone for days and nobody heard from you?" Judy asked coldly. She said they had even filed a missing person report on her the day after she left. Not that they were worried about her; it was the first step to take before filing the papers.

Judy again told her that she didn't live at their house anymore; she was not a member of their family.

Theirs was the ultimate betrayal to Kelli, who wouldn't even treat an injured stray dog that way. She was one of them, and she was injured and bleeding.

She had no home. She had no place to go. She had no family.

David offered to take her away with him. That was fine with the Murphys. They didn't care what he did with her.

Uncoordinated, stumbling and doubled over in pain, Kelli meekly, helplessly left the Murphy home with David Parker Ray.

Preface 2 – Angelíca

Angelíca Montaño, Cindy Hendy and David Ray had partied together around T or C and Elephant Butte for months. Angelíca had lived in Sierra County for several years and had the reputation locally as a prostitute who indulged in drugs. She had visual problems and her mismatched eyes—one was artificial—made her distinctive.

On February 17, 1999, she told Hendy and Ray that she needed to borrow a cake mix to bake a cake for her boy friend's birthday. Together, they went to David's home—where Cindy also lived—at 312 Bass Road. Cindy invited her inside to get the mix, while David remained outside.

Soon Ray joined them inside. He briskly walked up to Angelíca, grabbed her suddenly and held a knife to her throat, threatening to cut her. As he did, he said in a peculiar tone of voice that she'd never heard him use before, "You are being abducted against your will."

That sounded funny to Angelíca and she giggled; she thought he was teasing her. She didn't take him seriously; she didn't understand what "abducted" meant anyway. She quickly discovered, however, that neither of them was kidding her. The situation suddenly changed from friendly to hostile. Nothing funny about it.

She only had time to think, "What did I do to make them mad?" before David Ray slammed his fist into her stomach. Taking advantage of her shock and breathlessness, he and Hendy stripped off her clothes and bound her, spread-eagle, with chains on a narrow bed in the large add-on room of their residence. They padlocked a metal collar around her neck and Hendy forced her to swallow an orange pill. They told her she had to listen to a recording. It was David's recorded voice telling her in chilling detail what he was going to do to her. That further immobilized her.

Two days later, they took her outside to a nearby windowless trailer of some sort that they called their Toy Box. There they beat and brutally tortured her sexually with electricity and objects.

Angelíca believed they would eventually tire of her and kill her. She expected she would never again see her two little boys. On the fifth day, she tried to talk them into letting her go. She pretended that she enjoyed rough and painful sex, even the perverted sadism that they used on her. She promised she would tell no one what they had done to her, and reminded them she had been seen with them before they took her captive.

For some reason, David agreed to let her go. Cindy wasn't happy about it, argued, saying that was a dumb thing to do. Still, Angelíca didn't believe they would set her free until they actually did.

David bathed and cleaned her, inside—with douches—and out. That was so she would carry no trace of his DNA, he told her. They allowed her to dress, and drove her some distance on I-25 where they let her out of Ray's Toyota truck.

On Sunday, February 21, Gary Leyba, an off-duty detective with the Luna County Sheriff's Office, saw Angelíca walking along I-25. She tried to flag him down.

Knowing "there are plenty of crazy people in the world," as he later said, he didn't like to see females hitchhiking. It wasn't safe. He stopped and gave her a ride.

He later said she had seemed upset, but at the time, he wasn't interested in hearing her problems and asked her no questions.

After they rode in silence for a short while, she spoke. "If I tell you something, you're not going to believe me."

Unaware he was a law enforcement officer, she said, "An old pervert and a woman" held her captive for five days; they had just released her before he picked her up.

Angelíca was right; he did not believe her. She could see he thought her story was crazy.

He told her she should write a report and take it to the police. He offered to drop her off at the State Police station in Socorro.

Leyba later reported that she had looked like she was crazy or on drugs.

She knew he did not believe her. She could hardly believe it herself.

She asked him to pull over and let her out of his car.

He did.

For several weeks, Detective Leyba forgot about the strange woman and her stranger tale.

Chapter 1 – Cindy

On the cool brisk morning of March 20, 1999, Cindy Vigil lingered with a business associate on the sidewalk in a known sex-for-hire area of Central Avenue in the Albuquerque heights, near the University of New Mexico campus. The pretty, slender twenty-two-year-old Hispanic woman with brown eyes and mid-length brown hair could have passed for a sorority sister.

As she had countless times, she was offering to sell her body to strangers. It was the fastest way she knew to make enough money to buy the heroin her body craved.

She thought she knew, and could handle, the risks.

A small brown Toyota RV pulled into an adjacent parking lot, its driver beckoning. Her friend sauntered towards it. He soon called Cindy over, introduced her to the man in the vehicle, and walked away.

A lanky mustached man with a craggy face and leering grin sat in the driver's seat. He reminded Cindy of a Shar Pei dog with his small eyes and deep wrinkles in his forehead and folds in his jowls. He seemed harmless, she thought, weather-beaten and well into his seventies. Rode hard and put away wet, she thought, like she'd heard a cowboy describe some of the girls she hung with, as if they were horses. Well, he looked that way too: misused, like she often felt herself.

A long lock of blondish hair fell over his forehead, and large work-roughened hands gripped the steering wheel. He boldly stared at her and, by jerking his head, told her to get in the front seat with him. She instantly disliked him, but after all, this wasn't the start of a long affair. Grin and bear it; it will be quickly done and you'll get the money you need, she told herself as she usually did to get through it.

He told her what he wanted her to do. She leaned across the seat, face in his lap, and complied. He seemed unimpressed by her efforts.

Just as abruptly as he'd told her to get into the cab with him, he next ordered her to climb into the back of the little camper. She knew what to expect but that was all right; that would cost him extra and she wouldn't have to go out again for a day or two. She hoped he had condoms; her stash was depleted. A girl can't be too careful in this business.

She got out of the cab, walked around and ducked her head to climb in through the little rear door. He followed her inside, closing and latching the door. He nearly filled the little camper with his tall frame.

What happened next was not what she expected. It took her by surprise.

The man pulled out a badge and said she was under arrest for soliciting. He tried to handcuff her. He cuffed one wrist before she began to squirm and yell. Instincts told her he was no cop. She fought, twisting, pulling, jerking, trying to escape his grasp.

Everything happened too fast. A small, thin middle-aged woman with sparse, wispy blond hair rushed out of the tiny enclosed bathroom. She shocked Cindy with a stun-gun, punched her in the stomach and held a handgun to her head. She and the man threatened to use more powerful electrical devices if she didn't keep quiet.

Unable to make her limbs respond, tingling all over from the effects of the electrical shock, Cindy whimpered and twisted as they wrapped silver duct tape over her mouth and eyes and around her head. They bound her hands and feet with straps attached to eyebolts secured in the corners of the vehicle.

She was helpless and speechless in the back of the enclosed camper. The window dividing the cramped living quarters from the cab was open. The front occupants could hear, and turn to see, the rear occupant; Cindy could hear them. She felt and heard the pickup being started, then pulled into traffic.

She heard snatches of conversations. The man's name was David; the woman's was Cindy, like hers.

When they were a distance out of town—she knew by reduction of traffic noise—the driver slowed and then pulled the vehicle onto the shoulder of the highway. The odd couple climbed in back and cut off all of Cindy's clothes while she struggled helplessly to free herself from her bonds. She fought with every bit of energy she had, which was little. They kept zapping her with the stun-gun and some other long-handled electrical device. They put a knit hood or mask over her head; she felt a metallic zipper click against her teeth. The head covering smelled rancid. They again tightly secured her feet and hands with the straps fastened to eyebolts in opposite corners of the camper. She felt as if her legs would pull out of their hip sockets. She was loosely covered, her head included, with a smelly blanket.

The couple drove the rest of the way to their destination. Wherever that was, it was a long distance away.

"Why me? Why me? Why are they doing this to me? I've never done anything to deserve this. God help me!" Cindy cried silently. Lying on her back, her tears ran down the sides of her face, filling her ears then spilling into her hair.

She was chilled from the cold air and fear. She needed to pee, but that was the least of her worries.

To lessen her physical and emotional misery, she willed herself to relax her body and mentally remove herself from this time and place. It was a technique she had used many times before to escape unpleasant experiences, of which she'd had many in her life. But this was already the worst, knowing the horror of it was only just beginning.

The man and woman cheerfully chatted during the road trip. They sounded like an ordinary happy couple out for a pleasant afternoon drive, making it even more bizarre and frightening. Cindy did not know in what direction she was driven. She just knew it was a long journey that seemed unending. She didn't want it to end, fearing what would happen to her when it did. She was terrified.

Her costly addiction had driven her to live off of the streets, to sell her body, during which she'd had many unpleasant, even scary, moments. But none compared to the terror she now felt. She knew something especially bad would happen to her this time. This was no game, no prank; no one behind a mock candid camera would jump out and cry, "Surprise!" while everyone laughed, like when she was a child at Grandmother's house.

Grandmother. She tried to fill her thoughts and mental visions of her.

As she was sped through her own private darkness behind the tape and mask, she longed for the comfort of her rosary that her grandmother had taught her as a child. She silently said it over and over in her mind, imaginatively counting and handling the smooth turquoise beads, pressing the cool and soothing Jesu Cristo medal to her lips.

At last, Cindy felt the vehicle slow down, turn several times, then stop. She vaguely smelled marshy water reminding her of the willows by the Rio Grande.

She felt the tensions in the bindings of her legs and arms released, heard rude commands to get up and get out. She was still blinded by the mask covering her head, and her legs, having been tied and immoveable for hours, were full-of-pins painful and uncoordinated. The couple roughly pulled her out of the back of the camper, prodded and led her into what seemed to be a dwelling. She stumbled several times, falling hard onto her knees.

Inside, they pulled the hood from her head, roughly ripped the duct tape off her mouth and eyes, taking skin and eyelashes with it.

Disoriented from being blinded for several hours, she had little time to examine her unfamiliar surroundings in a darkened room before they shoved her down, bound her—still naked, onto a narrow bed. They tied her hands and feet, with her legs pulled apart in the same extremely painful position as in the vehicle. They put a rough metal collar around her neck and locked it on with a padlock, which they attached to a chain attached to an eyebolt in the wall.

"Oh my God! Please sweet Jesus, get me out of here." She spoke her words in her mind. "Or let me die quick. I don't care what they do to me after I'm dead. Just let me die first."

The woman forced her to swallow an orange pill without water while the old man held a handgun to her temple.

"Now I bet you feel stupid, don't you, bitch? You never should have trusted me, huh?" he said, leering into her face with his foul cigarette breath, while the woman hovered nearby, a smug smile on her mean pinched face.

The man commanded her to listen to something he was going to play for her.

"This audiotape contains very graphic, sexually orientated [sic] material for adults only. The tape is designed and created to be used for entertainment purposes," the man's voice on the audiotape began.

Why did he speak to her on a recording when he stood right there?

"Hello there, bitch. Are you comfortable right now? I doubt it. Wrists and ankles chained, gagged, probably blindfolded. You are disoriented and scared too, I would imagine. Perfectly normal under the circumstances," the man's mocking voice said.

"For a little while, at least, you need to get your shit together. You've got to listen to this tape. It is very relevant to your situation.

I'm going to tell you in detail why you have been kidnapped, what's going to happen to you and how long you'll be here."

She wet the bed.

"This tape is being created July 23, 1993, as an advisory tape for future female captives. The information I am going to give you is based on my experience dealing with captives over a period of several years. If at a future date there are any major changes in our procedures, the tape will be upgraded.

"Now, you are obviously being held against your will—heavily captive, don't know where you're at, don't know what's going to happen to you. You'll wait here until this will stop. And I'm curious to see you try to get your wrists and ankles loose. You know you can't. You're just going to have to wait to see what's going to happen next ..."

There was much more to the tape. It was unbearably long but, except to pray, Cindy had no choice but to listen with growing horror as her body, drenched with sweat that ran off of her like tears of anguish, soaked the already wet sheet beneath her.

Chapter 2 – Lucy

The morning of March 21, 1999, 79-year-old Lucy Schmidt* called to her neighbor, David, over their dividing chain-link fence. She had looked out the small window in her door and saw him getting something out of his Toyota camper truck parked in his carport by his front door.

Because the land undulated here near the lake, her property was slightly uphill from David's on Bass Road, and she had a good view into the front of his yard and his carport. But she was not the kind of nosey neighbor who entertained herself by watching what her neighbors were doing. She minded her own business.

One day some years ago, David had pulled his white cargo trailer up into the front of his yard. It was usually parked, with its axles supported on blocks, close to the north side of his dwelling, but set at an angle, more accessible from his back yard. It was the enclosed trailer portion of an 18-wheeler diesel tractor-trailer rig like those seen hauling commodities down the highways across America. That day, Rolf*, Lucy's husband, and David had chatted aimlessly about it through their dividing chain-link fence. Rolf asked David what he was going to do with the trailer. David said he was thinking of selling it and getting something newer, better.

He offered to sell it to Rolf, who could see it had been modified from its original state. It had one steel-reinforced household-type door, and a small air conditioner unit attached to the upper outside wall of one end, and louvered openings on the side for additional ventilation. Rolf presumed it was David's workshop. He was very handy with his hands and Rolf didn't doubt it was well appointed inside.

He told David he might consider buying it and asked how much he wanted for it. Naturally, before deciding, he had said, he'd want to see inside.

"A hundred thou," said David.

"Huh! You sure don't want to sell it, do you?" It must be pretty fancy inside, but nothing that started as a cargo trailer could be worth

---

**denotes a fictitious name*

that much. Rolf figured David had just been chatting to shoot the breeze, as he often did. He liked to talk.

Not long after that, the same trailer, not a newer one, was on blocks back where it had been before. Rolf wasn't sure if maybe David had turned it around, or maybe moved it to a more convenient position. He couldn't remember at which end he had earlier seen the small air conditioner unit and door. Like Lucy, he never paid much attention to the details of his neighbors' lives. He had better things to do.

Rolf promptly forgot about the cargo trailer and it was no longer a subject of idle conversation between him and David and, therefore, between Rolf and Lucy.

Now, she could barely see a small portion of that trailer from where she stood at the fence. David's dwelling nearly hid it from her view.

David was a quiet neighbor. Sometimes she saw that he had friends over, but Lucy never noticed much going on over there. He was a good kind of neighbor to have.

She and her family had lived here more than thirty years; they bought the ninety-five-year lease on the land in 1975. Rolf had worked at White Sands Missile Range until he could no longer get down off the towers.

Before that, she had spent many years traveling all over the United States with him and their children. She liked to tell people that she had wanted four children, and she got four—but four each, four girls and four boys. Twice what she had asked for, but she loved them all.

The insecurity of not owning the land she'd lived on and paid taxes on for decades was becoming worrisome. The land belonged to the State Park. There had been talk there might soon be changes about that; she didn't know what was going to happen. She was growing old and some of her children were encouraging her to move away from Elephant Butte and get a newer mobile home. But she believed as long as she lived here by the lake, her children would come visit her and stay on weekends and holidays. She didn't think they would if she lived elsewhere.

Watching David tinkering around, she thought how small his RV was compared to the one she used to drive, and still owned, parked on a nearby lot. She supposed his had little more than a bed in back, and maybe one of those little porta-potties or toilet compartment. She didn't suppose a park mechanic and maintenance man could afford anything bigger. But, since he worked for the Park and probably had access to all of the state parks in New Mexico, perhaps federal ones too, he didn't need much more than that for himself. He was the kind of guy who could rough it, didn't need conveniences.

Lucy believed he now had a woman living with him, who had been with him several months, maybe a year. But for most of the fifteen years he had been her neighbor, she thought he mostly lived alone. She often wished David would find himself a nice girl and marry so he wouldn't be alone so much. She was a motherly type and fretted about him.

Well, until recently, he'd been mostly alone except for that tall, lanky daughter of his, built so much like him. She sometimes lived with him. That girl was a strange one, not feminine. Seemed more like a man, wearing that leather jacket and riding that motorcycle and all. Even her name sounded like a man: Jesse. Lucy wasn't sure whether that one liked men or women; she suspected women. She hadn't reached her age without knowing about people like that, who were so uncommon in her own youth. When she thought about it, which was seldom, she wondered what made people turn out that way.

Lucy thought she'd heard Jesse had lived with her father at his farm at Magdalena or wherever it was David had lived before he moved to Elephant Butte. She knew Ray also had at least one son in the service or working at a military base in Albuquerque.

David was a pleasant older fellow, a mechanic who worked for the State Park Service. He seemed good-hearted and helped his neighbors. Lucy felt lucky to have him living next door. He was so handy; he could do almost anything with those big hands of his, fix or make just about anything. He wasn't only mechanical. Years ago, he'd added onto the rear of his mobile home. She thought he did all of the work himself, maybe even the wiring and plumbing.

He was a scrounger. She'd seen him come home with stuff he must have scavenged, picked up beside the road or in the park, or maybe leftover material from his job. His garage, mobile home, storage sheds and trailers had to be full of junk, she thought. A few times when his garage door was up, she saw a tremendous amount of clutter inside. She wasn't being nosy; David's garage faced her kitchen window, she couldn't help but see inside. That's why he parked all his vehicles outside: no room for even a small one inside the garage. Probably a lot of the odd things he made were from bits and pieces and scraps, stuff that didn't cost him anything but his ingenuity. They probably didn't pay mechanics, even at the state park, all that much.

David was a genius, no doubt about it. Rolf, now deceased, was a smart man and he often wondered aloud why a man like David only did maintenance and such at the Park; he could do so much better for himself. But Lucy figured he was smart enough to do whatever made him happy.

Lucy's neighbors across the street, the Washburns*, were particularly fond of David. They often hired him to do things around their place. Like her, they were up in years and grateful when he was available and willing to help them.

Lucy had a red pickup that wouldn't run anymore and she had been meaning to talk to David about that for several weeks. She hadn't seen him around his place much recently, not even when she knew he must be home, according to his parked vehicles—the white four-wheel-drive Dodge Ram out in his yard that looked so much like a State Park vehicle but wasn't, and the Toyota RV now parked close to his front door.

When she'd looked out that morning, she saw him in his yard, and then tinkering around in the carport and in his Toyota. Maybe he was fetching his toolbox.

Now, standing at their dividing fence, she called him over so she wouldn't have to shout. When he approached, she asked him to look at her pickup to see if he could fix it.

She noticed, not for the first time, how thin he was. Maybe it was his lanky build, tall with long arms and legs, that made him seem skinny. She wondered if he was eating right. She had to be careful and not let him know she fretted about him. Men were funny about things like that and too often got the wrong ideas.

He smiled at her, saying he would look at her pickup first chance he got. "Maybe this afternoon. We'll see," he halfway promised.

She knew he was busy, always doing things. She hoped he would get around to looking at it soon. She had a project that would require that pickup.

Her kids had fussed at her, wanting her to tear down the old building behind her mobile home. It had been on the property ever since she and Rolf settled at Elephant Butte. If she did give in to the kids and have it torn down, she'd need that pickup in good running order. She'd need to haul off lots of stuff she stored in there. She hoped the kids or grandkids would want some of it. She guessed she'd have to put the rest in a yard sale.

Among the stuff she should get rid of were several tanks of butane and bundles of welding rods. Her husband had been a welder. David had already bought one of her butane tanks; she could see it sitting on the other side of his mobile home, in front of the white cargo trailer. Maybe he'd buy some more of them from her. Or better, maybe he'd take the tanks in trade for working on her pickup.

Joe, her son who lived with her, wasn't interested in welding.

Whenever she was away from home for a few days visiting her children, or when she had spent so much time at the hospital with Rolf when he was dying, she'd asked David to look out for her place. And he did. He even came over and watered her plants, including the small pomegranate trees by her front door. Whenever he said he'd be away for a while, she looked out for his place, the outside of it anyway; she was glad for the chance to reciprocate.

Neither she nor any of her family had been inside his home, far as she knew, nor had he been inside hers. Their relationship was strictly outdoors, over the fence or in their yards.

She had all those daughters; several often visited her and didn't like him. They did not like his looks or his bold stares. They couldn't quite explain why, they just felt uneasy around him. When they arrived for a visit and David was in his yard, they rushed inside so he wouldn't have an opportunity to engage them in conversation.

Now her son-in-law, James, married many years to one of her daughters, was different. He wasn't shy or afraid of anyone, and was polite to David just like he was to everyone.

David knew James had also worked for the state and he'd talk to him over the fence, comparing employment benefits with him and such. James would eventually find some excuse to end the conversation so he could join his family inside, otherwise he'd be stuck at the fence all day with David.

David really liked to gab; that seemed to be one of his favorite things, and she thought he particularly liked talking to James. Perhaps it was because he knew James had once been Deputy Chief of the State Police. That impressed a lot of people.

Lucy was proud of James; he'd once headed New Mexico State Police's plainclothes division. That meant their detectives, the state's narcotics and criminal investigations department.

As Lucy stood at the other side of the fence from David, she noticed his big rough hands as they clutched the top wire. Was that rust, that dark red stuff on his hands and under his nails? He was probably tinkering with his plumbing. He could do just about anything he wanted to do with those hands.

Chapter 3 – It Begins

On the afternoon of March 22, 1999, a bloody, naked woman, wearing only a metal collar padlocked to her neck with a long dangling chain, ran down a road in the tiny lakeshore community of Elephant Butte in southwestern New Mexico.

Thus began an international-media frenzy, New Mexico's largest FBI and State Police investigation of the year, and a case, because of its unique and bizarre nature, that became indelibly inked in the annals of criminal profiling.

That afternoon, in rapid succession, central dispatch received several related calls.

Generally, central dispatch calls were picked up by all area law enforcement agencies, at least those whose personnel had their scanners and radios on.

The first call—at 3:30 p.m.—was a 9-1-1 hang-up. The enhanced "caller-ID" showed that call came from 513 Bass Road near Elephant Butte Lake. Background sounds of commotion before an abrupt hang-up warranted a check on it. Sierra County Deputies David Elston and Lucas Alvarez, available at the sheriff's office in Truth or Consequences when the call came in, responded.

As they headed to that address several miles away, dispatch called them to say she had contacted someone at that Bass Road residence. The woman who answered said there was no problem at that location.

Before they found a place to turn their units around and head back, a second dispatch call came in. A female caller named Patricia, who said she lived in Albuquerque but was calling from Elephant Butte near the lake, had told dispatch that a naked woman running down Springland Road tried to open her car door and jump in. The caller said she was frightened and kept driving. The dispatcher recognized that location as being near Bass Road. She told Patricia that officers were on their way and asked her to wait in the area for them. She asked for an identifying description or color of her car.

"Green," said Patricia.

Dispatch received a third 9-1-1 call. That woman, named Doris, said she lived in El Paso but also had a place in Elephant Butte. She, too, said a naked woman had frantically tried to get into her car as she drove down the road in the same limited area as the prior caller.

Then came the fourth 9-1-1 call. The caller was a resident at 301 Hot Springs Landing Road, at the lake end of Springland Road. She said the door to her enclosed porch was open and a bloody, naked, terrified woman ran into her residence crying for help. The startled caller said the woman was only wearing a padlocked metal collar with an attached chain.

Those 9-1-1 calls sounded as if they were for Animal Control about a stray dog, not for law enforcement personnel about a human being.

Dispatch-to-car and car-to-car calls kept the units' lines loaded.

At the corner of Hot Springs and Ridge Road, Sierra County Deputy Peter Bowidowicz saw an idling green car fitting the description broadcast by central dispatch. He stopped to question the woman inside, named Patricia, who was the first of the two callers to say a naked woman had tried to get into her car with her.

Deputy Alvarez later wrote in his report, "When we arrived in the area of Springland and Hot Springs Landing Road, I saw Deputy Bowidowicz walking away from a little green car."

Alvarez and Elston proceeded to 301 Hot Springs Landing where middle-aged residents, Donald and Darlene Breech, lived.

Mr. Breech waited anxiously outside beside the road when the officers arrived. He told them the naked woman was inside with his wife. Mrs. Breech had given the woman a pink bathrobe to cover her nakedness, he said.

When the deputies had arrived at the address, they found, arriving ahead of them, Elephant Butte Lake State Park Rangers Mike Lanford and Chris DeGasse—responding to a call about a possible problem on state park lands. Border Patrol Agent Bob Johnston was also there. Deputy Bowidowicz soon joined them.

Since there was enough available manpower to cover two locations, Elston dropped off Alvarez to assist Bowidowicz and Agent Johnston, and he and State Park Rangers Mike Lanford and Chris DeGasse proceeded the short distance to 513 Bass Road, from where—they had been told—the naked woman had escaped.

Alvarez, who remained at 301 Hot Springs Landing, later wrote in his report: "Inside the residence I saw a Hispanic woman looking out a sliding glass window at us. She came outside. She was wearing a pink robe. She had blood and scratches all over her legs. She was wearing a black metal collar with a chain attached to it that was about four feet long. The female came towards us asking for help, saying she had been kidnapped. She approached Bowidowicz first and turned away from him and went towards Border Patrol Agent Johnston and turned away from him too. She did this in the manner of being afraid of the officers. Then she saw me and grabbed my arm and said she needed help. I noticed she had more blood coming from her head and other parts of her body."

The woman was hysterical and seemed confused. She kept crying out, "I broke free!" And, "They raped me!"

When Bowidowicz tried to question her, she continued to cry out, "I'm alive, yes, I'm alive!" And, "They hurt me!"

When Bowidowicz asked her where she came from, she answered, "I don't know where I'm at." He asked her where she lived, and she finally answered, "Albuquerque."

At last she gave her name, Cynthia Vigil, and her date of birth. The woman was twenty-two years old.

She seemed less fearful of Alvarez. She grabbed the chain and pulled on it, asking him to take it off. Alvarez looked at the chain, the collar and padlock and told her he could not because the lock fastened the collar on her.

Alvarez reported that the woman said she had been "beaten and tortured by a man named David, and that he and his girlfriend, Cindy, had done all kinds of sexual acts to her that hurt."

From Alvarez's mobile radio fastened on his shoulder, the victim heard a call saying the Bass Road address was the residence of a state park employee. The victim became excited, saying David, the man who had kidnapped and abused her, worked for state parks. She told them she had been held at a mobile home that had boats in the yard, which she had seen when she escaped.

She told the officers that she had freed herself by reaching the key that went to the lock on the chain attached to her collar. While she was trying to escape, the woman called Cindy walked in, saw she was loose and began beating her with a lamp. The victim said she struck her back, hitting her in the head with an ice pick, and ran.

If her story was true, the officers knew her life could be in danger until the suspects were in custody, because they wouldn't want her to testify against them. The law was opposed to violent rape, even if she was a prostitute. And kidnapping was of much greater importance, if indeed she had been kidnapped in the beginning, and hadn't willingly gone with them. Regardless, if the man and woman later held her against her will, as appeared to be the case, it was kidnapping, a federal offense, which could warrant years in the lock-up.

The officers heard enough to suspect this woman was a prostitute, but even if she were normally game to kinky stuff if the price was right, she did not welcome what was done to her in this case. She seemed terrified and untrusting even of uniformed officers. Her eyes were huge and bruised, pupils enlarged, she was trembling and wobbly, barely able to stand, she had deep cuts and bruises encircling her wrists and bare ankles indicating she had fought against restraints. Blood flowed down her legs. Then there was the collar around her neck and the dangling chain, which they could see despite the robe that covered her. She seemed to have experienced no ordinary S and M crap, sadism and masochism. At any rate, the officers believed it ended up not being something she had agreed to endure. How could anyone in her right mind, even a prostitute into S and M, agree to something like that?

She kept crying out hysterically, "Don't let them get me!" and, "I'm alive! Yes! I'm alive!"

Alvarez and Agent Johnston took the woman to Sierra Vista Hospital, the forty-three-bed medical and surgical facility in Truth or Consequences. All the way she kept crying, "Don't let them get me!" And, still in apparent disbelief, "I'm alive!"

At the hospital, Alvarez remained outside the door of the examination room while Dr. Mitova Radosveta, the emergency room doctor, assisted by nurses Johnna Brady and Lynn Cummings, used a rape kit on Vigil.

Then Dr. Radosveta and the nurses began treating her injuries.

The victim, Cindy Vigil, pulled on the chain and cried, "Take it off!" She demanded, then pleaded with them to remove the collar.

Alvarez asked the doctor to first photograph Vigil wearing it, and all of her surface injuries, for the investigation report.

Afterwards, the doctor called for the hospital maintenance man to come with bolt cutters. When he arrived, he and Alvarez, with the physician's help, carefully cut off the collar, trying to not further injure the fragile Vigil.

Alvarez remained at the hospital with her until a State Police officer could arrive to question her. While they waited, she told him that David and Cindy had gone to Albuquerque to kidnap her, pretending to be police officers.

Chapter 4 – The Scene

When they responded to the dispatched calls, and after he dropped off Deputy Alvarez to assist Bowidowicz and Agent Johnston with the victim at Hot Springs Landing, Deputy Elston, along with Rangers Lanford and DeGasse, drove the short distance to 513 Bass Road.

The rangers considered the accusations against Ray with skepticism. DeGasse didn't really know him, but recognized the name. David Parker Ray did maintenance on the Park's vehicles and property, where he had a reputation as a talented man who won a monetary reward and a commendation, maybe two, for useful things he designed and built for them, which they and other state parks continued to use.

In front of the property near the gate was a wooden sign on wooden posts: "David P. Ray, 513 Bass Rd. K8." Because the land under the residences in that area around the lake belonged to the State Park, addresses were shown as block and lot numbers, like Ray's "K8," which meant block K, lot 8.

A chain-link fence surrounded the rectangular lot that was twice as deep as it was wide. The doublewide front gate could accommodate RVs. An unlocked padlock hung from the gate. The officers entered and crossed the half-acre dirt yard, larger than some other properties on the short winding road. Parked inside the fence toward the back of the lot, on either side of the dwelling, were a sailboat with mast, a silver-colored cabin cruiser, a tow trailer, and other recreational vehicles and equipment. Enclosed within the property, besides the residence, were other prefab structures, including storage trailers, two of which were under a wide metal canopy roof.

The residence, an older model singlewide mobile home, had a high tower above it—a citizens' band ham or short-wave antenna. Attached to the front of the home was an open carport facing Bass Road; on the backside, an addition almost doubled the structure's size. At one end of the structure, an add-on garage with two closed overhead doors faced south. The land at the rear of the lot sloped downwards, and a portion of the rear add-on living area and long open porch was elevated above ground level. Some brickwork terraced the back yard. Three additional short roads running parallel to Bass Road, with a few residences, obstructed the lake view. Lower and closer to the lake, roads named Trout, Catfish and Pike meandered south between Bass Road and the lakefront. An unoccupied very small, rounded, old model trailer-home, pale pink, huddled like a featherless baby barn owl on the other side of a chain-link fence just beyond Ray's property.

Some reporters would later write that Ray's property fronted the water, and that he could see the rock formation, Kettle Top, from his residence. Neither statement was true.

Because Ranger Lanford and Deputy Elston believed there might be an injured suspect or an additional victim inside the 513 Bass Road residence, lawful reasons to enter, together they made the decision to go inside for a security check while Ranger DeGasse remained on guard outside, standing at the best vantage point to watch the majority of the property.

Elston and Lanford approached the dwelling with drawn weapons held at low ready. They knocked on the front door and announced themselves, then tried to open it. The door was locked.

They walked around to the back of the residence and climbed the steps to the covered porch. To their ears, their boots clomped loudly as they walked across the poured concrete slab floor.

They found an unlocked sliding glass door. Deputy Elston quickly noted the time in his little spiral pocket notebook. After knocking and announcing themselves as police officers, and receiving no response, they cautiously entered.

Although it was still afternoon, inside it was dark because heavy drapes and woven Mexican blankets shut out exterior light. Elston pulled his long black flashlight from the ring of his Sam Browne and shined his light around the first room they entered, flashing it on and off with the button, ducking and moving as he did to make himself less of a target as officers were trained to do.

They were nervous, as anyone would have been under the circumstances.

A hollow voice and a crackling sound startled them; then they saw a small horizontally-moving red light glowing in the darkness.

After the initial moment of panic, they recognized an activated police scanner on a low table. Apparently the person or people who lived there regularly listened to dispatched and car-to-car calls of the local fire department and law enforcement agencies. That did not mean the occupant was a cop or firefighter. Citizens' possession of police scanners had become common. Still, that, like radar detectors in vehicles, prejudiced many officers against those who, they thought, had no legitimate reason to have them.

When they later completed their security check throughout the residence, they would find, in different rooms, several groupings of electronics—each with ham and short-wave, police scanner and citizen's band radios. And each unit had a hand-held mike.

The first room they entered was large, perhaps a den, that was added onto the back of the original mobile home. Cheap paneling lined walls; self-stick squares of brown carpet covered the concrete floor.

Something glittered like emeralds in the flashlight's rapid bursts of light. Closer examination showed that it was green bits of glass—the remains of a broken lamp—on a narrow bed and on the floor. Also on the floor lay a bloody ice pick. Dried blood splattered the bedding and paneling beside the bed.

Attached to the wall by the bed were restraints—rings, clamps, hooks, eyebolts, some with chains and leather straps attached. Overhead, the ceiling bristled with hooks and eyebolts. On shelves and a table near the bed lay sex devices, including packages of prophylactics, as well as a hand-held unisex urinal. On a bedside table were Polaroid photographs. In one photo, the officers recognized the victim restrained naked on a table or bench. On the floor a short distance from the bed was a knocked-over soiled white plastic bucket, obviously used as a portable toilet.

It took the officers several moments to digest the significance of what they saw. If they had questioned it before, they no longer doubted the woman from Albuquerque had been an unwilling victim of violence.

In front of them, on a slightly higher level, was the living room of the mobile home.

The officers slowly proceeded to look in all areas of the residence, flashing their beams as they hugged walls and other concealment and protection. After beginning with the add-on room at the back, they moved forward into the original mobile home portion.

In the original area, the master bedroom opened at the end of a narrow hall.

The hallway's middle door led into a small bathroom. Inside the tub sat a pink hospital-type bedpan. Full. It needed emptying. Dried blood splotched a small rug in front of the toilet. Even this room had restraint devices.

As they proceeded, each area they saw was more incredible than the last. The officers opened the third door off the hall, to the front bedroom. Attached to the ceiling, dangling down, casting grotesque moving shadows in the bursts of light like something in a cheap B movie, was some kind of pulley device with weights. A large array of sexual devices and various means of restraint filled the small bedroom. An assortment of lubricants, dildos, pliers, knives, scissors, toggle bolts and other items were arranged neatly side-by-side on a dresser top, eerily like surgeon's tools laid out for surgery. Hanging on the wall above were leather harnesses, several with large dildos attached, and chains and leather straps. On the floor were piles of nylon straps, cords and ropes, and devices with bars that had labels neatly painted on them with white paint: Knee spreader – 17"; Ankle spreader – 17" to 24". Tacked on a wall was an artistically hand-drawn illustration of a naked and gagged woman, tied in what they thought was an impossibly spread-eagled pose.

On another wall a poster said, "I'm rather busy—would you PISS OFF!"

After somewhat recovering from the shock of the scene from the doorway, Elston slowly walked into the bedroom while Lanford covered him. He peeked under the bed and looked inside the closet. Absence of probable cause, even after incriminating evidence was found, was a legal loophole too often used by clever defendants' attorneys. However, Elston believed he had probable cause to look in places "not in plain sight." Their probable cause included a diligent search for more injured victims.

They found no one after carefully looking throughout the residence.

Deputy Elston later wrote in his report that the officers saw "an array of sexual devices along with various restraint-type devices, and various photographs on the walls and several types of hand tools on a counter in the room."

The reports he and Lanford, and later other officers, wrote were composed of simple, unemotional statements. They did not convey what they thought and felt, nor did they include their exclamations and comments to each other, while and after looking inside the dwelling.

After a cursory but careful examination of the entire residence, taking care to touch nothing but doorknobs when necessary, Elston and Lanford went outside into welcome fresh air.

Sierra County Sheriff Terry Byers arrived at Bass Road in his Jeep. He, too, looked inside. The enormity of what he saw made him also believe the case involved multiple victims. He knew this case would be beyond the limited abilities and resources of the Sierra County Sheriff's Office.

Byers called the State Police to come take over the case.

Deputy Bowidowicz arrived at the scene on Bass Road while the sheriff waited. He and Deputy Elston put up yellow crime scene tape around the residence and strips of blue tape sealing the doors. Once tape was up, no one, including law enforcement, was allowed to enter the home or the marked-off area until crime scene investigators arrived.

State Parks Ranger Bryon Wilson pulled up at the gate. Byers walked to his unit to explain the situation to him. Wilson said he had just passed David Parker Ray driving on Warm Springs Boulevard.

Byers ran and jumped into his Jeep and sped off, throwing gravel. Wilson followed close behind.

Soon thereafter, Elston received a radio call from Byers, asking him to meet him on nearby Springland Road. Leaving Bowidowicz and Lanford to keep the crime scene at 513 Bass Road secure, Elston drove off to meet the sheriff.

On Warm Springs Boulevard, the sheriff, joined by two park rangers in their own units, had detained a small brown Toyota RV. A man the park rangers recognized as David Ray had been placed in a patrol unit.

A tall, thin man with moustache and unkempt sandy hair, Ray had lots of wrinkles, even on his arms, an undefined jaw-line and loose skin on his neck. He looked harmless and much older than the nearly sixty years indicated on his driver's license.

Elston recognized Cindy Hendy, a woman also detained and handcuffed, from prior domestic calls from or about her. She was a thin, nondescript, mousy-looking woman, almost forty years old, with a high forehead, wide-set eyes, long straight nose, thin mouth, shallow chin and sparse shoulder-length light-colored hair. She had once been pretty but was no more.

Sheriff Byers told Elston to read the Miranda warning to both Ray and Hendy. That and the handcuffs were standard procedure although they were not yet charged with anything.

The sheriff left the task of questioning the suspects to the State Police when they arrived, but he thought it was important to read the Miranda warning to them in case they blurted out something that could later be used in their prosecution.

The law requires the Miranda warning to be given to a person being questioned who is the subject of the investigation, whether or not he's been arrested. (In a February 2007 telephone conversation, retired federal law enforcement instructor Howard Goetsch commented that defense attorneys have used, as a ploy in the courtroom, the claim that an officer had not read the defendant his rights before he blurted something prior to his arrest. Goetsch said judges who do not know the law have upheld the defense's claim and disallowed acceptable information or evidence.) "Excited utterance" is the legal term used when someone says something in the passion of the moment that may implicate himself or someone else in a crime. The Miranda warning is not required for excited utterances to be lawfully used in a court of law.

Officers towed the Toyota RV to the nearby State Parks Training Center, placing it inside a locked fence, and encircled it with crime scene tape, until state investigators arrived.

Elston noticed Hendy had blood in her hair and recalled what the victim had said about stabbing her head with an ice pick. He and Ranger Johnston took her to Sierra Vista Hospital in Truth or Consequences, where she told a nurse she had been hit with a lamp. The cut was more like a puncture wound, but appeared to be minor, requiring little medical attention. She refused anything beyond examination, and cleansing and painting of the wound with a topical antibacterial ointment.

The officers transported her back to Elephant Butte, to the State Parks office on Rock Canyon Road, just off Warm Springs Boulevard, not far from Bass Road. They detained her there until state investigators arrived.

The deputies had also taken David Parker Ray to the State Parks office, holding him under guard separately from Hendy. Later, Ray would be held at the Sierra County jail in Truth or Consequences. In the lower backside of the Sierra County Courthouse—a white two-story building with burnt-brick coping—on Date Street, the jail's door faced the sheriff's office housed in a separate small building across the rear parking lot.

Later still, to keep them fully separated, Hendy would be transported to the Dona Ana County Detention Center at Las Cruces.

A deputy arrived at 513 Bass Road at 6:15 p.m. to replace Deputy Bowidowicz, who had held the crime scene area secure. Bowidowicz briefed the oncoming-duty deputy, pointing out areas of concern requiring special focus because of limited view.

He went home at 7:30 p.m.

^^^^^^^

The little community with the strange name, Truth or Consequences, was seven miles south of Elephant Butte.

Chapter 5 – Elephant Butte

Low vegetation composed of mesquite, sage and desert willow, accompanied by the sour odor of marshy, stagnant water, surrounded the lake. There was a lot of traffic, even that early in the season. Pickups and SUVs towed boats. Boat trailers and cars, train-like, were coupled behind many large motor homes.

Elephant Butte had only one stoplight and few commercial enterprises besides filling stations, rental storage units, and open yards for sales or storage of RVs and boats of all kinds. Many out-of-towners stored their boats and travel trailers there year around.

Interstate-25 paralleled a portion of the lakeshore. From the Interstate, one exit took motorists to State Highway 195, which passed by commercial yards and the Blue Waters Saloon, a corrugated metal prefab building without windows. Another exit from I-25 led to Warm Springs Boulevard. Both 195 and Warm Springs took travelers to Rock Canyon Road, a perimeter road on the west side of the lake. Springland Road, one of the roads that led from Rock Canyon Road, quickly became Hot Springs Landing Road, which abruptly ended at concrete abutments with nothing beyond but sand and the lake's receding shoreline.

From Rock Canyon Road, the land dropped gently downward to the shore of Elephant Butte Lake and Reservoir. Trailers and similar types of prefabs huddled right up to the outer edge of the sandy beach. Many of the residences were old model trailers.

Warm Springs Boulevard and Rock Canyon Road were paved. Springland Road was paved until it abruptly became Hot Springs Landing Road, which was unfinished and washboarded. The short Hot Springs Landing was, when the water was higher, originally only what its name implied: an access from the paved road enabling boaters to drive to the water's edge to launch their craft. The water had receded from years of drought, revealing a wide sandy beach, where the road now ended, much further from the water. Hot Springs Landing also led to a few short roads, mostly going to the right or south of it, to residences on leased land closer to the shore.

According to the 1990 census, taken more than eight years earlier, the average age of housing in Sierra County was thirty years. The average housing was probably older yet in Elephant Butte. Until fairly recently, there had been little new development in the area in the past twenty years. Despite the tourist attraction, the 1990 census said this county was poorer than the state average.

Since that 1990 census, new development had begun.

Rolf Hechler, New Mexico State Parks southwest regional manager, on March 30, 2007, said that the U.S. Bureau of Land Reclamation had owned the land around Elephant Butte Lake, which it leased to the New Mexico State Parks until 2023. That included 350 one-quarter-acre lots intended for vacationers. People began to live permanently on that leased land by setting up mobile homes or prefabs. People would not want to build costly permanent-type structures where they did not own the land underneath. The residents' rent, perhaps a few hundred dollars annually, was amazingly low and they paid property tax only on their modest appurtenant structures. That explained the predominantly low-scale housing of Elephant Butte, one of the state's largest recreational places.

In 2003, the Bureau of Land Reclamation entered into an agreement to sell those land parcels to the Elephant Butte Homeowners Association. The association in turn sold each parcel to that property's tenant at fair market value—that is, market value of desert land, not of lakefront property—that averaged $3,000 or $4,000 per lot. Since that transaction, the property values have considerably increased and new construction reflects the residents' confidence that they now own the land.

By 2003, Elephant Butte visitors would see several large, new, expensive multi-storied homes along Springland Road.

Bass Road was a narrow curving road fronting a jumble of prefab dwellings squatting among the mesquite and willow bushes, reached by turning right off Hot Springs Landing.

When newcomers settled this area off Hot Springs Landing, there was no zoning ordinance. They parked their mobile homes where they had a good view of the lake, until others came and parked in front of them. Some had built double-car garages into the hillside for their boats and vehicles, and put their mobile homes on top, with high overlooking porches to provide them better lake views.

Casual add-on porches, roofs and awnings extended many of the prefabs, making them seem less transitory. Owners had enclosed some properties with fences, but most of the lots were open and undefined. Few of the yards in Elephant Butte, or even in nearby Truth or Consequences, were adorned with lawns or cultivated yards. In Elephant Butte, there was just loose wind-blown sand, and most of what natural plant-life there was, was still dormant because in mid-March of 1999, spring had barely sprung.

Besides tourists and retirees, the arid land seemed to nurture mainly creosote, mesquite, walking-stick *cholla, ocotillo*, prickly pear cactus, salt cedar, plus desert willow bushes that midsummer adorned with pink blossoms. Although Sierra County and some surrounding New Mexico counties are part of the Chihuahuan Desert, much of that is not as barren as this area, with its rocky or loose sandy soil and, in places around the lake, marshy areas.

In many places, the Chihuahuan Desert is alive with vegetation, and blooms with wild flowers in the spring and summer after rain. Annual rainfall is usually less than ten inches, so droughts are common, but rangeland plants grow in brief spurts after rain when soil and moisture conditions are right. There are few perennial streams in the mountains to the west, but some creeks drain areas of Sierra County to the Rio Grande. Accelerated erosion creates *níchos* and *arroyos*, nature's drainage systems caused by intense storm runoff. New Mexico is known for its rare sudden, brief but intense storms.

Besides the few developed places, basic land characteristics of Sierra County are the riparian areas—vegetation around permanent bodies of water—plus alkali flats, foothills, mesas, escarpments and volcanic formations.

Throughout New Mexico, stands of trees mark almost every community and humble adobe and clapboard abode, even abandoned ones on desolate wind-swept prairies. But the community of Elephant Butte was essentially treeless.

Still, the sparkling lake, reflecting New Mexico's usual clear blue cloud-dappled sky and pale blue and lavender hues of the surrounding mountains, provides a spectacular panoramic view. It is a huge star-sapphire set in the jagged platinum prongs of the Fra Cristobal Range to the east and the San Mateo Mountains to the west.

Like anywhere, all kinds of people lived in the lakeshore area of Sierra County, which included Williamsburg and Truth or Consequences as well as Elephant Butte. Because they seemed to run together, it was difficult, except for their residents who well knew, to tell where the village of Williamsburg ended and Truth or Consequences began.

In late 2002, Kathy McClean, Seventh Judicial District Court clerk, said, "I've lived here for twenty-one years. I choose to live here; I wouldn't want to live anywhere else. Reporters and writers describe T or C like the area back there, all prefabs," she said, sweeping her arm back in a southerly direction, "but up the hill are $100,000 homes."

In 1999, Pat O'Hanlon was a sheriff's office dispatcher while waiting to become the community's public library director, a position she held in 2002. She, too, was unhappy about the negative descriptions of the area by outsider reporters and authors after this case broke in the media. It made her angry. After she was employed at the library, she wanted to file some of the books about the Ray case that described her community under the fiction category.

However, most law enforcement officers and investigators temporarily assigned to the area, or who visited it during the extensive investigations of this case, described it as a lawless place, with a disproportionate number of aging 1960s hippies caught in time warp, druggies, transients living in buses, and just plain old "white trash".

One investigator said, "Half of the females are older, retirees; they're decent ordinary folks like you and me. Many of the others are a subculture. They are crack- and meth-heads, perhaps in their thirties, living in their cars with their poor little kids, prostituting themselves to the older guys, including residents." Perhaps an unfair generalization, it nonetheless showed how outsider law officers regarded, and were affected by, the case and its setting.

Everywhere, police regularly deal with, and are accustomed to, sleazy life styles. However, officers were understandably sour on this community because it appeared that many residents knew, and apparently condoned or ignored, what David Parker Ray, Jesse Ray and Cindy Hendy were doing. They believed some of the locals, including "higher-ups" in the community, were involved with them. Investigators thought many of those who knew could have, by reporting it, brought it to an end years earlier, and so doing, spared many victims agony and death.

The 1990 census found almost three-quarters of Sierra County's population to be Anglo, an unusually large ratio for New Mexico. A quarter was counted as Hispanic. A negligible number were American Indian, Black or Asian.

Except for one elementary school in Arrey, the only public schools in Sierra County were in T or C, which had one each elementary, middle and high school. And, according to that earlier census, only about sixty percent of the adult residents of Sierra County had completed high school; fewer than ten percent had graduated from college.

Elephant Butte—with a permanent population of 2,500 and incorporated less than a year earlier, in July 1998, as New Mexico's newest "city"—was in a little pocket, like loose change, near New Mexico's largest body of water, the forty-three-mile-long Elephant Butte Lake.

The Bureau of Reclamation created Elephant Butte Dam and Reservoir on the Rio Grande, from 1911 to 1916, for irrigation and recreation.

The influx of tourists on summer weekends swelled the little Elephant Butte community to 80,000, even 110,000 or more on holiday weekends, temporarily making it, by head-count, the second largest community in New Mexico. Its law enforcement capability was woefully inadequate. The fixed population of Sierra County was no more than 11,000 and most of that—7,500—was in the nearby town of Truth or Consequences. Therefore, huge holiday crowds, mostly camping around the lakeshore, made for mob-scenes and all kinds of crises.

Through the 1980s and well into the 1990s, the Elephant Butte Lake area was considered undesirable because of the lawless type of people who lived there or frequented the place. Groups of them, looking for trouble, drove down to the beach looking for friends or mischief. They ultimately gathered at Jet Boat Cove where the biggest "rumbles" seemed to occur. Jet Boat Cove developed a reputation as the place for bad action; those looking for trouble drove straight to that Cove.

Around the mid-1990s, the Park's rangers began to change tactics and use subtle psychology. Rolf Hechler said in late March 2007 that, as one of those tactics, they had changed the name of Jet Boat Cove— including on their maps—to Hot Springs Landing. When troublemakers arrived asking for directions to Jet Boat Cove, rangers said they didn't know where that was, or that there was no such place.

The Park also bought a quantity of three-thousand-pound Jersey wall barriers and lined them up, creating pathways from the road straight down to the water. Now, instead of being able to freely wander from group to group, the barriers forced them to drive or walk back up to the road before heading down to another campsite or group, slowing their momentum, preventing them from freely mingling. The cove's name change and those barriers effectively altered some of the lake's negativity. Those and other tactics the Park began using reduced misbehavior and violence.

After those changes, the park rangers were able to exercise firmer crowd control and could more strictly enforce the codes. The image of Elephant Butte Lake State Park began to improve, and it became a better recreational place for families with children.

Still, in late 2002, T or C resident, librarian Pat O'Hanlon, said gangs used Elephant Butte on weekends and holidays as a setting for confrontations with other gangs. "Several times a year they come here to kill each other," she said.

This area of southern New Mexico, along I-25 and the Rio Grande, was a major international drug corridor. In March 1999, there were federal Border Patrol checkpoints on either side of Truth or Consequences on I-25. One was just a few miles north, and the other was between T or C and Las Cruces. Large drug busts, including dangerous meth-labs in residential areas, were common.

Vast open spaces and a sparse population characterize Sierra County. The eastern half of the county is the federally owned no man's land of White Sands Missile Range and Proving Grounds, where the first atomic bomb was detonated. A smaller portion is state-owned. What little private land there is has few people, not counting the temporary tourists around the lake.

Elephant Butte was one of three incorporated "cities" in Sierra County. Truth or Consequences was the largest of those, and the only one with a municipal police department. Small, poorly financed and understaffed even for a community of its uninflated size, the police department was constantly stressed.

In addition to the small Truth or Consequences city police department, the law enforcement of Sierra County was comprised of one or two State Police officers stationed in the area and the chronically understaffed County Sheriff's office. Additional law enforcement could come from U.S. Border Patrol, U.S. Forest Service rangers,

State Game and Fish officers, plus state and federal park rangers, whose jurisdictions were the areas inside their parks.

Elsewhere throughout New Mexico, only municipal police officers, or county deputies or State Police officers, respond to calls within their own specific jurisdictions, unless they call in other agencies to assist them. That forest and park rangers and border patrol agents routinely responded directly to calls from central dispatch reflected the shortage of police officers in Sierra County.

All firefighters were volunteers.

^^^^^^^

On the afternoon of March 22, 1999, Border Patrol Agent Bob Johnston and Deputies Peter Bowidowicz and Lucas Alvarez were the first to see and question Ray's victim, Cindy Vigil, who had been kidnapped in Albuquerque.

That same afternoon, Deputies David Elston and Bowidowicz, their sheriff, Terry Byers, and Elephant Butte Lake State Park Rangers Mike Lanford and Chris DeGasse were the first to see the crime scene at the residence on 513 Bass Road.

Very soon, however, an even more important and bizarre crime scene would be discovered.

For months after the case began, the name and identity of Cindy Vigil, the first of three to claim to law enforcement that she had been kidnapped and sexually abused by Ray, was redacted (blackened) from legal documents seen by the public. The media and the public only knew her as the Albuquerque Woman, Jane Doe Number One or "the first known victim".

Vigil told the first officers on the case that David (David Parker Ray, fifty-nine) and Cindy (Cynthia Lea Hendy, thirty-nine) forcibly abducted her from Central Avenue in Albuquerque three days before her escape from their trailer home at 513 Bass Road. During her three days of captivity, she said, she endured hours of unbelievable sexual torture at the hands of David, accompanied and assisted by his live-in girl friend, Cindy.

Chapter 6 – Cindy's Escape

Late on the afternoon of March 22, when a New Mexico State Police officer—Agent Wesley LaCuesta—arrived at the scene at Bass Road, the sheriff, deputies and park rangers gave him their reports. He learned the suspects were already being held for questioning, and he saw the scene was secured. Therefore, he believed his first duty was to question the victim while she was available, and before she might be too medically sedated to talk. After briefings, he rushed to Sierra Vista Hospital in Truth or Consequences.

Agent LaCuesta, stationed at the State Police's district headquarters in Socorro, automatically became the primary or case manager because he was the first State Police officer to arrive on the scene.

He was the first to fully question Cindy Vigil.

New Mexico's law enforcement officers, and many of its residents, knew that the Albuquerque area, from where Cindy Vigil said she had been abducted, was noted for prostitution and pornography outlets. Vigil admitted to LaCuesta that she was a prostitute.

He expected her to be an unreliable witness; but looking at her and the physician's medical report and the Polaroid photographs taken at the hospital showing her injuries, he did not doubt that something terrible, beyond the realm of her normally awful life, had happened to her.

Getting details from a sexual abuse or rape victim was always difficult; it could even be with someone whose primary livelihood was sex.

Victims who report rape must subsequently give—to officers, investigators, and perhaps later in courtrooms before the public and media—specific details of what was done to them, adding to their feelings of indignity and shame. It is little wonder few rape cases are reported. From the onset, such cases required a trained officer, preferably female, to question victims. But no female state officer was stationed in Sierra County at the time.

Flooded with relief by her escape from the horrifying experience, Vigil was talkative. She described her experience in detail to LaCuesta.

On the third day of her captivity, she said, she was tied to a bed in the large add-on room of the dwelling, with the metal collar around her neck connected to a chain padlocked to a restraint fastened to the wall. Ray and Hendy had restrained her, most of the prior time they had her in another smaller, but more horrible, room completely filled with torture tools.

She was coming down from a bad heroin trip and was terribly sick, with vomiting and diarrhea. Ray became tired of unfastening her and taking her to the bathroom. When she did go, Ray forced her to crawl on her hands and knees, holding onto a leash attached to the neck collar as if she were a dog.

That day, he had to return to work and leave her alone with Hendy, which he knew was a potential disaster because Hendy was dumb.

Vigil knew Ray's thinking by the way he talked to Hendy, as if he thought she was an idiot. And she knew it by signs tacked on the walls in the bedroom of horrors where they had kept her most of the time. "Never trust a captive," a sign warned in large letters. Vigil, later also some of the investigators, thought Ray addressed that warning to Hendy.

Early on Vigil's third day of captivity, Ray had moved her to the den and attached a longer chain to her collar, giving her just enough slack to get off the bed by herself and reach a nearby bucket. Ray did not like unpleasant messes; those made him angry and even more punitive, almost as much as when a captive tried to kick or bite him. He said he always warned his victims that those behaviors could lead to deadly punishment.

Ray had put on his uniform—green pants and beige shirt—and left early that morning. Vigil supposed he went to work. Her only hope to escape was while she was alone with Hendy. All that day while Ray was gone, she pestered Hendy to let her go.

"Please! Please let me go," Vigil repeatedly begged her. "He's going to kill me, you know he is. He told you he's going to kill me; I heard him tell you. You know it.

"And you'll be locked up for murder with him. My friend saw you and him take me from Central. He knows you took me. He knows who you and David are. He introduced David to me. He remembers your license plate number; he always does that to look out for me. He'll know how to find me. You have to let me go."

Indeed, Vigil had overheard Ray tell Hendy that they would kill her when they were through playing with her.

Hendy sighed and told Vigil to behave and endure the pain; it would soon be over. "Then we will let you go," she said.

Vigil knew Hendy lied.

Even while she had hung by her wrists and ankles from the ceiling yesterday, Vigil never stopped trying to persuade Hendy to set her free. She was in pain, and terribly ill. Besides her other miseries, her captors hadn't fed her and she badly needed a hit of heroin; Ray said she wasn't worth wasting any of his on her.

Despite her pain and sickness, she never let up on Hendy while she was alone with her that third day.

Trying to make a break was worth dying for or killing Hendy. She'd die anyway. She had to get away no matter what.

Early that afternoon, while Ray was still gone, Hendy came into the room where Vigil lay tied to the bed. While Hendy busied herself around the room—Cindy supposed the bitch thought she was cleaning house—she dropped onto a nearby table the key that locked the chain anchoring her to the eyebolt in the wall.

She lay still and kept quiet, watching and waiting for her opportunity. Hendy left the room, probably for only a few minutes. With the slack given to her in the chain only that day, Vigil was just barely able to slip off the edge of the bed and reach the small table with her feet, dragging it towards her with her toes until she could reach the key. Once she got it in her hand, she shoved the table back in place so Hendy would not be suspicious when she returned. She also picked up a nearby ice pick.

Vigil managed, with some panicked fumbling and dropping the key several times, to unlock the chain's lock just as Hendy walked back into the room. Vigil hid the ice pick behind her and lay very still, trying to will her heart to stop pounding. She avoided eye contact, willing Hendy to notice nothing unusual.

"Oh no you don't!" Hendy suddenly yelled when she saw the key missing from the table. "You ain't going nowhere!" she screamed as she lunged at her. Vigil jumped from the bed and started to run on rubbery legs, but fell to her knees. Hendy grabbed a nearby lamp and began smashing it on Cindy's head.

Just thirty minutes earlier, Vigil believed her tortured pelvis and legs, after being bound for three days in an extreme position, would never let her walk again.

Adrenalin and determination pumped into her from deep reserves she thought were empty. She got on her feet and stabbed at Hendy's face and head with the ice pick. Hendy turned away, throwing up arms and hands to protect herself from the sharp instrument Vigil wildly wielded.

Vigil managed to punch Hendy in her stomach with her elbow and stab her in the head with the ice pick. Hendy went down, her breath knocked out of her. While she recovered from the shock of the blow and her profusely bleeding head injury, Vigil smashed the glass of a window behind a heavy drape. She saw it was too jaggedly sharp an exit, and it didn't offer freedom anyway. Something still covered the window from the outside. She found the patio door open and ran, naked, out of the residence, stumbling and often falling hard onto her knees as she went across the porch and yard and down the road as fast as her legs would let her.

She told the officer that her ordeal in Ray and Hendy's house was mostly in a bedroom filled with torture things, but she heard them say they intended to take her to a nearby trailer that Ray called his Toy Box. There, they promised her with glee, the torture and their fun and games would be even worse for her. That was where she expected to die.

She told LaCuesta things already done to her included mechanical rape, electrical shock, puncturing her labia and breasts, and being hung from the ceiling by her breasts attached to a pulley with weights.

LaCuesta questioned Cindy Vigil for several hours, before releasing her to her father and grandmother, who had come to take her back to Albuquerque.

Chapter 7 – Warrants

LaCuesta, as head of the investigation, had much to do and a large responsibility. Only a portion of his problems was securing the property's large perimeter and protecting the crime scene in the dwelling until state crime investigators and crime scene analysts arrived. That security alone required considerably more manpower than was available. He had seen, heard and read enough reports to know that this would be a big case with multiple victims.

There had already been five persons wandering around inside the residence: two deputies, two state park rangers and the sheriff. A deputy and a state park ranger were the first to enter, having no idea what they would find, or that the scene would be an important one. How much training did any of them have about protecting and preserving crime scenes? All of their fingerprints, even footprints—shoes or boots—would need to be added to the case file for comparison. They had to report everywhere they touched or stepped to eliminate their own trace evidence. The importance of not disturbing the scene should have been repeatedly hammered into them. But was it? The average state uniform cop often received even less crime scene training than deputies and community police. Not seniority, skill or experience, only fate—timing and place—had made LaCuesta the State's primary on this case.

Candid cops are the first to tell you that cops are the greatest cause of compromised crime scenes and, ultimately, of unproven courtroom cases. That is one of the main reasons bad guys go free. That and their wily defense attorneys.

The Nicole Brown Simpson and Ronald Goldman murders—better known as the O. J. Simpson case, the Martha Moxley and JonBenet Ramsey murders were some of the recent, better known and—in 1999—unsolved or legally unresolved cases; in part because investigators allowed the crime scenes to be compromised, and because the suspects had excellent teams of attorneys defending them.

Police know a case that stands up in court largely depends upon that rare thing: an uncontaminated crime scene. LaCuesta hoped the first responding officers had immediately understood this was a major crime scene, requiring more expertise and credentials than any of them possessed.

Hell, it required more experience and equipment than anyone within one hundred or two hundred miles possessed, certainly himself included.

To head a case of this magnitude—LaCuesta could see it would not be a simple one—required an officer with considerable management skills as well as experience in handling criminal investigations.

When this case broke, Wes LaCuesta had been a uniformed state patrolman for eight years and a plainclothes agent for only three months. He had no supervisory experience.

Within the New Mexico State Police, prior specialized investigative training or experience was not required when officers became agents or detectives straight from training academy or by transfer from uniform division. Nor was training necessarily given to them after they became detectives.

Because at the time there was no available investigative supervisor in Socorro or Las Cruces, LaCuesta called State Police Sgt. Keith Clayton Rogers. LaCuesta knew Rogers' specialty was narcotics and criminal investigations, and that he was an experienced investigator and case supervisor who had managed cases.

Among the elitist State Police, Sgt. K. C. Rogers had a no-nonsense reputation. He was known for getting the job done whatever it took, even if, in the process, he angered many, including others in law enforcement. His ramrod techniques might be offensive to some, but they were often effective.

Late that afternoon, LaCuesta and others in his State Police district in Socorro called additional state investigators besides Rogers. That called-up state crime investigative team included: Special Agent Lou Mallion of the Department of Public Safety, special investigations division; Agent John Briscoe, New Mexico State Police criminal investigations unit; State Police Agent Jennie Tafoya, stationed in Albuquerque; and State Police Agent Frank Jacoby from Santa Fe.

Rogers, Mallion and Briscoe were stationed in Roswell. But Mallion was in a meeting in Albuquerque in the late afternoon of

March 22 when his beeper went off and he was told to proceed without delay to Elephant Butte.

That State team was accustomed to receiving short-notice calls requiring immediate take-offs to crime scenes anywhere in New Mexico, and was always prepared. After receiving their calls, the team members packed their few necessities not already in their units and rushed to Elephant Butte and Truth or Consequences in southwestern New Mexico.

From Albuquerque, the trip was 149 miles. The trip was 208 miles from Santa Fe, about 59 miles further north than Albuquerque. From Roswell, it was 217 miles to T or C.

LaCuesta hoped summoned expertise would arrive soon. This case was already much too large for him to manage alone.

Larger New Mexico cities, such as Albuquerque, Santa Fe, Las Cruces and Roswell, had their own well-trained investigators and technical equipment, processed their own crime scenes and sent the gathered evidence to the state crime lab in Santa Fe for analysis. Smaller communities and rural areas like Sierra County had to call in state investigators.

Cameras—a basic and vital tool for working crime scenes—were not standard issue to New Mexico State Police officers in the uniform division in 1999. Their limited budget did not provide for them. Besides, crime scenes required costly cameras with high resolution.

A few city police departments, such as Carlsbad, had begun carrying digital cameras to expedite the processing of mug-shots, accidents and crime scenes by 2000, but they were still not issued to the average State Police officer.

Quality cameras were only one of many types of forensic-gathering tools required to properly analyze a crime scene.

Upon arrival, the state crime scene investigators would minutely record the scene by photography, measurements and other means, and carefully gather the evidence—fingerprints, blood and hair samples and all those other delicate traces that must be lifted and analyzed—and take or send them to modern, well-equipped forensics laboratories in Santa Fe and Albuquerque.

There are two national parks or forests nearby, the Gila Wilderness and the Cibola National Forest. One of the paradoxes of New Mexico is that close to this barren desert area are high mountains and large expanses of woodland forests. That one was named a wilderness signified that area's ruggedness. LaCuesta was relieved the two suspects had been quickly apprehended. That was a great advantage to this case.

Available officers, needed to help secure the perimeter of the scene at 513 Bass Road and other unspecialized but essential assignments, could include uniformed State Police assigned to the local and outlying districts, the County Sheriff and his deputies, U.S. Border Patrol, U.S. Forest Service rangers, Game and Fish officers, and State and Federal Park rangers.

Elsewhere in New Mexico, law enforcement agencies are very territorial. Federal Border Patrol agents, state Game and Fish officers, Federal and State Forest and Park rangers, even if available and capable, would not respond to police calls unless they were asked to help, or something about the situation indicated one of their agencies should be involved. An undocumented alien, an untagged deer carcass in a car trunk, or a kilo of heroin could bring in officers of one of those agencies. The initial sighting of a naked woman running down a residential road would not. Except in Elephant Butte.

That such diverse agencies did respond to routine police calls in Sierra County was just one of that county's many anomalies. Sierra County had little money and few law enforcement resources. The few municipal police, county deputies and assigned state officers could always use outside help; in fact, they depended upon it. The various agencies backed up each other and worked together, sometimes compatibly and sometimes not.

With the known suspects already arrested, LaCuesta knew officers should quickly go to Elephant Butte Lake State Park to gather David Parker Ray's employment records, and begin interviewing his work associates, neighbors and other people who might know him.

Primary were arrest warrants for David Parker Ray and Cynthia Hendy, yet to be served on them while they were held at the State Park office and sheriff's office. LaCuesta would have to write an affidavit and arrest warrant for each of them, along with the initial affidavit and warrant for search of the premises. He would write them, but Magistrate Judge Thomas Pestak in T or C must sign and officially issue them.

LaCuesta expected to write more affidavits and search warrants, and perhaps more arrest warrants, as the investigation progressed. He suspected that process had only just begun.

Search warrants might include other areas of Ray's premises besides inside his residence, as well as inside his vehicles. The victim had mentioned a nearby trailer. Those warrants had to be in-hand before crime scene discovery and analysis could begin. LaCuesta knew correctly and legally writing those affidavits and warrants was critical.

Many officers are intimidated by having to write those documents that are filed, usually becoming public record and vital parts of court proceedings, especially in an important criminal case. Besides, a literary aptitude seldom figures among cops' skills.

It never fails to amaze cops how easily criminal defense attorneys find legal ways to block evidence that even they know prove their client's guilt. Protesting improperly executed warrants are some of their ploys.

Soon, probably before investigators arrived, it would be too dark to see inside the dwelling, buildings and trailers and to carefully search the grounds inside the chain-link fence. Initial responders had assumed the primary scene and evidence was confined to inside the dwelling, but there could also be evidence in adjacent trailers and recreational vehicles, including boats, in the yard.

Excitement and getting in a hurry can and does cause as many problems at a crime scene as plain carelessness. Calm and patience are vital.

Judge Pestak, in his T or C office on Date Street a few blocks from the courthouse, approved the affidavit for the search warrant and signed the search warrant, and approved the affidavit for arrest warrants and issued those warrants. His job was just to analyze and agree that what the officer had written on the documents presented to him was just and right, that there was probable cause for the arrests or search. He signed them and his job was done. For the moment.

It is the law enforcement officer, usually the primary on the case, who creates and manually writes both sets of documents he presents to the judge. If the judge approves them, the officer is required to give oath swearing everything therein is correct and accurate. Then the officer and judge sign the affidavits, and the judge signs the warrants.

Next, the officer delivers the search warrant to the scene or to the person to be searched. If it is a scene, ideally the officer gives the owner of the property a copy of the warrant and he is present to witness the search to assure his rights are not violated. That also protects the officers so the suspect cannot later claim his personal possessions were stolen or damaged during the search. With Ray and Hendy, however, that wasn't going to happen. They were in custody.

The requirement for the search warrant comes from the U.S. Constitution's Fourth Amendment. It became binding over two-hundred years ago, guaranteeing citizens' rights to privacy and to be safe in their persons, houses, offices, vehicles, papers and effects against unreasonable searches and seizures. Its purpose is to keep the government from being unfairly invasive.

There must be probable cause for a search or seizure, and the affidavit sworn to by oath or affirmation. The place to be searched and the things to be seized must be explicitly described. An uninvolved judge—a neutral person placed between the person whose property is being searched or seized, and the law enforcement officer—issues the warrants. While it is a precious citizen's right, for cops in need of search warrants in a hurry, the Fourth Amendment's time-consuming red tape can be frustrating.

If the documents do not clearly specify the items to be searched for, if the descriptions are too broad and sweeping, the defendant's attorney could say the search warrant was aimless or a "fishing expedition" and, therefore, items found would be inadmissible in court, even if they were vital to the successful prosecution of the case. Yet, the officer narrows his field of discovery if the itemized items are too specific in the warrant; unlisted items found in the search may not be taken. Those sometimes vital unmentioned items found must be left where they are until another affidavit and warrant are issued. That requires the scene to be secured by at least one officer while another goes for another warrant.

The scene cannot be left unsecured. Evidence is likely to disappear, or the defendant's attorney could say evidence is inadmissible in court because others had access to the unguarded scene. With the warrant, there must be reasonable belief that the specified items to be searched for will be found, that they will be found where they are expected to be, and found within the specified time frame.

The items to be searched for and, if found, seized for evidence, are listed on the documents. Those items must fall under one or more categories.

"Contraband" is something unlawful to possess, like narcotics and other illegal drugs, or a sawed-off shotgun. "Fruits of the crime" are monies or stolen goods, as in the case of a robbery, burglary, or embezzlement. Generally, "instrumentalities of the crime" are tools necessary to commit the crime, such as facemasks, gloves, lock picks and crowbars in the case of a burglary. "Weapons" are those used, or to be used, to cause bodily harm while committing the crime.

In this case, the line was fuzzy between "instrumentalities" and "weapons." Tools and other devices of torture seen in Ray's residence fit either one. However, it did not matter which they were for the sake of those documents, as long as the sought-for pieces of evidence fit one or more of the required categories.

Last, but the most difficult to list prior to a search, and what seemed to be the largest category in this case, is what is called "mere evidence." That is evidence or proof that supports the probability that the crime was committed, and committed to the suspected victim or by the suspected person. In this case, the list should include traces of blood that could be Cindy Vigil's, another victim's or Hendy's—as Vigil said she had injured her. Since this was to be a sexual abuse or rape case, it could include traces of semen, hair, victims' clothing and other personal effects, photographs depicting torture of victims, and sex abuse devices.

The initial search warrant would only be for topical searches; in other words, investigators could not tear into walls and rip up floors.

LaCuesta could not, at least not yet, include a search warrant for the grounds because he had no specific reason to search there. He knew those five responding officers had already walked across the grounds and circled the dwelling, as well as entered it. Then the sheriff had the wisdom to put up his crime scene tape around the perimeter of the residence and hold it secure, keeping out everyone including other cops, until more qualified officers arrived. Hopefully, no one else, besides those initial five, had gone beyond where the tape was placed.

Before the investigation was completed, the crime scene tape would be expanded to include the entire 513 Bass Road lot, not just around the residence.

Since the first of the specialized investigators wouldn't arrive until late in the day, probably after sundown, they might postpone further search of the property until the next morning.

It was almost dark by the time LaCuesta obtained the signed warrants from Judge Pestak in T or C and returned to Bass Road.

The sun setting behind the San Mateos lit the western sky in a final burst of spectacular color, and illuminated Fra Cristobal's jagged mountaintops. A cool wind blew off areas of the lakeshore, bringing the scent of desert willows and marshy water. That added surrealism to the crime scene.

Chapter 8 – DPS

LaCuesta dispatched many calls before the next daybreak.

One of the calls went to his district commander stationed in Socorro sixty miles away, who in turn called his boss, Frank Taylor, Chief of the New Mexico State Police, and Taylor's boss, Darren White, Secretary of the New Mexico Department of Public Safety.

Because of LaCuesta's limited experience with criminal investigations, NMSP Agent Rich Libicer of Las Cruces was called in to share the management of the case with him. Therefore, early into the investigation, the case had two primaries. Among other responsibilities, Libicer would write many of the affidavits and warrants.

The political structure of the state police varies in different states. In New Mexico, the State Police Division is under the jurisdiction of the Department of Public Safety, but was not always that way.

As with state agencies in most states, their heads are usually politically appointed.

Until the early 1970s, the boards of commissioners, made up of individuals appointed by the sitting governor, governed their various state agencies. Each agency was a stand-alone entity, subject only to its respective state board of commissioners and the governor. That included the State Police agency.

Then a new governor, Toney Anaya, reorganized the state's structure. He made all of the boards that governed their individual state agencies—including such diverse groups as livestock, beauticians, public schools, highway, oil conservation—advisory only. In the process, some of those agencies were moved from under one cabinet to another. The State Police was placed under a new cabinet, the Criminal Justice Department. The Department of Motor Vehicles, Motor Transportation Division and Alcohol Beverage Control (which included what later became Special Investigations Division) were under Tax and Revenue.

Then along came another governor—Garrey Carruthers—who again reorganized the state's structure. In 1987, the legislature created the Department of Public Safety, under which several state agencies were placed, including their own Special Investigations Division (SID) and the much larger State Police Division. The Motor Transportation Division was later added to this group. The boards of each of those groups remained advisory only.

Despite that, many New Mexico State Police officers considered themselves a stand-alone agency and a power unto themselves.

Of necessity, State Police are trained from the onset to have high-level self-confidence. Usually alone on highways with backup a half-hour to an hour or more away, uniformed officers must act as if, and fully believe, they are in control of any kind of situation.

Many State Police officers never fully accepted being under the Department of Public Safety. Along with that resentment was an attitude of superiority towards their smaller sister agency, Special Investigations. "They're not one of us," is a common refrain by many uniform and plain-clothes state officers when speaking of SID. "They didn't go through SP academy," is a reason given by some State Police officers for discounting the value of Special Investigations Division agents.

SID agents still specialize in the enforcement of alcohol, tobacco and gaming laws. However, they are also trained to investigate crimes and analyze crime scenes, and often their agents have more training and experience than their State Police counterparts, and far more than uniformed State Police officers, who generally received little during academy, and none following it.

Some State Police officers believe themselves superior to any other branch of law enforcement, such as county deputies and municipal police officers, some with much more experience and training. A city uniform cop in one of the larger municipalities might see more action in a week than a state uniform officer might see on the highway—chasing tail-lights as other police describe it—in a month or year, depending upon where he is assigned. Domestic disputes, dealing with gang problems and drug busts usually put city cops over the top in all but the most rural neighborhoods. However, the State Police officer assigned to outlying areas might be the only available law enforcement and must handle alone all situations as they occur.

Darren White was another State Police bone of contention concerning DPS. White, Gary Johnson's neighbor, was a uniformed sergeant with the Albuquerque Police Department. When Johnson became governor, as is often standard procedure with new governors to build their own handpicked administrations, it was out with the old and in with the new. He appointed new cabinet heads and state advisory boards. Johnson chose Darren White, with no prior supervisory experience, as DPS secretary—New Mexico's top cop over the state's various law enforcement divisions, including State Police.

Throughout the case's investigation in 1999, the media frequently quoted White; his impulsive comments often irritated investigators as well as the defense.

^^^^^^^

By late afternoon and early evening of March 22, the crime team—comprised of DPS' Special Investigations Agent Lou Mallion, and State Police officers and agents K. C. Rogers, John Briscoe, Jennie Tafoya and Frank Jacoby—arrived in T or C.

New Mexico, and Las Cruces in particular being so close to Mexico, had its alien problems; but Rogers, Mallion and Briscoe took a ration of teasing from the other officers about being from Roswell, known for a totally different kind of alien, the gray or green variety.

Mallion, a trim man with the build of a runner, which he was, with dark hair and sharply defined facial features, was a pilot and had a military background in special ops. He still flew Civil Air Patrol search and rescue operations. Prior to this case, he had more than a thousand hours of training in crime scenes. Before he joined SID, he had been a Roswell Police Department criminal investigations officer and had worked for years on crime scenes and criminal investigations, accruing extensive experience.

After beginning to work for the state, he was the only SID agent and the only non-State Police officer called to serve on State Police investigations to process state level crime scenes. He was probably the most qualified and experienced.

However, some State Police officers did not want DPS agents having any involvement, beyond routine perimeter security, with the Ray case. Because the State Police was in charge, this intra-departmental conflict limited Mallion's overall involvement to one area.

"You have to understand something," said K. C. Rogers in an interview in late 2002. "DPS agents are not one of us. They didn't go through our Academy. But I told the guys that Lou was all right."

State Police Academy, once twelve inclusive weeks of training, is now sixteen weeks.

Training in the academy had some similarities to that of Army boot camp. Some of that stressful training had lessened in recent years, as it had in Army boot camp, military academies and schools and, to a lesser degree, hazing in college fraternities. Reducing some of that became necessary at the academy because of the large dropout rate. State Police already had trouble getting enough applicants to pass background checks and tests—drug, psychological, written and physical—to even qualify. They could not afford to have a large attrition rate at the training academy, further reducing numbers of their potential recruits.

Some NMSP recruits who would have been valuable, especially older ones and those who had served in the military, decided they did not have to "go through that degrading bullshit" to become a police officer, and dropped out of academy.

The State Police Training Academy was not just physically, but also emotionally, stressful for recruits. In-your-face instructors routinely intimidated them. However, those officers who completed the academy, especially even tougher earlier sessions, had a shared experience that bonded them, adding to the creation of an elite brotherhood. State Police officers who fully experienced and graduated from academy felt superior to other law enforcement officers who had not experienced it.

^^^^^^^

When the state's investigative team individually arrived at Bass Road, no other State Police officer besides LaCuesta was at the scene. Rich Libicer had not yet arrived. The team stood around waiting for LaCuesta to process the initial affidavits and warrants.

When he returned and they had the search warrant for the premises, the team carefully entered the residence.

"We began searching the house. It was a typical singlewide trailer layout. There was the living room and kitchen, and a hall leading to two bedrooms with a bathroom separating them. As you came inside through the front door, to the right was a railing and step-down to the big open room of the add-on," said Mallion. "When we looked around, we could see it was a place of bondage."

"Cindy's clothes were found piled in the bedroom at the end of the hall." They quickly looked around the residence. "I thought I knew everything about sex, but I didn't have a clue! I was flabbergasted, everyone was flabbergasted, at what we saw in that place."

Mallion added, "Do you know what a drink glass with a hole drilled in the bottom would be used for? I didn't either until I later saw Ray's illustrations."

"Eyebolts everywhere, even in the kitchen, in the ceilings, in the walls. There were all kinds of sex tools and devices. I didn't realize I was naïve. I had no idea what many of them were for until I later saw Ray's illustrated journals and charts that told how they were used. Ray made most of them himself. There were straps, chains, whips, dildos of varying sizes. We just backed up, collected ourselves and decided we had to get out of there and regroup."

The detectives quickly saw that Cindy Vigil was not Ray's only victim.

Within the first hours, the Elephant Butte Lake State Park loaned their headquarters' training center and hangar near the lake as the investigation's command control post. It was a perfect set-up; a stationary building, completely enclosed by a fence and locked gate, and close to Bass Road.

"It was a secured post," said K. C. Rogers in late 2002. "First time ever the State Police was set up so fast to work a case. In less than 24 hours we had eight phones. Everybody recognized what kind of case it was, and the need to get as many people involved as quickly as possible," he said.

Via the media, the police asked citizens to call with information through New Mexico Crime Stoppers and to the phone numbers at the case's headquarters.

K. C. Rogers, the first State Police officer with supervisory experience at the scene, was in charge of the command post.

He said, "I'd spent a lot of years in state narcotics. We were trained to speak up. If you don't speak up, you're the only one to blame. So we're very fast to say we don't like something or to say we do like something. We don't have a problem telling supervisors what we think, all those things that tend to hinder investigations with everybody else. In Narcotics, we have to make decisions fast that involve many different details. We know it needs doing so we say 'Do it!' Criminal investigations move much slower. At first I spent a lot of time [working this case] saying 'We need this,' and they'd say, 'Why?' and I'd say, 'Because I say we do!'"

By early the next morning, March 23, the State Police crime team began methodically processing the scene in the residence. "In the add-on part was where the victims were initially taken," Mallion later said. "Then they were taken into the front bedroom, the bondage room. Everyone was flabbergasted," he said, repeatedly using that word, by the assortment of sexual tools and devices they saw in that room. "Pure bondage and S and M stuff."

A small female dog, part Boston bulldog, wandered aimlessly around in the dwelling, underfoot and confused, while investigators began their searches.

Chapter 9 – The Dwelling

Crime scene investigators entering the dwelling by the front door found themselves in the orange-carpeted living room. On a shelf sat a small white ceramic devil's head, with stuck-out tongue and horns. That and an upside-down cross hanging on the wall in the next room made officers think of witchcraft or satanic worship.

On a bookcase resided an array of family photos, including of one of Ray's sons, a young man in Army uniform. The lower bookshelves contained many books, including a multiple-volume set titled *Man and Woman*. Inside a drawer they found a pearl-handled gun and many tubes of Super Glue. They later learned that Ray used the glue to attach ropes to his victims' breasts while practicing what he called breast bondage.

Because the surface of the land dropped away towards the back of the lot, the original part of the dwelling—the mobile home—sat on a higher level than that of the rear add-on portion, or den. Despite the nearly three-foot difference in floor level, a large portion of the living room and den were open to each other.

In the den, a bed snuggled in a corner against the elevated floor of the living room, the top surface of the bed nearly at the same level as the floor of the living area, with only an open wrought-iron railing separating them. Officers photographed and documented the green glass from the broken lamp on the floor and on the light blue quilted floral bedspread. They also photographed the nearby table with the unisex urinal smeared with blood, and the unopened packages of prophylactics. Beside the bed on the floor, nearly hidden by the drooping bedspread, they saw an icepick, a prescription bottle and two bunches of long strands of brown hair. And the dry blood-spatter on the wall paneling beside the bed; hooks, eyebolts, chains and padlocks attached to the walls beside the bed; and the hooks and eyebolts attached to the ceiling.

Woven Mexican blankets covered a window near the bed and large shards of glass sparkled below it on the floor. When investigators pulled back the blankets, they found a broken windowpane; however, wooden paneling nailed outside the window rendered it purposeless. That confirmed what Cindy had said. A brass-colored crucifix hung upside down beside a calendar on one paneled wall; and a flat-topped iron potbellied stove, its pipe passing through a leak-stained ceiling with missing tiles, hunkered near one wall.

Two green Elephant Butte Lake State Park jackets, and two light-colored straw western-cut hats above them, hung against the wall, giving investigators the eerie feeling of two people watching them from the end of the room. A nearby door led into a storage area.

Once officers knew to recognize them, they noticed hooks, eye-bolts, and restraint devices everywhere.

The large partially opened sliding glass door leading to the back yard was heavily draped. A small white teddy bear lay on the floor of the threshold, as if dropped by a fleeing child.

Returning to the original mobile home portion of the dwelling, a door opened at the end of the hall to the master bedroom. On the bed's headboard was a quantity of paperback novels and sex devices. In the room, investigators found and documented what they called a rape kit: an attaché-type case containing a toggle bolt, chains, and various-sized dildos. They found three handguns around the room and in the closet. They also found a Sam Browne belt, a stun-gun, a computer and a sound system with a varied collection of mostly commercial audiotapes, especially by western music artists. The closet held women's and men's clothing, including Elephant Butte Lake State Park uniforms.

In the small bathroom, crime scene investigators documented the blood-smeared overflowing pink hospital-issue bedpan sitting in the bathtub and the bloodstained rug in front of the toilet.

The investigators' adrenalin really kicked in when they opened the door to the front bedroom. They knew it was Ray's primary bondage room.

On the top of a dresser, neatly set out in rows, were all kinds and sizes of dildos, rolls of tape, pliers, scissors, clamps, bolts and a bottle of Hot Damn! liquor. Above the dresser hung straps, chains, handcuffs, whips, and leather harnesses—some of which were motorized. Like snakes about to strike, a large quantity of chains, ropes and nylon straps coiled on the floor. They saw and photographed the neatly labeled 24" to 41" Ankle Spreader, the long black bar with stirrups at either end; and also photographed the similar device, the 17" Knee Spreader—a black bar with curving pieces attached at either end. A black padded bench or table, with legs folded, leaned against one wall; on the floor sat a box with knobs to control electrical flow and amps. Also on the floor lay large lead fishing weights and sinkers, a gun holster and a wide wadded strip of silver duct tape, apparently a used gag.

Contents of what investigators regarded as another rape kit included a bottle of Hot Damn! liquor, a large stainless steel fixed-blade knife and an official-looking star badge with "State of New Mexico" and the state's seal in its center. The two "ribbons" on the metal badge, where the name of the agency and officer's rank would have been engraved, were blank.

A freestanding object, which the officers dubbed "the rocket" because of its shape, stood near a wall. It was a large, white upright dildo attached to the top of a pipe on a pedestal. The height of the dildo was adjustable. It had neatly marked inch measurements in red, and two rows of delicate but sharp white steel spikes surrounded the uppermost portion of its base—each spike meticulously tipped with shiny red nail polish. Illustrating its evil purpose, a naked woman was depicted in a drawing, standing on her tiptoes, hanging from the ceiling by her wrists, with "the rocket" positioned beneath her, between her legs. When she relaxed her feet, as eventually she must, she would impale herself.

Mallion said a photo of a naked woman, strapped to a bench on her back, made him think she had two cherry-red balloons sitting on her chest until he saw Ray's how-to illustrations explaining the evil purpose of the drink glasses with holes in the bottoms. By aid of the hole, each of the woman's breasts was mechanically suctioned into the glass; then Ray tightly bound the base of each of her breasts, and removed the suction and the glass. The woman's severely constricted breasts looked like two separate red globes.

Investigators ultimately found several bottles of Dekuyper Hot Damn! Besides in the "rape kits," they were found in other areas of the dwelling and, the next day, in a trailer. Crime lab analysis later found drugs laced the liquor's contents. Hot Damn! was Ray's medium of choice for administering drugs to his victims. Investigators also found mind-altering pills inside writing pens.

In the dwelling, they discovered a nautical map of Elephant Butte Lake with large Xs marked on it. They drew conclusions from those maps.

^^^^^^^

They had just gotten accustomed to yesterday. Then along came today.

Later that morning of March 23, Agents Mallion and Briscoe approached a trailer, close to the dwelling, that had a padlocked door. First they had to call a locksmith.

"Holy shit!" thought Mallion, when they were able to look inside.

Seeing the residence and its contents should have prepared them for what they found in the trailer, but it did not. Nothing could have.

The interior immediately hit the two investigators with feelings of revulsion. Inside was a distinct aura of evil; they were nearly overcome by it. Although they found no one, dead or alive, inside, it contained a powerful odor of terror and death.

"A giant leap off the edge of reality," was what K. C. Rogers thought when he saw it after Mallion and Briscoe called him over. "Edgar Allan Poe on speed and worse."

Rogers later said, "Nobody would believe what we found unless they saw it for themselves. You could describe it but it doesn't have the same impact as being there and seeing it for yourself. We opened the door and it had an aura, an actual odor that smelled like very bad things happened in there. It damn sure smelled like death to us in there."

He continued, "We opened the door, we started to step in; we knew this was the number one piece of evidence, the main crime scene. We knew we needed to regroup. We decided: don't touch anything; let's get out. Briscoe and Mallion were the first who saw it; they just stood in the doorway, and then called me over to see it. I had the exact reaction they did: flabbergasted. No one else had seen it yet. After the FBI got there, Lou led the show in there," Rogers said.

"Right away, I knew to do this right, we needed to involve the FBI. I knew that would be a very unpopular decision, the State Police wouldn't go for it. The FBI has the reputation of taking over investigations and cutting the State out of the loop. All take of information, but no give. But to do the case right, I knew we needed them."

The FBI could not just come in and take over a case unless the local authorities called them in, or unless the case clearly showed it involved federal offenses. They needed a formal invitation.

K. C. said, "We ended up getting the New Mexico State Police captain and lieutenant of criminal investigations—Capt. Carlos Maldonado and Lt. Mark Weaver—to come down and walk through the crime scene. We ended up with the Deputy Chief, Herman Silva, coming down, too. Herman said, 'if this [the FBI] is what you believe we need, we'll give you approval for it.' I already had the wheels in motion; I knew it needed to be done. It was just a need to get the State Police to say 'Yes' and I could pick up the phone and say, 'Okay, get over here, you're invited.' They got in their cars and made the drive. The first of the four FBI guys arrived at one, the morning of the third day."

Initially, Rogers said, he called FBI Special Agent Dennis Kentigh, stationed in Roswell. He told Kentigh that the FBI was invited to come and assist with the case, but they had better tread carefully. If they took over the case and made him look bad with the State Police for calling them in, "I will tear down your house," he warned. "This is a State Police case, we are in charge and we will remain in charge."

Rogers asked Kentigh whom to call. Kentigh notified New Mexico's office of the Federal Bureau of Investigation in Albuquerque, and talked to Doug Beldon and Dave Kitchen, FBI's supervisory agents in New Mexico. They were among the first four FBI agents to arrive at the scene within twenty-four hours.

Long before daybreak on March 23, several units had gathered on Bass Road and officers already began to have trouble finding places to park on the narrow dirt road. In various uniforms, law enforcement officers stood just within the fenced property, keeping the scene secure, waiting for special investigators and additional warrants.

By early that morning, more than a dozen uniform and plain-clothes officers had gathered at 513 Bass Road. Those included Elephant Butte Lake State Park rangers in khaki and green, State Police agents in plain clothes as well as uniformed officers in black woolen uniforms with gray accents. Two New Mexico Mounted Patrol volunteers added a western touch with their gray shirts, black jeans, and black western boots and hats. There were Truth or Consequences cops, including T or C Police Chief David Bryant and

Sierra County Sheriff Terry Byers in plain clothes, and his deputies dressed in black. When Byers had taken office on January 1, 1999, just two-and-a-half months earlier, he decreed the Sierra County sheriff deputies' uniforms be changed to black from brown.

Also present was Sierra County Sheriff's Office Lt. Bobby Parks, with his large trademark moustache. Parks would soon retire, on June 30, after a thirty-year law enforcement career in Sierra County that had begun as a state park ranger.

The number of law enforcement officers working the case would grow tremendously, and the extent of the investigation would be beyond anyone's imagination.

Chapter 10 – The Toy Box

Most murderers kill only once and their crimes are impossible to anticipate. Mentally-ill killers are easy to catch because they are inept and usually not repeat offenders.

However, various renowned criminologists say serial killers seldom know their victims, which they choose randomly; and that type of killer is often very intelligent, making them much more difficult to identify and capture. Profiling is a law enforcement technology, not used by psychologists. Psychologists believe serial criminals cannot control what they do; they are psychologically driven. Law enforcement believes such criminals do make choices; it is their obsessions that push them towards the criminal choices they make.

Police and FBI invented profiling, which is only a pre-indicator. Serial killers, who are intelligent and plan ahead, also use profiling when they choose their victims. They are more concerned about being successful than about being caught.

Serial killers have three characteristic needs: control, dominance and manipulation. They also tend to have inadequate personalities, are underemployed or unemployed or have trouble holding jobs, and they have chronic problems with parents or girl friends. Many had been targets of bullying or teasing in their youth, feel a sexual inadequacy, and are determined to get what they want to fulfill their needs. Serial criminals have methods of operations (MOs), but can change them to make themselves more successful. They also have their own unique signatures wherein they leave some kind of marks or evidence, or take certain things with them for trophies.

There tend to be two kinds of criminals: organized and disorganized, which is a kind of MO in itself, but one they can change. A criminal may begin by being disorganized, but by continued practice, might become organized to make himself more successful. Once their cruel fantasies are set in motion, once they begin to act out, they cannot stop until they are stopped. It is a compulsion. Their actions gratify their egos. When they are stopped, they tend to credit themselves for their deeds because they need that ego gratification. According to criminologists, most serial criminals are male because the strong male sexual orientation is tightly tied to ego.

Serial killers have told investigators that they *had* to kill their victims. "I had to kill her to own her." Or "I had to kill her to possess her."

Something in their personal lives, usually a specific event, pushes them to begin acting out or to accelerate their actions, which are fantasy-driven.

Cruelty to animals is a usual early behavioral trait of those who become serial killers. Another early trait of some is self-mutilation. Profilers find that law enforcement tends to fascinate those types of criminals.

^^^^^^^

The axles of the white cargo trailer parked diagonally on the north side of the dwelling rested on blocks; two propane bottles sat on the tongue at the front end of the trailer and a small house-type air conditioner unit was placed high on the rear end, near an entrance door. Agents had seen a louvered ventilation insert at the upper center on the side of the trailer. A sharp-witted officer also noticed that the large TV antenna dish behind the trailer was aimed the wrong direction to benefit the resident's television transmission. Its placement effectively screened the view of the trailer's entrance from neighbors. The cargo trailer looked as if it was used for more than storage. It was that thought that had drawn officers to look inside it before looking in the other trailers and storage buildings on the premises.

A local locksmith had been called to break open the lock on the modified door of the trailer for the agents.

When they had looked in, Agents Lou Mallion and John Briscoe instantly knew they'd found Ray's Toy Box. This trailer topped the house of horrors.

That was when Mallion and Briscoe called K. C. Rogers over to see it, and then they waited for the FBI to arrive before proceeding further.

Looking in from the doorway, the officers had seen signs and posters on the wall. Directly in front of them, on the wall at the opposite end of the trailer, hung a sign printed in large red letters: SATAN'S DEN. Near it hung another sign, "Bondage Room," made with a freestanding office-desk-type nameplate. Grotesque, yet artistically rendered illustrations of how to sexually torture women covered the walls.

A peculiar chair was the trailer's centerpiece.

After FBI agents arrived, they and the state crime team first superficially examined the interior of this trailer.

They considered the enormous size of the task of cataloguing everything at the 513 Bass Road premises—including, besides this trailer, each room of the dwelling, the garage, other trailers and storage units, boats and vehicles.

They assigned a team to each area.

"The FBI have this polite, subtle way of telling us to stay out of their way," Mallion said with a small self-deprecating smile three years later. "Tony assigned me to the Toy Box," he said, as if FBI Agent-in-charge Tony Maxwell expected the assignment to keep Mallion occupied for a while. It did. This trailer, where Mallion spent the majority of his time, proved to hold the case's greatest amount of evidence. He became an expert on it and its contents, where the small team assigned by Maxwell to evidence recovery in the Toy Box, catalogued more than one thousand pieces of evidence there alone.

The large, odd-looking chair, unlike anything they had seen before, dominated the inside of the trailer. It took no imagination to realize that it was a unique, custom-made gynecological chair intended for no properly sanctioned purpose. The chair consisted of two separate pieces of padded black vinyl: a wide back and a seat. In front, where the back of a seated person's knees would rest, were two padded parts, apparently leg spreaders, that also provided means of immobilizing the legs separately with straps. The chair had foot stirrups, and various forms of restraint were attached to the chair and the overhead pulleys. Large and small weights (similar to the fishing sinkers seen in the dwelling) hung from the pulleys. The larger ones were used to lift or suspend the victim. Smaller weights attached to certain parts of her body were other devices of torture, as illustrated by Ray's records and drawings.

Among other things, it was an electric chair that must have brought death to some who sat in it. Attached to it were various devices. A black box, with lights and toggle switches, allowed the parts of the chair to be tilted and elevated or lowered into various positions. Multiple coils and wires ran from another box. Clamps and probes attached to the victim at the other end of the wires allowed the one controlling the box to apply varying degrees of shock and motorized torture.

An enclosed wooden cabinet, with doors and a sliding-bolt lock on the outside, stood against one wall beneath a small portable stove. Inside were two pullout shelves, the upper one of plywood. Investigators recognized the lower one, with bars surrounding heavy blue canvas and tie-downs; it nobly began life as a search and rescue basket. Both shelves were the length and width of a cot; the headroom above both was minimal. Eyebolts were strategically placed inside the cabinet where Ray stashed his victims. The shelves claustrophobically held two victims at a time. He simply closed the doors and locked them until he later chose to get out his live dolls to play with again.

An expensive stainless steel cabinet, the type used in physicians' examination rooms to hold equipment, was against another wall. The upper half or hutch portion had two glass doors. Inside, three shelves held various surgical instruments, tools, and sexual devices including dildos of varied sizes, some electrically powered. In the center of the lower shelf sat an object of witchcraft or Satanism: a three-candle candelabra with a small white replica of a human skull in its center. A blood-pressure cuff lay nearby. The cabinet also contained books—from published medical textbooks to activity logs written by David Parker Ray. The cops found more published books, as well as records meticulously kept by Ray detailing his exploits and his victims, in the lower portion of the cabinet and in other parts of the trailer.

A large array of cutting tools, including razors, knives, packets of extra blades, scalpels and scissors, lay in the two waist-high drawers of the stainless steel cabinet. Investigators found more instruments of torture in the lower portion of the cabinet, behind closed doors.

Three strategically-aimed cameras were set up close to the ceiling at opposite ends of the trailer. A video screen was suspended above where the victim was bound in the chair, placed where both she and her tormentor could watch what was done to her. One screen was a closed-circuit TV that transmitted the scene live—sight and sound—into the nearby residence. Ray could stay inside, comfortably relaxed on his couch, and view his victim being tortured by automated devices.

A large flesh-colored dildo, attached to a small windshield wiper motor and car battery, sat nearby on the floor.

Ray had been an avid anatomy student. He learned the marvelous human body comes equipped with built-in mechanisms for self-preservation. Everyone has a threshold, a point at which pain becomes unendurable. If the pain is continuous for a period of time at a constant level, the body adjusts its threshold to make it endurable. Knowing this, Ray designed his automated machines to deliver pain at variable levels. His victims could never become—psychologically or physically—accustomed to the pain he dealt them. He either gradually pushed up the pain level a notch, or his evil contrivances delivered intermittent pain.

Eventually—after searching the entire Bass Road property—investigators found only one recorded video cartridge pertinent to the case. That surprised them. With the elaborate video equipment, and given Ray's profile—one who would want to later relive his dirty deeds—they knew there must somewhere be a large quantity of videos. Finding his stash, which would help identify many of Ray's victims, became a primary concern, even an obsession, to the officers.

The cameras led investigators to conclude that Ray made porn, including videoed child pornography and snuff-films, to share with or sell to other perverts, as well as to personally enjoy.

Eyebolts were everywhere, attached to walls and ceilings. Agents found a leather mask, a black cape, chains, restraints and leather whips. Ray made many of his sophisticated devices; he probably scavenged some of the material from his job. Recovered records showed that he also sold some of his homemade *objets de Sade* to outlets catering to sadism and masochism.

In November 2002, Mallion said he had no idea what many of the devices were for, how they were used, until he began to study David Parker Ray's meticulous records, illustrations and written instructions.

Ray, with his considerable artistic skill, had filled journals and posters with graphic artwork in minute clinical detail on every inconceivable type of torture—like a surgeon impersonally, objectively writing a procedure for his medical students. On pages of a record book was advice to the torturer (himself) on how to deal with the captives—like a biology teacher instructing his students how to dissect a toad. It told how to frighten the victims (as if they weren't already terrified), how to position their bodies, how to totally immobilize them, and how to inflict on them extreme forms of pain. Instructions detailed how to tell victims how they would be raped and tortured.

In other words, in two separate steps, he told himself how to tell his victims, and then he told them.

Officers found a written script that Ray read to the victims at the beginning of their abduction, telling them graphically what was about to be done to them. Its purpose was to build their terror. This text, and audiotapes that he later recorded, showed how Ray's methods evolved.

In Ray's earlier days of criminal activity, he ad-libbed to each victim what would happen to them.

Being a perfectionist, he wanted to be sure he didn't omit an important detail or step, and that the fear-inducing information was perfected and identical each time he gave it to, or used it on, a victim. He also wanted to improve his efficiency. By now, he was snatching many girls and women. He tried to make each process identical to the last one, but it was easy to forget something. Therefore, he wrote a script that he read to each victim. Officers believe they had found one of those early scripts. Eventually, when he believed his torture methods and his script describing them were perfected, David Parker Ray recorded the text, in his own natural voice, on an audiocassette. Now, all he had to do was play it for each new victim. He had eliminated the effort of memorization but retained the fun part of watching their terrified reactions.

Somewhere along the way, Ray decided to tailor the monologue to victim type. One tape was designed for a school-age girl, a young, virginal type. Another was for prostitutes. In the Toy Box and in his residence, officers found nine somewhat different audiotapes, known as his "terror tapes." In one, a screaming victim could be heard in the background while he spoke into the mike.

Building suspense, adding to the victims' terror, was an important element of his bag of tricks. Ray tortured their minds as well as their bodies.

When officers first saw the audiocassettes on a small table, they recalled the Polaroid photographs they had seen in the dwelling. They supposed the audiotapes contained the sounds of women screaming.

The officers had mixed emotions when they later listened to those chilling recordings wherein Ray told his victims what would be done to them. The good news was, the tapes were more useful than they expected. The recordings, spoken in Ray's soft articulate voice, described in detail what he did to his victims. They would be effective "smoking guns" in a courtroom, guaranteeing his conviction.

After investigators saw all of Ray's records and posters, the exact purpose of each torture device became graphically, sickeningly clear. He also labeled many of his tools and devices, leaving no question as to their evil purposes.

Mallion later said, "Some devices were in twos, matching pairs, like the sets of water glasses Ray used for breast bondage."

He commented that the evolution of Ray's skills was evident, when comparing Ray's more ready-made devices found in the residence to those in the Toy Box that he had uniquely designed and created. Over his many years of experience, and by trial and error, Ray devised more sophisticated tools for his Toy Box. Officers would soon conclude that the "electric chair" was a recent one, more outfitted and useful than the modified weight bench he had previously used.

All of the case investigators recognized that, while Ray had a very sick, perverted mind, he was intelligent and a gifted artist.

The universal question was what causes a man to apply his brilliance and artistic abilities to evil instead of good?

Shelves and tables held sexual and torture devices, and also published textbooks on self-help medicine, sex and psychology. Among them were: *Sexual Behavior of the Human Female, Emergency Victim Care, Family Medical Guide, Human Sexuality* and *American Psycho*. One medical book, an advanced first-aid text, included how to resuscitate and how to perform an emergency tracheotomy. There were also texts on witchcraft and voodoo practices.

A display box, mostly of glass, held prominent view. A miniature panoramic torture scene with small, shapely female dolls naked and enhanced to appear anatomically correct, in various spread-eagle poses, depicted extreme torture scenes. Most of the dolls had unusually large breasts, with ropes tied to them, wrapped around the base of each one, with painted red and blue swollen veins to show the effects of that particular torture.

This display was yet another way Ray built his victims' terror towards climax, to add to their already fearful anticipation of what would happen to them.

A large, oblong wooden box gave agents another jolt. It was longer than a standard casket, about seven feet. Padded and carpeted inside, it had ventilation holes and a battery-powered fan, a pillow and a blanket. And of course eyebolts. The agents believed, after learning he kidnapped victims from distances away, that Ray used this box to transport them to his domicile. With them, he had to pass through Border Patrol checkpoints. One flanked each side of T or C on I-25.

Ray, believing himself smarter than any law enforcement officer, no doubt enjoyed passing through with his kidnapped victims undetected.

After examining it inside and out for trace evidence, Agent Mallion spent days sitting on this box while meticulously cataloging the other contents of the Toy Box.

Near a narrow bed, the agents found several batteries with metal clips attached, and dildos of varying sizes and kinds, some huge with measurement markings (to show depth of insertion), and others attached to small electric motors and batteries.

They also found a square-shaped wooden box with hinged lid that could be padlocked. On one end of the box was a cutout for the woman's neck. Ray placed the box on the back of her head and closed and locked the lid of the box over her face. Keeping her from identifying him was not its purpose; the box was to heighten her sense of helplessness and crescendo her terror.

Ray later told an FBI agent who interviewed him that he acquired the idea for the "head box" from a true crime book he had read.

Officers found a respirator and an inhaler in the trailer. Ray took his victims to the brink of death, and then medically revived them. Prolonging their agony extended his pleasure, doubled his fun. Ray used the respirator and other life-saving techniques, some gleaned from his medical books, to save his victims from death, so he could continue playing with them.

Dead victims were his failures.

A serial sexual sadist like Ray wanted his victims alive, writhing in pain, screaming. If she died while he had her, he'd have to go to the bother, not to mention personal risk, of abducting another.

The Toy Box interior stunned all who saw it. Those ultimately included prosecutors and defense attorneys. Afterward, many stood outside the trailer in stunned silence, or took deep gulping breaths of fresh air, or lit cigarettes with trembling hands. Police, like morticians and doctors, keep their sanity by employing dark humor to lessen the emotional impact of their jobs. However, dark humor didn't help in this case, at least not initially while they still reeled from shock.

One officer stuck a cigarette in his mouth backwards and lit the filter. When he sucked in the acrid smoke, he choked and coughed until tears ran down his cheeks. Those standing nearby laughed, and he joined them, laughing and coughing, with more tears pouring down his face. Their laughter, instead of amused, seemed hysterical. More than one hardened cop or attorney was physically ill, retching or so overcome that he could not stand after exiting the Toy Box.

Ray's written records found in that trailer showed he had more than one hundred victims. Ray, age fifty-nine, had begun recording his sadistic activities in 1955, when he was fifteen. Investigators believe he killed his first victim before he was twenty years old. Over at least forty-five years, he had run amok, wrecking countless lives, until he was finally stopped when he was almost sixty.

In November 2002, K. C. Rogers said, "If Cindy Vigil hadn't been street-smart, if she hadn't been sick because she was coming down from a heroin trip that caused David to give her some slack in her chain, and if Cindy Hendy wasn't an idiot, David would still be out there doing his thing. There's no doubt in my mind about that."

It was those seemingly minor circumstances that finally stopped David Parker Ray.

That, and because of Ray's advancing age, he had targeted those he thought were the easiest victims. He believed prostitutes were easier to snatch than girls and housewives. They were, because of the nature of their lives. However, schoolgirls and housewives were unaccustomed to humiliation and pain. They were quickly overwhelmed; they easily surrendered as helpless victims. Conversely, prostitutes were tough and street-wise. They had already experienced humiliation, pain and dangerous situations; those did not disarm them. They were less likely to give up without a fight to the end.

Law enforcement officers involved with this case admired Cindy Vigil's tenacity, despite all she endured and the overwhelming odds against her. They applauded her for never giving up her survival instincts.

^^^^^^^

Within the first days of the case, investigative presence at the scene, now including FBI, grew from four or five to seventy, then exceeded one hundred officers representing multiple law enforcement agencies.

How many more victims would they find?

Chapter 11 – Ray's Documents

Over the many years of his practice, there seemed to be no pattern to Ray's choice of victims, except that they were young and convenient or easy to take. And, according to his records, they were attractive and "had good bodies." When he was younger, they were more varied. They were all kinds, and from different backgrounds. She might have been a woman he picked up in a bar. She might have traveled alone and, because of car trouble, stood on the side of the road until he came along. She just happened to be at the right place at the right time for him to grab her. She might have been your friend, neighbor, sister or daughter. However, most of his victims were trusting, vulnerable, drunk or on drugs, or prostitutes. In the latter years of his practice, prostitutes comprised a larger percentage of them because they were easy pickings. They required less energy and he was less likely to get hurt and fail to catch his prey.

He knew he was growing old.

David Parker Ray was not a strong man, and he had become an aging man. He often used a stun-gun to overpower his victims.

According to Ray's records and what he implied later during interviews, his kidnappings picked up momentum by 1994. He snatched several females a month to appease his "urge" and fulfill his "fantasy," to use his own words. He had directed his interest towards ten-year-old girls by early 1999. There was a particular young girl he had begun to stalk just before he was caught, according to Cindy Hendy in a later interview. She said he wanted that child "real bad."

Almost from the beginning, Ray placed his victims in painful positions where their struggles against the pain he inflicted caused them to hurt themselves. He tied up many of his early captives on their knees, with their legs folded back and immobilized, and kept them that way without relief for days. Besides the position adding to their pain, if they managed to get loose, they could not run away because their legs wouldn't work.

Agents found a journal in the trailer, entries neatly typed, detailing twenty-nine abductions, ending in 1995. The entries gave place, approximate age of the captive, the length of time he kept her, and a quality rating: "1 = very pretty, excellent body;" or "2 = average face or average body;" or "3 = below average or overweight."

According to this and other records, the number of victims he nabbed and the degree of torture increased over the next years, as did the length of time he kept them. Many of his captives were teenagers. Ray did not indicate what he did with them afterwards. The entries left investigators with unanswered questions. Who were the victims? What happened to them after Ray finished misusing them?

Police searched old police records—in the areas and during the dates Ray indicated in his journals—for complaints by victims who reported being kidnapped and sexually abused. Absence of such complaints suggested the majority of Ray's victims did not live to talk about it.

Ray's first recorded entry in this typed journal was for 1955. Under place he had typed "Ranch-Grove;" approximate age of his captive, fifteen; he kept her for four hours, and he gave her a quality rating of "2 = average." Included in his written comments: "First sex! Experimented with light bondage ... pretended it was rape ... tied her spread-eagle between two trees while I played with her. I didn't use S&M but it was still nice." His notes indicated that she enjoyed the experience.

Date of his second entry was 1956; under place he wrote "Pine Shadow-Tent;" his victim's approximate age was sixteen; and he wrote that he kept her for a weekend. He rated her "1 = very pretty, excellent body" and wrote: "First kidnapping. First rape. I was as scared as she was." He detailed what he did to her. There was no pleasure in it for her.

There were four entries for 1957. For all of those he gave "BLM Cave-Scholle" as the place, and said he kept each of his recorded victims through a weekend.

Of the first one, a sixteen-year-old high school girl, Ray wrote: "Shirley helped me ... we made a lot of mistakes. The girl almost got away. ... There were a lot of experiments performed on the girl." The second one was a twenty-year-old college student. "Shirley set her up for kidnapping. A GORGEOUS blonde." In this entry, Ray detailed several types of sadistic tortures, including using "needles and fish hooks on various sensitive parts of her body." His third 1957 victim was seventeen. Ray wrote: "Getting her was a fluke. The girl had a flat tire. Shirley and I was [sic] on our way to the cave. We tied her up and took her with us. … The S&M was more violent." The fourth entry was of an eighteen year-old girl. "We got her at a bus stop. … We kept the woman tied to the table with her legs folded back most of the weekend… I spent a lot of time practicing breast bondage. … Shirley pulled most of [victim's pubic hair] out. … The girl passed out several times." As with all of his entries, he detailed using various forms of cruelty.

Ray first mentioned using electro-shock on his victims in 1963. Both entries for that year showed "Jemez-Tent" as the place, and "weekend" as the duration of captivity. A twenty-two-year-old woman was a "bar pickup … very drunk," and a twenty-five-year-old woman was a "hitchhiker."

In 1973, he picked up two hitchhikers, Navajo Indian sisters age fourteen and fifteen; he said he held and tortured them together at "Church Rock-Motor Home" for five days. In addition to these two girls, he claimed he nabbed three others in 1973. Their ages were nineteen, twenty-two and thirty. One was kept at the same location as that of the two Navajo girls. He kept the other two at "EB-tent-E. Side." (A tent on the east side of Elephant Butte Lake?) Two, each kept through a weekend, were entered as "bar pickup." He kept the other, a "hitchhiker," for five days. This hitchhiker had an eighteen-month-old baby with her. "The kid was a pain in the ass but Mama wasn't bad," he wrote. He said he invited "Russ" to join him in the abuse of one of the bar-pickup victims.

Two entries for 1974, victims' ages twenty-five and seventeen, showed each was kept over a weekend in a tent on the east side of Elephant Butte Lake. One was a prostitute; the other was a hitchhiker: "We got her on the way to the lake. Russ was drunk and dangerous," he chortled.

An abduction and torture entry for 1978 showed "Alb.-SB" as the place. "Russ got her in the truck. We took her to W. Mesa … then we took her to the camper. The first time with a fully equipped bondage room." This entry described using some new electronic torture devices and "small winches to spread her pelvis…" The victim was eighteen and they tortured her for six days.

In 1979, Ray grabbed a sixteen-year-old girl from a school bus stop. He wrote that she was "very small, about 4'6". Scared and very easy to handle." Under place he wrote "Bernardo-SB Camper" and he detailed torturing her for eight days. Another entry for 1979 showed the same place; this victim, a prostitute, was kept for three days. "Johnene was with me... She ... eventually joined in" the torture of the seventeen-year-old girl.

In 1980, Ray grabbed a twenty-five-year-old hitchhiker; place of bondage was "S.F. Tx.-Land Cruiser." Ray complained, "Very cramped in a jeep." He described tying her hands to the vehicle's roll-bar and using another bar to immobilize her legs behind her back, leaving her in that position all night. In another 1980 entry, place "Temple-Land Cruiser," he said he immobilized a twenty-seven-year-old drunk "bar pickup" all night with the vehicle's roll-bar and the "knee bar behind her back." In this entry he described his "suitcase full of equipment."

In 1982, a twenty-year old "very small" prostitute let him "tie her to the bed. Big mistake and very easy." He detailed torturing her for two days at "Avondale-SB Camper."

In 1986 were two entries; both places were shown as "Phx.-Trl." The first victim was twenty-five, and she was kept for two weeks. "Prostitute – needed a place to sleep. On drugs. She woke up gagged with chains on her wrists and ankles. Really pissed off. I kept her a long time and subjected her to extensive sexual torture. She had heroin withdrawl [sic]." He said he hung her by her wrists with her legs spread most of the time. The second entry was a fifteen-year-old girl hitchhiking from school. He kept her for one week. "Very pretty ... Small and very easy to handle, like a Barby [sic] Doll."

The journal had two entries for 1989 and both showed "Phx.-MH" as the place. One victim, eighteen, was a prostitute who "let me tie her to the bed for $75.00. Dumb." The other was a sixteen-year-old runaway. "Gave her a ride. She wanted a shower and to crash on my couch for a few hours. I let her use the bed. Had only one wrist cuffed to the bed when she woke up. She fought like hell." He kept the girl for two weeks and he said he shared her with a friend a couple of times.

He had two entries for 1993, "Phx.-B Trailer" given as the place for both. They were prostitutes; one was twenty, the other seventeen. He tortured one for four days, and the other for five days. He again wrote of using "ankle winches" to open her pelvis, and added details of using new devices, including a barbed steel bra, nipple screws, and weights.

In 1994, he said he grabbed a nineteen-year-old prostitute. "High class. It took $300 to get her out of the club. Hah! I kept her a long time" (two-and-a-half weeks) and "I did it all." He wrote that she often passed out during her ordeals. The place indicated was "Phx.-EB." This was the first known recorded time when he apparently grabbed someone in Phoenix and took her to Elephant Butte. Also in 1994, he recorded a two-week abduction of a hitchhiker, nineteen, taken from Phoenix to Elephant Butte. "She passed out a lot but was strong," he wrote. "Really hard to handle."

The last entry in this journal was for 1995; the victim was a small prostitute, sixteen. He grabbed her in Albuquerque, took her to Elephant Butte, and kept her a month. "Winter. Plenty of time," he wrote. He described the many tortures he subjected her to and wrote, "Totally used up. Last two weeks was like playing with a rag doll. A month is too long."

Who were Shirley, Russ and Johnene? K. C. Rogers had said Cindy Hendy and Ray's daughter, Jesse, were not the only ones involved with him in the kidnapping and torture of women over the years. Rogers said he believes there were many others, including some of Ray's ex-wives—while they were married, and various girlfriends.

In this journal, entries jump from 1957 to 1963 with nothing recorded for the years between them. After increasing his abductions to four a year, it seems unlikely Ray stopped his activities for six years. And there were no entries for the ten years between 1963 and 1973. Entries again jumped from 1974 to 1978, with only one entry for 1978. There were two entries in 1979, two in 1980, none for 1981, one for 1982, and none for 1983, 1984 or 1985. There were two for 1986, none for 1987 or 1988, two for 1989, two for 1993 and 1994, and one for 1995, when the entries end.

Absence of entries does not mean there were no abductions; they were just not recorded in that journal.

Another book found in the Toy Box also logged abductions. Its entries began in 1994, with five dates of kidnappings for that year, and ended on September 27, 1997. Each of the dates—day, month and year—were followed by hash marks. He had used the simple, time-old method of counting by making small strokes: four with a fifth across them, increments of five resembling sections of a picket fence. These bundles of five filled each line following a date. They signified counts from twenty-five to more than fifty as the number of times he abused that victim. A long "fence" trailed each entry.

Ray's unusual practice of keeping copious records should have made identifying his victims easy for investigators. But nowhere did he give their full names, descriptions or identities. On some records he gave their first names. On others, he wrote their ages, and the dates and places he grabbed them.

On a clipboard hanging in the Toy Box were pre-printed forms with blank spaces he manually filled out on each of his victims. One form was a medical record. He took his victims' medical histories that included her age when she began menstruation, age at her first sexual experience, whether she had given birth and if so, how many times. He took playing doctor to a sick new dimension.

Ray envisioned himself as a writer. He wrote lengthy third-person "stories" about sexual escapades—multiple rapes and sexual torture—of a woman by an unnamed man.

One of those began: "As he stepped out of the motel room for a breath of fresh air, he thought of the young woman tied to the bed inside. It had been so easy. He had known the location of her car when she came out of the bar. Her senses were so alcohol-numbed that she was unaware of his presence until he was upon her. The quick stomach punch left her gasping for air as he tied her hands and feet. After she had been blindfolded and gagged he drove her to the motel. She had been tied in a small neat bundle with her hands drawn up behind her back and no one noticed as he rolled her in a blanket and carried her into the room. His special suitcase was well equipped and the cloriform [sic] had worked well. He only had about two hours before she woke and he lost no time as he untied her and removed her clothing. After placing her body in the middle of the bed he raised her arms and securely tied her wrists at the upper corners of the bed."

Except for minor spelling and typo-error corrections, that was exactly how he began his detailed single-spaced five-page treatise. Ray seemed educated, or at least had read enough to write better than the average high school graduate.

His records also showed how bold and confident he was, and how easy his victims were to take. Too often, they were at the right place at the right time and in the right condition for Ray to grab with ease.

During later interviews with Ray, agents asked him about this and other "stories" he had written. He claimed they were fiction, or just his fantasies that he wrote down for his own enjoyment. He often spoke of his fantasies. Profilers said that his crimes, as with all sexual predators, began with fantasies that he eventually acted out.

Ray claimed that, in his youth, *True Detective* and other types of pictorial magazines, including *Playboy*, first fired his fantasies. Later, various books added fuel. He told investigators that he had a large reading library of books and magazines. In fact, he offered to share them with the agents.

In an effort to identify Ray's victims, the FBI and State Police used a computer program to try to track Ray's movements over the years prior to his arrest.

Between 1960 and 1963, Ray served in the U.S. Army, where he developed some of his auto mechanic skills that later provided him a means of livelihood, and also a convenient way to prey on vulnerable, unsuspecting women.

He was stationed in Korea some of the time he was in the Army.

Korea was a lawless frontier. "With prostitutes throwing themselves at U.S. servicemen, there's no way to know how many victims he might have had there," said K. C. Rogers.

Did those easy successes add to his belief that he would never be caught?

Chapter 12 – Angelíca

News of David Parker Ray's arrest upset many of his coworkers, acquaintances and neighbors, including Lucy Schmidt and the Washburns. Mr. Washburn, Lucy's neighbor across the street, called her, insisting she go to the police and appear in court to testify on behalf of David because he was physically unable to do it himself. The news devastated the Washburns, but they remained staunchly convinced of his innocence. Because Mr. Washburn was so overcome by the news and she worried about him, Lucy was noncommittal about his request, but she had no intention of doing what he asked.

At first, she, too, believed in David's innocence, but she kept her opinions to herself. She seldom even discussed the subject with her family. She read and listened to everything being reported. Soon her conviction of his innocence began to weaken and then was gone. Still, she just walked around shaking her head, and seldom talked about David to anyone.

When news reporters swarmed Elephant Butte, anxious to interview people, a German journalist offered Lucy a large sum of money if she would talk to him. She refused to talk to him or anyone else. (She first consented to be interviewed—for this book—almost three years later, partly because she knew the author had already interviewed her son-in-law.)

The many civilians with scanners that cover all channels included news media. That enabled them to hear dispatched and intra-unit conversations among various law enforcement agencies.

By mid-morning of March 23, several reporters from newspapers, radio and television stations—mostly local but a few from farther distances—had come, as well as a growing group of curious onlookers. This case had begun to be a breaking-news story. Bass Road was crowded, which didn't take much on the short, narrow dirt road.

By morning of March 24, officers had gathered enough probable cause to take to the district attorney's office and charge David Parker Ray, and Cynthia Lea Hendy as his accomplice. Early that afternoon, members of the Sheriff's Department and NMSP Agent LaCuesta accompanied Ray and Hendy to the Magistrate Court for their arraignments before Judge Thomas Pestak. Albert Costales of T or C was their first court-appointed counsel.

Like uninvited ants whose antennae tell them when a picnic is in progress, several news media were present in court.

Ray and Hendy were each charged with seven counts of kidnapping and rape of "the Albuquerque woman." Each of them could face up to ninety-three years and $85,000 in fines. Assistant District Attorney Lee Huntzinger recommended bond on each of them be set at $1,000,000. Pestak complied.

Cindy Vigil testified about being fully restrained and about the padlocked metal collar and chains. She said they made her swallow an orange pill and forced her to listen to a recording in Ray's voice telling her what he was going to do to her. For three days, she said, she was restrained, beaten, shocked with an electrical device attached to her breasts by clips that sent shocks through her body, and suspended by her breasts with a pulley from the ceiling.

She said she was sodomized and otherwise personally assaulted sexually by David Ray and by him using motorized objects. She told the court that she was penetrated with electrical devices that "hurt so bad that I screamed and screamed. They put a tape on my mouth." All the while Ray abused her, she said, Hendy watched and part of the time held a handgun on her. Her experiences had been limited to the front bedroom and den. She said they had told her that they would soon take her to the "Toy Box," but she escaped before they did.

She quoted Hendy as saying: "I've only been kidnapping, raping and murdering girls for a year. David's been doing it many years." According to Vigil, Hendy also claimed that Ray bragged about murdering fourteen women, and either buried them around the area and the desert, or dropped their bodies into Elephant Butte Lake.

Hendy's testimony—in court and during her earlier interviews with agents—gave significance to the maps of Sierra County and of Elephant Butte Lake with many Xs marked on them that officers had found when they searched the residence.

As is usually done for the privacy of rape victims, Vigil's identity was kept confidential; her name was redacted on affidavits or other documents released to public view.

From the beginning, Cindy Vigil was to only be known to the public as "the Albuquerque woman" or, after more victims were found, "the first known victim."

Because most visitors to Elephant Butte are weekend tourists at the lake, they tend to come in motor-homes or with fifth-wheel trailers. The immediate area offered few decent sleeping quarters for incoming investigators, including FBI. And they had to compete for what there was with media coming from faraway places, more each day. Agents scrounged around for places to stay, expecting to be there for an indefinite period of time. Some FBI agents booked rooms at the Black Range Motel in T or C because it was nearby, fairly low priced for the area, and had a small restaurant.

In their newly-established headquarters at Elephant Butte Lake, now equipped with cassette players, a television set and VCR player, agents listened to several audiocassettes, which they began to call Ray's "introductory" or "orientation" tapes, or "terror tapes" that had been recorded several years earlier.

A soft male voice, Ray's, told each victim what was going to happen to her. "You're being abducted against your will. I bet you're scared." The agents imagined the girls' fear as they listened. " … The proceedings are based upon my experience in dealing with captives for many years." Many years! That confirmed evidence they had already found, including in Ray's logs.

"You probably think you are going to be raped. You are right. Thoroughly, repeatedly, completely," the almost monotonous voice droned on. "… It's no big deal. My lady friend and I have been doing this for years. We prefer to snatch young girls … you're just a piece of meat." Again he indicated that he'd had female helpers over the years. He'd only known Hendy for a year.

The voice said, "If I killed every bitch we kidnapped, there'd be bodies strung all over the country." All over the country? Not just around Elephant Butte? Shit!

"We're going to play with you for a while." The voice told the listener in chilling detail exactly what would be done to her.

"After we get through with you, you're going to be drugged up real heavy. You're going to be kept drugged for a couple days while I play with your mind. You won't remember anything afterwards and you will be cleaned up so there won't be any DNA evidence."

In Ray's residence and the Toy Box, officers had found used and unopened boxes of disposable douche kits.

"Once we get tired of you, we will get rid of you." First, he had said he didn't kill all of his victims; was that an admission that he killed some of them? Now, he was saying he would get rid of her when he finished with her, which had a permanent ring to it.

These audiotapes were part of Ray's cruel game of cat and mouse; in Ray's game, he clearly wanted his mice to know they had no hope of escape.

Among the vast amount of evidence on Ray's premises were hundreds of videos and audiocassettes. But the investigators soon learned the majority of those were not homemade tapes. Most were commercial movies and music.

Despite the cameras in the Toy Box, officers later found only one video that showed a Ray captive. They knew there had to be a large stash of those somewhere. They had to find them.

NMSP was the presiding agency and Agents Wes LaCuesta of the Socorro office and Rich Libicer of Las Cruces had taken joint control of the case. They assigned Agent John Briscoe as the crime scene manager and put Case Agent Norman Rhoades in charge of intelligence. Sgt. K. C. Rogers, with supervisory experience, had already been assigned to run the command post at the lake.

^^^^^^^

On Friday, March 26, four days after the case began, the investigative team received a call from T or C Police Chief David Bryant. He said another victim of Ray's had contacted him. Chief Bryant brought them up to date before officers interviewed her.

Weeks earlier, before this case broke, an unknown woman called the Sierra County sheriff's office. They traced the call to a public phone. The caller did not give her name but she asked to speak to a certain female officer. The caller must have thought the named officer was a sheriff's deputy; she was, instead, a T or C police officer. The caller told the SO dispatcher that she had been kidnapped and sexually tortured. "I need to report it because nobody believes me," the caller said, but she would only talk to a certain female officer. Sheriff Terry Byers called Chief Bryant.

When the call had come in, the requested officer was attending a service. The chief called her away from that, told her to wait at the SO for the caller to come in and talk to her. The officer waited there the rest of the afternoon and into the evening, but the caller never showed. Neither the SO nor the T or C police department heard from that woman again—until now. They had concluded the caller was a prankster or a nut, a not uncommon occurrence.

The chief related that incident of a month earlier to the investigators. That woman, Angelíca Montaño, twenty-five, had now come forward.

In the past few days, the case of the Albuquerque woman, who accused David Parker Ray of kidnapping and torturing her, had been broadcast and printed in newspapers. Those caught the ears and eyes of T or C residents John and Jean Branaugh. They told their acquaintance, Angelíca, to report to the police her own experience—what David Ray and Cindy Hendy had done to her, that was so similar to what the news said they had done to that Albuquerque woman.

The Branaughs had dismissed the whole tale back on February 28, when Angelíca had told about her experience at the hands of David Ray and Cindy Hendy. They knew Ray and Hendy, especially Hendy. In fact, Hendy and her then-boy friend, John Youngblood, were witnesses at Branaughs' wedding a year earlier. They were also acquainted with Angelíca, a woman they knew to have a serious drug problem.

Now, after hearing the news of a case that sounded similar, the Branaughs called the T or C police chief, who recognized the importance of the call. He sent an officer to the alleged victim's home to bring her to the station to make a full report.

Police knew Angelíca Montaño, a sometimes-prostitute and drug user.

Investigators were elated to have another victim to interview, but the question begged to be asked: why didn't the Branaughs come forward when they first heard about this and let police decide whether there was any truth to it?

During her interview, Angelíca told officers that on February 17, 1999, she had gone to the residence of David Ray and Cynthia Hendy, people she knew. She related about going in the house with Hendy for a cake mix, and while the women rummaged around in the kitchen, Ray had come in, threatened her with a knife and punched her in the stomach. She said they stripped and restrained her with a neck chain and collar, handcuffs and shackles. They forced her to swallow an orange pill that made her fall asleep. When she woke up, they made her swallow another pill and listen to a prerecorded message, in Ray's voice, that said, "I bet you're scared." She was.

The voice said, "We're gonna play with you a while. When we are finished, we will wash you to remove DNA, drug you, play with your mind and make you forget what happened, before you are released."

She said Ray sexually tortured her, while Hendy watched and held a gun on her part of the time, for five days. On the third day, she said, she was taken to another place nearby, a smaller trailer that Ray and Hendy called their Toy Box. There, she saw a large array of restraint devices and medical and sex tools. She was tied to a table and sexually abused while Hendy watched. She was later returned to the main residence because Ray said he wanted to watch the second half of a television program.

On February 21, five days after they had taken her, Angelíca said she convinced her captors, primarily David, to let her go. Perhaps one of the things that saved her was that she pretended to like it and acted like they were friends, which she had originally thought they were.

"You do what you gotta do. If I hadn't, I'd be dead or I'd still be there," she said with a shudder. "I thought I'd never see my little boys again."

After Ray and Hendy had a lengthy discussion—Hendy hadn't liked the idea of turning her loose—they let her get dressed and drove her to a location on I-25 where they put her out on the roadside. A man stopped and gave her a ride. She said she told him about her experience but he didn't believe her. He told her to go home and write a report for the police. She said she asked him to stop and let her out of the car and he did.

That off-duty law enforcement officer, being skeptical, hadn't filed a report at that time, but after statewide publicity of the David Parker Ray case began, he contacted State Police and disclosed the story told to him by the unknown hitchhiker he had picked up.

The police were glad she had come forward.

Angelíca confirmed she later told her acquaintances, Jean and John Branaugh, about her Ray and Hendy experience, partly because she was aware they knew Hendy. She knew that, on several occasions in the past, Jean Branaugh had befriended Hendy. She allowed her to live, for a few days, in one of the rooms of the motel she then managed. Thereafter, claimed John Branaugh, Hendy expected handouts from his wife.

When Angelíca first told them in February about her experience, she knew they didn't believe her, she told the officers.

The Branaughs told Chief Bryant they had forgotten about it until they began to hear and read news coverage that sounded familiar. Then they pressured Angelíca to talk to police. They even called the police themselves.

The next day, Saturday, March 27, 1999, officers told the media that another unnamed victim of Ray's and Hendy's had come forward. An officer told the public this woman was from Truth or Consequences; they called her "the T or C woman," or "the second victim," although she had been taken earlier than the first one. The FBI spokesman gave the media details, that she had gone to Ray's trailer to borrow a cake mix and was restrained and tortured for five days. In his briefing, for the first time, the public information officer mentioned "the Toy Box."

The media likes catchy words and phrases. Thereafter, the Toy Box became an often used sound-bite. The PIO told the media that, because of this second victim, Sierra County prosecutors filed twenty-five additional counts against David Parker Ray and his suspected accomplice, Cynthia Lea Hendy.

^^^^^^^

Within the first days of the case, investigators found hundreds of leads, each of which led to a hundred more, many in places far from Elephant Butte. This case was becoming overwhelming. They were drowning in evidence and leads.

Chapter 13 – The Circus

It took considerable manpower to keep all of the scenes secure. Within the first forty-eight hours, New Mexico Mounted Patrol Capt. Von Weddige, a rancher from southeastern New Mexico near the tiny community of Hope, was put in charge of security of all crime scenes.

More than two thousand pieces of evidence were found at the Bass Road property, and another Pandora's box was discovered when storage units rented by David Parker Ray were discovered and their contents were catalogued. For days, volunteer New Mexico Mounted Patrol troopers, called in from around the state, guarded the rental units twenty-four hours a day. Investigators wondered how many more Pandora's boxes they would find? They still had not found the hoped-for stash of Ray's victim videos.

The long list of what law enforcement found on Ray's property was still sealed, not open to the public, but prosecutor Jim Yontz mentioned several items to the media. Those included as many as one hundred videotapes, not all of which had yet been viewed. (All but one of those proved to be useless to this case.) There were also identification cards for people not known to have connections to Ray, some of which were altered or false; police were searching for those individuals. He said boating items tested positive for blood. He told them they found maps of Sierra County and Elephant Butte Lake marked with Xs, including near Kettle Top. And he said they found photos of bound women. Hendy identified two of those as women she knew Ray had killed.

Agent Mallion later said those female victims in the still photos, with their eyes and mouths bound with tape, were not identifiable and it was impossible to tell whether they were alive when the photos had been taken.

On Friday, March 26, 1999, more FBI agents arrived in Elephant Butte.

By Saturday, March 27, thirty FBI agents from New Mexico and surrounding states, twenty New Mexico State Police—both uniform and plainclothes, assisted by volunteer New Mexico Mounted Patrol troopers—swarmed the half-acre lot leased by David Parker Ray. His mobile home, garage, storage trailers, and all other structures, boats, equipment and vehicles on the property were meticulously examined. Besides blood, they found other trace evidence on the boats and boating equipment. One boat was registered to one of Ray's sons.

The arrival of even more FBI agents signified to the media a substantial escalation of the investigation. For the first time, Elephant Butte Lake State Park rangers and New Mexico Mounted Patrol troopers blocked roads in front of and behind Ray's property.

Responding to a question, an Agency spokesman told a reporter that this large quantity of FBI agents had arrived several days after the case began because it took time to gather enough of them from many outlying places.

Officers blocked the roads to keep away the mob of curious onlookers and media, and to make room for all of the police vehicles at the crowded scene. State Police and FBI agents in white coveralls, wearing blue latex gloves, began to remove sealed boxes from the trailers. Those coveralls and gloves were to protect the integrity of the crime scene and its evidence.

When they observed reporters with cameras, they hung up blue tarps to block the view before they began removing other, larger, pieces of evidence that would otherwise be difficult to camouflage or hide. Behind the tarps, investigators set up picnic tables to work on, to tag and catalogue the mass quantity of evidence. Rangers and troopers shooed away persistent media and onlookers from the road, in front of and behind Ray's property, who had slipped through the barriers.

Officials transported David Ray's Toyota RV from where it had been kept at the hangar at their temporary command post at Elephant Butte Lake, by enclosed truck to the New Mexico State Police's crime lab where technicians could better gather and analyze evidence with their forensic equipment.

Two investigators from the FBI's Behavioral Science Unit in Quantico, Virginia—experienced in profiling serial sex-criminals and murderers—were expected to arrive the next day, Sunday, March 28. Those profilers and others like them have applied their psychological expertise to criminal minds like Charles Manson, Ted Bundy, John Hinckley, Jr. and the Unibomber; and tried to describe the probable suspect in the JonBenet Ramsey case.

Within its first breaking-news days, the T or C sex case, as many media dubbed it, became FBI's number one investigative priority in the state of New Mexico; and some prophesied that it would become a high-ranking FBI priority in America. Information already gathered from interviews with Hendy, and from David Parker Ray's diaries, journals and recordings, indicated that this case was far-reaching—in time and in space. It appeared that David Ray had been committing crimes of kidnapping, sexual torture, and also murder, for decades and in at least ten states.

Law enforcement had expanded the area blocked off to include all but about one hundred feet of Bass Road in Elephant Butte. Access to the area, including the block behind Ray's property, was denied to the public and media. Park Rangers and Mounted Patrol kept 24-hour security. Press lined the road waiting for a briefing all day Saturday, but by 5 p.m., there was no new information given by NMSP Deputy Chief Herman Silva or State Public Information Officer Randall "Randy" Bertram.

Darren White, NMDPS secretary, Doug Beldon, New Mexico's FBI supervisory special agent, and Frank Taylor, chief of NMSP, together visited Bass Road on Sunday, March 28, to be filled in on the latest developments of the case. The unusual at-the-scene presence of New Mexico's three top-ranking law enforcement officers proclaimed to the public the importance of this case. However, on this day, the three remained outside the fence surrounding 513 Bass Road.

Law enforcement held their first public conference on March 28 at the State Police headquarters at T or C. There was an unusually high level of cooperation among DPS, the State Police and the FBI. The agencies' spokespersons fielded questions and made additional comments.

"The purpose of this meeting is to address your concerns and fears," said DPS Secretary White. " … This is a safe community, and while this situation is a community's worst nightmare, I believe the nightmare is behind bars."

That was one of White's most widely quoted statements.

Within days, the number of FBI agents and other law enforcement officers involved with this case at tiny Elephant Butte and elsewhere would swell to more than one hundred, said NMSP's public information officer, Randy Bertram.

"It is paramount that we do not compromise this investigation," said White.

Beldon said, "The FBI's purpose is to support the State Police and the District Attorney, including our evidence response team, to collect evidence and protect the crime scene until the job is done. There are likely substantial federal violations, interstate, federal criminal sexual type crimes in this case. There's likely to be a prolonged intensive expansive investigation. Facts are known, terrible facts. The FBI Behavioral Science Unit handles crime profiling and evaluating suspects involved in alleged criminal sexual deviant behavior."

Chief Frank Taylor said the State Police, so far, had twenty agents assigned to the case.

"We are not going to rule out more victims, we are not going to rule out the possibility that this case involved homicides," said White. He told the media—and he was widely quoted—that investigators had already found an overwhelming amount of evidence in the trailers where investigators believed the crimes took place. "When we witnessed, first-hand, the evidence at the scene, it literally made my stomach turn," he said.

All of the investigative officers involved with the scene found the evidence overwhelming, horrifying and disgusting. Even veterans with many years' experience investigating crimes had never before seen anything like it, and they hoped they never would again. Probably for all but the FBI criminologists and profilers from Quantico, this would be their once-in-a-lifetime really big case.

Still, despite the horror of it, many of the officers and agents were intrigued, even excited, by their opportunity to work the case because it was such a huge learning experience.

More than two years later, K. C. Rogers said, "This case, we hated it but we loved it. We learned something new every day. I told the guys it was important that they understood what kind of guy David was, they needed to know what a sexual predator is, what a sexual sadist is. They needed to know David normalized what he did. You have to know he is a sick bastard and deal with it, and you have to normalize it yourself to an extent so you recognize this guy is a sick bastard. That keeps you from saying, 'Oh my God! This is the most horrible sight I've ever seen,' and lose sight of what it is. We have to deal with it, so we don't lose sight of the case, and don't get emotionally involved."

And Rogers said, "Nobody would believe what we found unless they saw it. You could describe it but it doesn't have the same impact of being there and seeing it for yourself." He called David Parker Ray "the King of Weird." He said studying this case would change anybody's view of normal life. Ray's goal was to cause his victims prolonged pain and total humiliation. He even assaulted the women mentally, said Rogers.

Several of the investigators assigned to the case later described Elephant Butte as having an established drug culture. They said many of the residents were longhaired, aging hippies and dopers living in Volkswagen Beetles and microbuses. In looks and behavior, Ray fit right in with many of them, one said. Many officers, especially those who interviewed residents, began to suspect that some of them were involved with Ray and Hendy. They knew many of them had played around together.

"More arrests are expected," a State Police spokesman told the media.

During that first media briefing on Sunday, Darren White said he had never before worked a case with so many investigators working it, when the suspects were already in custody.

Several times he said, "This case is disturbing."

"In regards to severity, on a scale of one to one-hundred, this case is a ninety-nine," he told the public.

Rumor in the community and among the media was that the case was moving towards becoming a murder case, but Beldon would not confirm that. He did say, "There are other victims out there; we want them to give us a call." He said the investigation had spread to other places where Ray was known to have lived or visited.

The drive to the property, Bass Road, was marked off-limits to all except authorized personnel by yellow crime-scene tape and guarded by officers, rangers and Mounties.

Neighbors told police that they had seen Ray digging up plants and bushes, and replanting them, as many as three times.

Around the yard, the FBI stuck many small red flags in the dirt, but they had not yet begun to dig.

Some of Ray's coworkers and acquaintances told officers he seemed so much happier since he had begun taking Viagra®, a sexual performance-enhancing prescription drug.

During a televised interview, John Branaugh told viewers that Hendy had spoken of Ray burying bodies around the prairie and that

Ray had also told her he'd dropped bodies into the lake. "When he's done, he gets his surgical tool or whatever and splits them down the middle, fills them with rocks and that's why they don't have no buoyancy," Branaugh told the KOB-TV interviewer.

Officers were annoyed. Why didn't he tell this to police long ago, instead of now to a public audience? As far as investigators knew, this was the first time Branaugh had spoken of this, and now he was telling it in front of a television camera.

In sharp contrast to what Branaugh said on TV, but almost as amazing, was what Hendy's former landlady, Dianne Lamm, told reporters. She said Hendy was a kind person. "She's into romance novels. She listens to the Christian radio station." Lamm also said that she had visited their Bass Road residence and saw nothing there that troubled her. "I never seen Cindy so happy as since she's been with David."

Officers continued to develop a growing skepticism of—even contempt for—many people they interviewed or who associated with Hendy and Ray. That included Ray's grown daughter, Glenda Jean "Jesse" Ray, about whom they had begun to hear so much.

Officers found many things at the Bass Road premises with her name on them, indicating she had lived there. They learned that Jesse was not her only alias. Her family called her Jean while she was growing up, but she used a variety of completely different names and aliases, including Sissy, Linda and Brenda. She now preferred to be called Jesse by her friends and family.

Truth or Consequences, Elephant Butte and little Bass Road swarmed with as many as fifty journalists, representing papers and networks from all over the country and beyond. Newspaper journalists included *The New York Times* and *Dallas Morning News*. TV networks included ABC, CBS, CNN, FOX and NBC; reporters represented TV shows like "Good Morning America" and "The Today Show."

To give themselves peace, investigators allowed reporters to walk up to the gate of 513 Bass Road for a few minutes for a closer look. Reporters kept asking why officials believed there were other victims besides the two who had come forward, and why they believed this case involved murders. The reporters were clearly frustrated because they believed the officers knew more than they were telling.

In the media, Ray's and Hendy's defense attorneys blasted law enforcement officials and investigators, especially DPS Secretary

Darren White, for public comments they made. They said that made it difficult if not impossible for their clients to have a fair trial anywhere in New Mexico.

Of course, each defense attorney continued to say his client was innocent.

Some TV reporters with camcorders offered Ray's neighbors hundreds of dollars to allow them to climb their trees and trellises to get onto their roofs so they could get better views and shots of Ray's property. Some in Ray's neighborhood began to profit from the case that was drawing national, even international, attention.

The case already had sideshows and showmen; the media turned it into a circus.

One agent said he felt like pleading "contemporary" insanity; the world he now lived in had gone mad.

Chapter 14 – Briefings

The temporarily-appointed local defense attorney, Albert Costales, was replaced on March 30 in T or C, in the court of District Judge Neil Mertz, at Ray's and Hendy's second preliminary hearing—this one about Angelíca. Mertz and the public defenders' office assigned Jeff Rein, an Albuquerque attorney, as counsel to Ray. They would soon assign another attorney to defend Hendy, but until then, her counsel was Javier Acosta of Las Cruces.

The state, in the person of Assistant District Attorney Jim Yontz, now charged Ray and Hendy each with a total of twenty-five criminal counts. If found guilty on all of them in a court of law, each could be sentenced to nearly two-hundred years in prison. A $1,000,000 bond was set on each of them. Ray and Hendy continued to be held at the Sierra County jail, in the Sierra County Courthouse on Date Street in Truth or Consequences.

On March 31, after interviews with Cynthia Lea Hendy, police began digging in the back yard of 513 Bass Road.

District Attorney Ron Lopez issued a gag order.

TV began repeating rumors of a possible link between David Parker Ray and Marie B. Parker, a twenty-two-year old woman who had disappeared about eighteen months earlier and was still missing. She was last seen July 5, 1997, at the Blue Waters Saloon.

David Parker Ray lied to the court when he said he had no aliases. County assessor's office records showed that he first leased the property under his mobile home dwelling in 1984 using the name of David S. Parker. It had also been leased using the name of one of his former wives, Lee Parker, and his water bill was still under that name. Officers learned other Elephant Butte residents had also known him as David S. Parker.

The case investigators began to hold daily media briefings. On March 31, they said that as many as sixty agents and officers—FBI and State Police—gathered on Bass Road and the surrounding area.

The public was told an assistant district attorney was on the scene at all times to write additional warrants and answer legal questions.

FBI Agent Beldon said, "There's an overwhelming amount of information, and many people assigned."

Secretary White commented, "No bodies at this point, no digging at this point … we're not at any of those stages yet. But we are prepared to dig. This man lived a very dark, disturbing lifestyle." When White was asked if videos of other victims had been found, he said, "No comment." When he was asked about Ray being involved in a cult or Satanic worship, he said, "No comment." When asked about the red flags in the dirt at 513 Bass Road, he told reporters to not "jump to conclusions."

Chief Taylor told the gathering that the case was the state's number one priority. "We are dealing with a small community … affected by the fact that we have literally converged on their town. The public is safe. It is important we are respectful and sensitive … this is a tourism town, a safe community, these people are in our custody and now we have an investigation to complete."

White added, "I think the unthinkable did happen to her [the Albuquerque woman]. I had not been at the crime scene until today. I was emotionally affected. … My stomach turned. I am very sorry that the things that happened to her did happen to her, and I am just grateful she was able to escape. She's a victim and we are going to protect her. … We want to ensure the mental health of our agents working this case is addressed. I worked crimes against children when I was with the Albuquerque Police Department … very dark and disturbing lifestyles in those investigations. Feelings I had at this briefing vividly reminded me of how I used to feel when investigating those crimes against children." He said, "Officers are being affected by the evidence found here. You don't have to ask them, you can see it in their faces."

Beldon told the crowd that areas under investigation included El Paso, Phoenix, Tucson and Victoria, Texas. He said agents had been sent out to investigate leads gathered from phone calls. "People are calling in. ... This case has caught the interest of our Behavioral Science Unit."

More than three years later, K. C. Rogers said the investigation at the command post involved sophisticated FBI software to coordinate case information. It included an FBI computer program, Rapid Start System, which compiled and cross-referenced, by age, race and name, leads they gathered at the crime scene and received from the many incoming phone calls. Those leads had numbered one-thousand and continued to grow.

On March 30, an agent had discovered an important tape in the Toy Box. It turned out to be the only video found that depicted a victim being held captive. After it was booked into evidence, FBI Special Agents Tony Maxwell and John Schum, and NMSP officers John Briscoe and K. C. Rogers, took it to the command post at Elephant Butte Lake to view it.

It showed David Parker Ray in the Toy Box with a young, blindfolded, naked, blonde woman strapped to a weight bench, her feet secured far apart in stirrups, her arms bound above her head. This video showed distinctive tattoos, especially one on her right leg. They believed that tape would help them identify another of Ray's victims.

David Parker Ray was shown touching and stroking her body while the woman tried to pull away. "Fondling" was the description later used by Sgt. Rogers in court, and he said the woman did not appear willing in the video.

Officers received a pivotal phone call at the command post. The caller, who now lived in Arizona, said she believed she'd made a terrible mistake. She—Janet "Judy" Murphy—said she and her husband, Steve, previously lived in T or C. Murphy told the officer on the phone that a young woman, Kelli Van Cleve, had been briefly married to her son. She said soon after the couple had married, in 1996, Kelli disappeared for several days and claimed David Parker Ray had kidnapped and hurt her. They found Kelli hard to believe because she said she had no memory of what did happen to her. At the time, none of the Murphys—the caller, her husband or her son—believed her. That is, not until Mrs. Murphy began to hear and read news reports about the sexual abuse case in T or C. She said it had been David Parker Ray who returned Kelli to their house after she had been gone several days. Because they believed Kelli was drunk or on drugs, they let Ray take her with him when he left. The caller sounded very upset.

Mrs. Murphy confirmed Kelli was blonde, her hair had been in tiny braids all over her head when she had seen her that morning before she disappeared for several days. And it was still braided, but unkempt, when she had briefly returned to their house. She had an unusual swan tattoo on her right leg. She added that Kelli now lived in Colorado.

Investigators were elated after the discovered video and the subsequent call from Mrs. Murphy. They believed they might have located another victim of Ray's who was still alive. K. C. Rogers said NMSP Officer Cary McPhearson was one of the first to go to Colorado to locate and interview Kelli Van Cleve.

FBI Agents Carrie Parbs and Larry Haulpt also went to Craig, Colorado, to interview the woman.

Ever since her experience with Ray, the young woman kept having flashbacks, bits of memories of what had happened to her. That, believed the agents, was because of the drugs—including phenobarbital and amitriptyline—Ray had used on her.

^^^^^^^

John Schum of the FBI's psychology unit interviewed David Parker Ray. Ray had told agents that he wanted to talk to an FBI profiler. "I've wanted to talk to you guys for a long time," he said. "I will finally be with people on my own level of intelligence." He believed regular cops could not match him intellectually. Some agreed that was true.

He claimed the events he detailed in many of his "stories" found at his property, and what he told the FBI psychologists, were fantasies. He did not admit that he had done those things, but that he had fantasized about doing them.

Based upon the evidence at the scene and through the profilers' expertise, a chilling profile of Ray emerged. Among the known serial rapists and killers the profilers had studied or knew about, Ray's type was rare, almost unique. His profile fit only a proportionate few in the world.

K. C. Rogers said FBI's Doug Beldon, Agent Mary Ellen O'Toole, FBI's expert on sex crimes, and he had extensively interviewed Hendy. One interview with Beldon, O'Toole and K. C. lasted nine hours. "It was a strange interview," said Rogers. "She's a very strange person. The whole interview was very unusual."

During that interview, Rogers asked Hendy what she was doing at a particular moment. Hendy said she was in the kitchen making potato salad.

Rogers asked her what Cindy Vigil was doing while she was making potato salad. "She was on the couch," said Hendy.

"She was just sitting there on the couch?" asked Rogers.

"Oh no, she was lying down, naked, tied up, with a big motorized dildo stuffed in her ass," said Hendy in a matter-of-fact voice.

"What! You were in the kitchen making potato salad while Cindy was lying there, tied up with a huge dildo shoved into her?" shouted K. C., incredulous at her casually uttered comment.

Hendy shrugged and said in a reasonable tone, "Well, yeah, I had to make potato salad, see. David and I was going to have a picnic and you gotta have potato salad for a picnic."

Her entire life, Hendy had been subjected to abuse by men. Living with David, and earlier, she had learned to normalize torture as a common way of life.

At that interview, Rogers, furious and disgusted with Hendy over her indifference about the pain and indignity she caused Vigil, jumped up and yelled at her.

Hendy reacted. She smiled at him, pulling her legs tightly together, hugging herself. He stormed out of the interrogation room and stood outside the building chain-smoking.

Soon O'Toole joined him outside. "That was brilliant," she said.

"What the hell are you talking about?" he asked, snapping at her.

"Using the masterful, bullying approach. Being dominated by men her whole life, that's all she understands. It worked. I bet you gave her an orgasm!"

Rogers glared at her. "I wasn't playing games, using any technique with her. Hell, she disgusts me. She makes me sick!"

Rogers commented that this was the first investigation he knew of in New Mexico in which many State Police and FBI "actually did a successful job working together, with no problems."

Sherry Doyle was the FBI's investigation supervisor, said Rogers. He later said he sat down with her the very first night she arrived, and talked to her. "I said, 'Look, I'm putting my ass on the line by asking you [the FBI] to come here, guaranteeing nothing will go wrong. The very first hint I have that somebody is going behind my back, interviewing people without communicating with my people, doing anything that might remotely look like you're trying to take over this investigation, I'm going to burn your house down. I'm going to stand you up in front of everybody, embarrass the shit out of you. I'm going to shut you down.' Yeah, I can, because I worked in Narcotics for so long, I know people. I can call their SAC, say 'Hey, nothing personal Jack, but if your people shit all over us here …'."

Rogers did not mention how Doyle responded to his comments.

He said, "The Toy Box trailer itself was a primary piece of evidence," and not very many people ever saw the inside of it. A few State Police, the FBI evidence techs, and the prosecutor of the case, Jim Yontz, saw it. "Javier, Cindy Hendy's attorney, went through it and said, 'What kind of deal do you want me to make?' He knew it was not just a little S and M game and he was immediately ready to deal. Jeff Rein, David's attorney, came and looked at it. Jeff got nauseous, couldn't take it, continually shook his head, turned green, had to get out, get air, sit down. It made a hell of an impact on him."

He added, "But David wouldn't even consider, wouldn't agree to plead guilty. He wanted to go to trial. Profilers will tell you that those kinds of people enjoy reliving it for however long the trial lasts. The victims get up on the stand to testify and David, reliving it, will thoroughly enjoy listening to them. You gotta understand, that's how those kinds of people survive, they relive their deeds over and over again."

He went on to say, "We believe he was a true serial sexual sadist, one of only twenty-five known. We believe he killed many victims, but we don't have proof, no bodies. We understood enough to work the case, but we could not put ourselves in David's mind. It's a learned behavior; it's not something he woke up with one day, deciding 'I'll find out what beating a woman feels like.' He started out at a low level and over time worked his way up. It grew and grew into what he became."

Rogers commented that, based upon investigations and profilers' observations, he believed he knew what had caused Ray to become a sadist, to act out his fantasies. "But I'll never tell," he said, tantalizing his interviewer. He added that he thought it was a relatively small thing that had pushed him over the edge.

Rogers said, "We were left with thousands of details that needed to be investigated, countless loose strings. There were a whole lot of other things going on out there. It became very difficult, the emotional ups and downs, for us investigating the case.

"We'd get a call at our command post. A guy would call and say, 'My sister disappeared eight years ago, she was riding her bicycle through your part of the country, her bicycle was found outside of Hatch, but no trace of her.' We'd listen to him with great interest, take notes, and then we'd say, 'Well sir, we don't have anything for you, sorry.' We'd hang up and say to each other, 'Well, we know David got that one,' based upon information the guy gave us, dates and places we had, we knew that was somebody David grabbed. We knew it but we couldn't prove it. There were *lots* of phone calls like that. That, all those phone calls, was the hardest part of working this case."

Looking back on the case three years later, Rogers said, "Ray was very intelligent. You have to understand … the average police officer has an IQ of 90; we believe David Parker Ray's was at least 130. He was way out there above and beyond the average cop, and he knew it."

He was bold. He'd drive his Dodge Ram—that looked like a State Park vehicle but wasn't—with his victims bound and gagged on the floor inside, through the checkpoints.

"Nobody really wants to know all the details of this case because it's sickening. It can stay with you and affect you the rest of your life," said Rogers. "It makes you examine yourself, makes you wonder. You ask yourself, 'Why did I do that?' Your own natural, ordinary sex practices suddenly seem, well, not ordinary. You end up uncertain, questioning yourself."

^^^^^^^

At a *Consequences* book signing in January 2007, K. C. Rogers disclosed what he believes caused David Ray to become sexually sadistic. He said that, at a young age, Ray had lived with an aunt who sexually abused him. That aunt also wanted him to hurt her during sex. From that early influence, he not only learned to disrespect women, he grew up equating sex and pleasure, for him, with pain and violence.

Criminologists also say sadists and habitual murderers come by their traits from a combination of heredity—bad genes—plus negative early childhood experiences—such as cruel parents who showed them no love. Combining those with certain personality flaws, like lack of conscience and unrestrained anger, heighten those cruelty traits. Each factor, alone, is found in a small percentage of the population. The percentage of those who have all of those factors in one person—bad genes, bad childhood experiences, no conscience and uncontrollable anger—are few, population-wise. Those people are rare but deadly.

^^^^^^^

Sunday, April 5, a cold wind blew off the lake, making life miserable for all exposed to it, saints and sinners alike.

Some of the press still interviewed locals. One interviewed-for-TV churchgoer said, on the steps of his church, "Unfortunately, the devil gets more press than God."

Hot Springs Landing, where boats were unloaded onto the water (beyond concrete abutments like the one in the foreground below the sign) before drought lowered water levels. Kettle Top is seen in the distance.

(Above) Sierra County Courthouse, front view from Date Street in Truth or Consequences.

(Below) Downtown Truth or Consequences.

Memorial to Kelly Clark, Sierra County Sheriff's deputy killed by a prisoner during transport in early March 1999. Memorial is in front of Sierra County Courthouse.

Black Range Motel and Restaurant where breakfast cook, Roy Yancy, was arrested for Marie B. Parker murder.

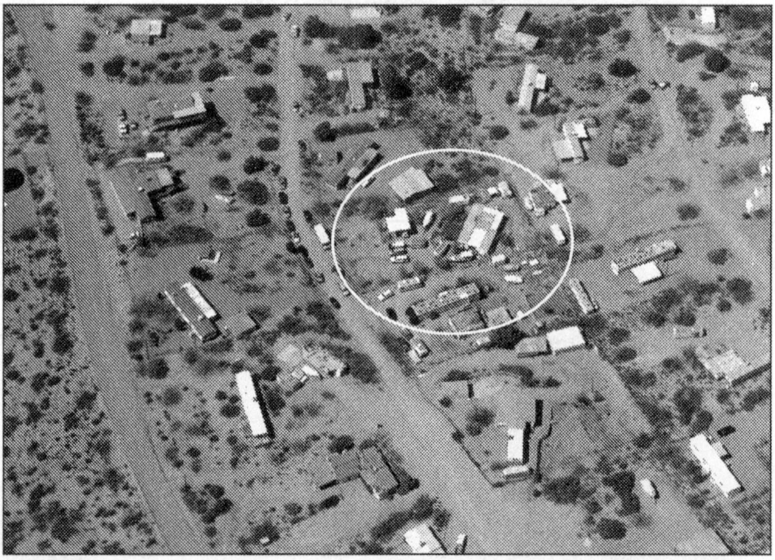

Aerial photo of David Parker Ray's property (center of photo, with many vehicles on Bass Road in front and inside his yard) taken after the case broke. Courtesy photo.

(Above) Ray's front yard after the crime scene tape was removed.

(Below) South side of Ray's home after the crime scene tape was removed.

(Above) "Coffin" box where Ray imprisoned his victims, probably while transporting them through border patrol checkpoints on either side of T or C. Courtesy photo.

(Below) One of David Ray's rape kits … that included a fixed-blade knife, bottle of Hot Damn! liquor laced with drugs and a law enforcement badge. Courtesy photo.

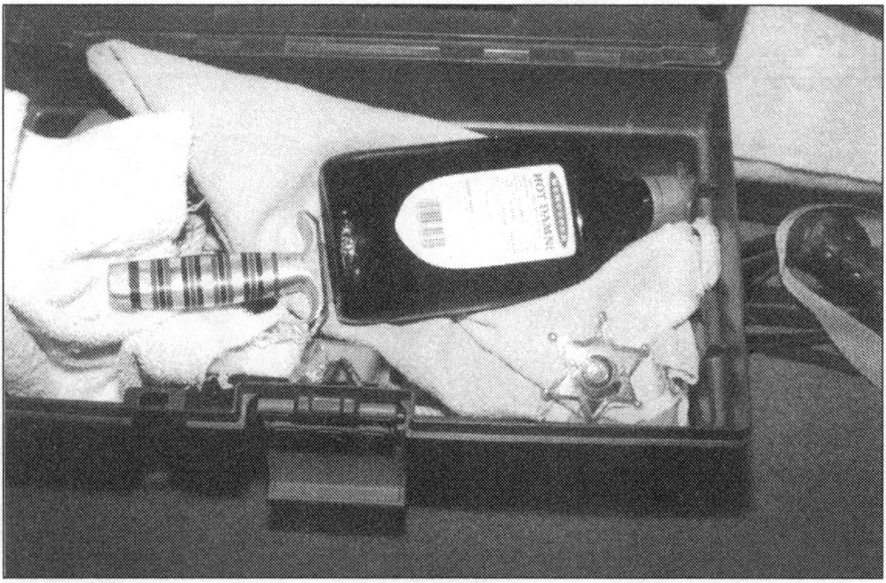

Ray's den (lower level) from where Cindy Vigil escaped March 21, 1999. Note the pieces of glass on the bed from the lamp that Cindy Hendy broke over her head when she was escaping. A bloody ice pick was found on the floor under the bedspread. Courtesy photo.

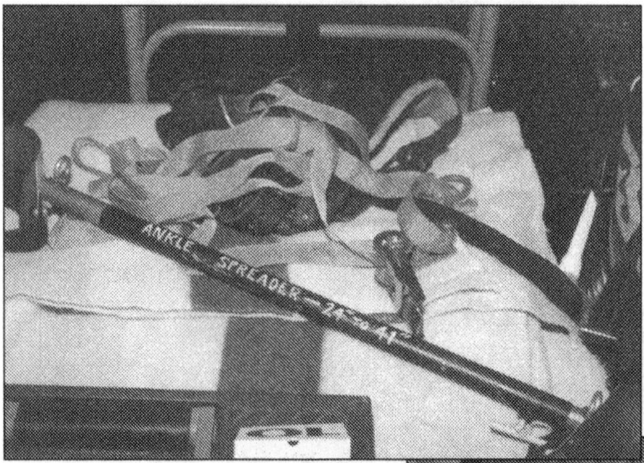

(Above) Some items found in the middle bedroom of Ray's dwelling. Courtesy Photo.

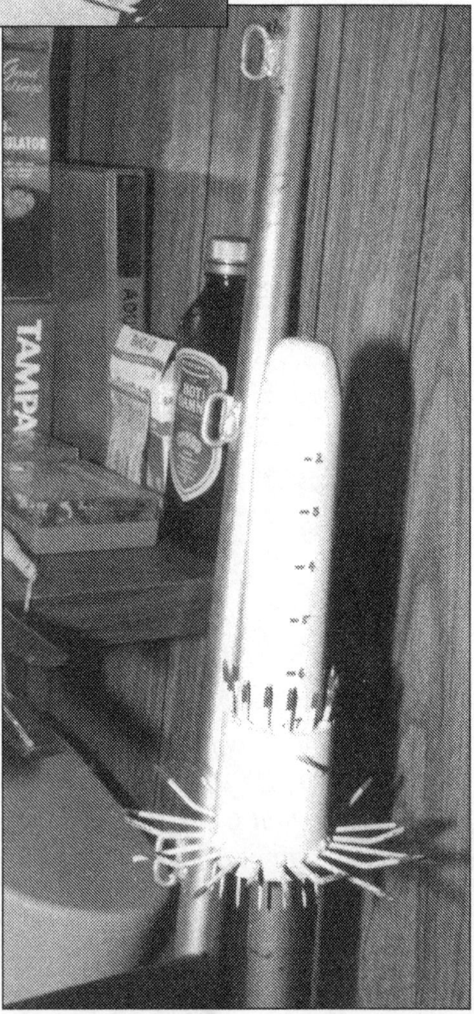

(Right) The "rocket" investigators found in the dwelling's middle bedroom. Note bottle of Hot Damn! in background. Courtesy Photo.

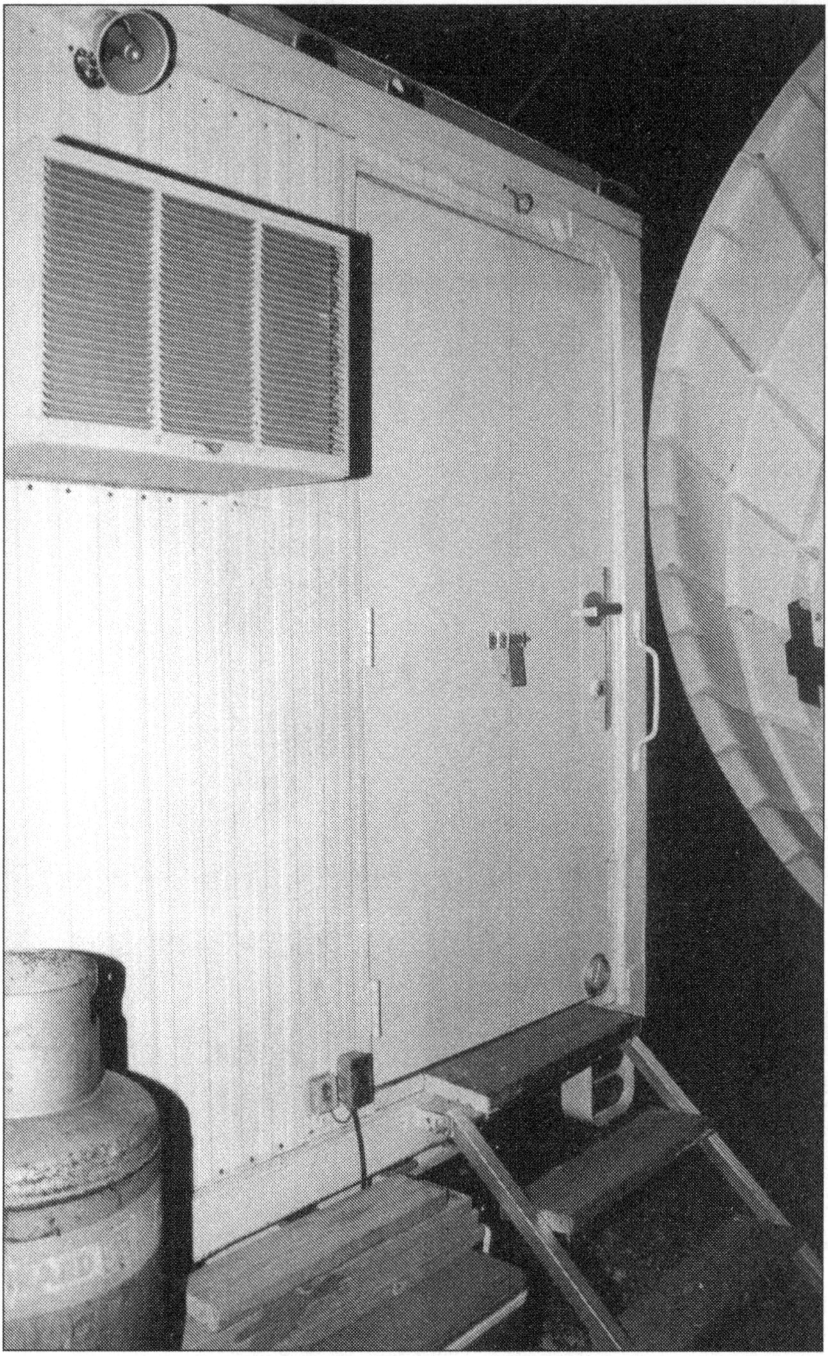

Door at rear of Toy Box trailer; note satellite dish effectively hiding its view from neighbors. Courtesy photo.

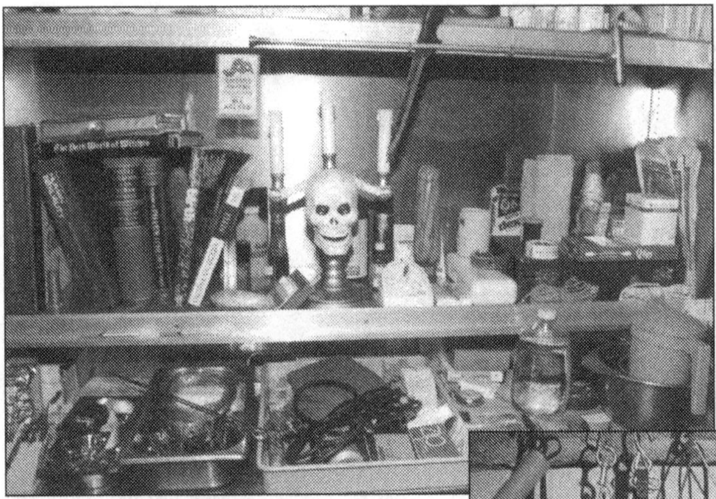

(Above) *Stainless steel cabinet in Toy Box trailer that held some of Ray's paraphernalia used on his victims. Courtesy photo.*

(Right) Items found in the Toy Box. Courtesy photo.

(Below) One of two shelves, one above the other, inside an enclosed cabinet where Ray stashed his live victims for extended periods when he wasn't abusing them. Courtesy photo.

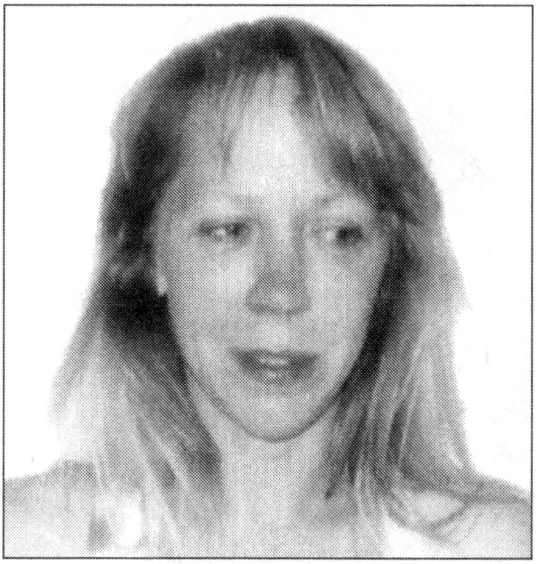

Mug shot of Cynthia Lea Hendy, 39, taken March 1999.

Photo courtesy of Brad Spencer, Sierra County Sheriff's Office Information Specialist, Records Division.

Mug shot of Glenda Jean "Jesse" Ray, taken in 2000. Initially arrested in April 1999 for her involvement in the kidnap and torture of Kelli Van Cleve, she was also implicated in the kidnap, torture and murder of Marie B. Parker, but never tried for either. Released on probation in a plea bargain between her father, David Ray, and the district attorney, she completed her probation in New Mexico in September 2006.

Photo courtesy of Brad Spencer, Sierra County Sheriff's Office Information Specialist, Records Division.

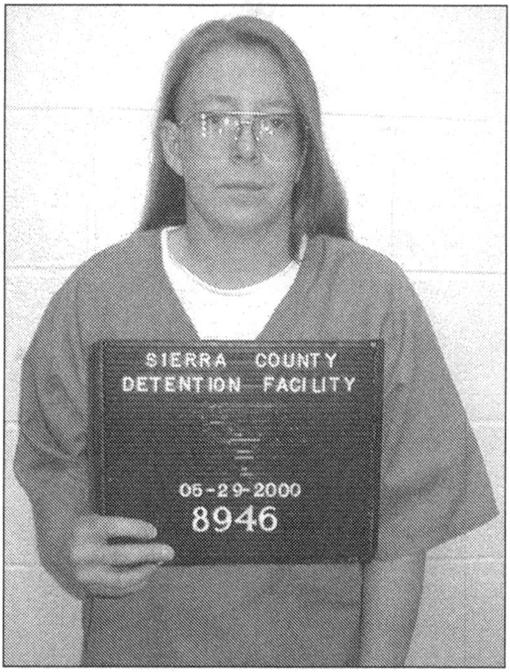

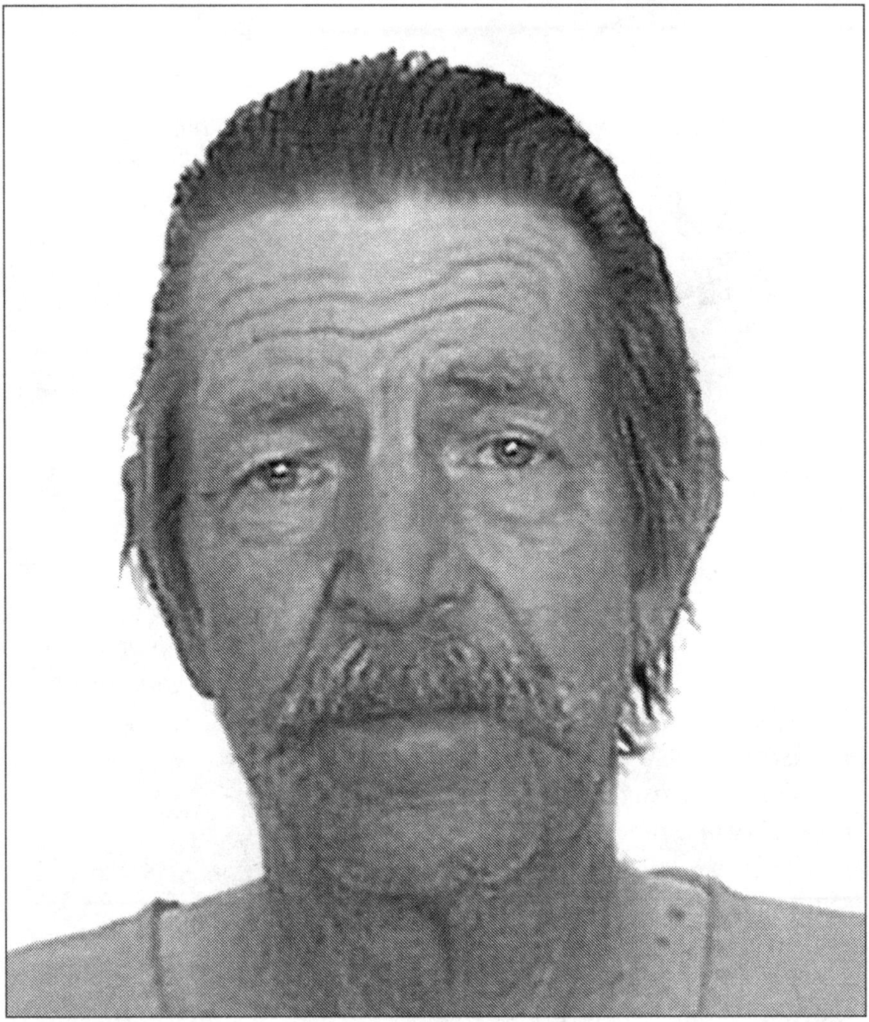

Mug shot of David Parker Ray, 59, taken March 1999.

Courtesy of Brad Spencer, Sierra County Sheriff's Office Information Specialist, Records Division.

Chapter 15 – The Cast

Early in the process of interviewing for this book, the author was visibly shaken by horrific details related by K. C. Rogers. He paused and said, "If you react that way when you hear something like that, you can't write this book." Many of the interviewed investigators said they wanted all of the ugly details included, "... to tell it right, because the public needs to know what David Parker Ray did." However, some details are best left to the readers' imaginations. Besides, the amount of information related to this case is enormous; it was necessary to focus in order to extract a compelling story.

Agent Mallion said, "There are thousands of pieces of evidence, countless boxes, volumes of files, records and reports; you'd be writing this book for years if you tried to cover everything in this case. It's not possible."

^^^^^^^

"Ray was methodical," said K. C. Rogers in a later interview in a Roswell restaurant. A handsome, masculine blonde man in his early fifties, Rogers habitually gripped a wooden toothpick with his teeth.

"A set routine was very important to him, and his methods and techniques progressed over the years." Rogers explained that was why Ray detailed how-to instructions to himself, and kept journals, records and logs.

He said, "Ray, being a state park employee, had access to all the state parks in New Mexico. Probably had keys to every park. This state is full of state and national parks."

He added, "Can you imagine being Ray's victim? When he took you, after you woke up, your life was changed forever."

He said, "Investigators admired David's intelligence. He was sharp and manipulated his victims. He also tried to manipulate his investigators and the court."

Rogers said the officers knew Cindy Hendy was weak and stupid. He considered her a totally disgusting woman. He believed she was not Ray's only female helper, that he had many assistants in his games of torture, including former wives and girlfriends.

What David did with any potential victim depended upon his mood at the moment. He didn't take many available women simply because he wasn't in the mood.

Rogers said Ray devised many ways of serving up pain to his captives, such as sandpaper rubbed on nipples, not just a few minutes but for hours.

"What's the worst pain a woman experiences? Childbirth, right? Some of Ray's tortures simulated childbirth," said Rogers. Ray would put a woman in such an extreme position, and insert such large things into her, that her pelvis separated. Over the years, David learned how to progressively push his victims' pain up another notch. Prolonging their pain without killing them became a science he studied in depth. David would never articulate exactly what he did with his victims when he was through with them. According to Rogers, he would only say, "I put her with the rest of them." But then add that he was just fantasizing.

As profilers found to generally be the case with serial rapists and killers, David Ray was a cop buff. In his home, officers had found scanners and other law enforcement trappings—including a Sam Browne belt and holster and various law enforcement badges that at first glance looked authentic. They also found several handguns.

In his 1985 white Dodge Ram, officers found many seemingly official articles. A list of the New Mexico law enforcement 10-codes was clipped behind his visor. Inside the Ram were a police scanner, a Realistic brand CB radio, a Federal brand control for siren and PA system, and a police radio—all with attached mikes. Also in the front of the Ram, on the floor, was a portable "Kojack light," an official-looking red light that flashed when activated, placed upon the dash or top of an unmarked law enforcement vehicle. They found an electric cattle prod on the floor beside the driver's seat, roadside flares in the back, and many tie-down devices including bars, eyebolts, chains and nylon straps.

On the Ram's rear bumper was a sticker: "DARE to keep Kids off Drugs." That probably amused David Parker Ray, a drug user and drug enforcer—that is, he forced his victims to take drugs.

His authentic Elephant Butte Lake State Park green and beige uniform alone would have lowered women's resistance when he approached them wearing it because, as an official, they would automatically trust him. Inside his home and the Toy Box, officers also found various other types of uniforms: a light-green uniform shirt with "Alamosa Fire Department" embroidered on the back; a light-blue short-sleeved shirt with an authentic U.S. postal patch on the sleeve; a short-sleeved light-blue shirt with a private security company shoulder patch: "Superior Security Agency;" and a long-sleeved armored car uniform shirt, gray with gold braid on the epaulets and a shoulder badge: "Armored Motor Service – Arizona."

Ray often used the guise of a vice cop when he picked up victims, but he wore other disguises as well to impart the public's confidence—not only victims he picked up, but also witnesses who might have seen him take them.

^^^^^^^

David Parker Ray, born in Belen south of Albuquerque on November 6, 1939, grew up with his sister, Peggy. Some say his mother and an aunt raised him. He claimed his father was abusive and almost totally absent from his life, and that he seldom saw his mother. According to recent information from K. C. Rogers, he had lived with his aunt when he was a boy.

Others said his grandmother raised him, and she was strict and neglectful of the children left in her care. Ray had no love for her; he believed she had none for him.

Ronald Hadley of Santa Teresa, New Mexico, had briefly met Ray at Elephant Butte Lake in the 1990s. According to Hadley in March 2007, David Ray said he had lived his early life on a ranch near Claunch, New Mexico. Claunch is a small, remote community, perhaps twenty-five miles south of Mountainair on Highway 55. Hadley speculated that, if Ray's parents had been poor, which was likely, he grew up learning how to improvise, to be resourceful as most ranch kids were anyway—traits he put to good use as an adult.

David and Peggy lived a few years near the small community of Mountainair in Torrance County, southeast of Belen off US-60. Some investigators believe he might have first murdered, while living there, when he was fifteen.

At a book signing event in early 2007, this author met Joe* (who asked to not be named), who had slightly known David Parker Ray when both were teenagers. Some of the following is from his Mountainair recollections.

From I-25, US-60 winds its way east from Bernardo, which is south of Belen, through the Abo Pass between the Manzano and Los Piños mountains. The road twists and turns between the federal lands of the Sevilleta National Wildlife Refuge and the Cibola National Forest. Between the tiny settlements of Blue Springs and Dripping Springs, a ranch road intersects US-60.

At that intersection every school day for a few years, David and Peggy, like other students from ranches in the area, gathered to meet the school bus that took them into Mountainair.

Joe had been one of those students. He recalled an elderly couple named Parker owned a small piece of nearby land, a portion of a section. He said the Parkers, an older man and woman, lived in a shack on the property that was too small to sustain livestock. Locals did not know what they did for income.

The west line of the Parker property backed up to Los Piños Mountains and the Sevilleta National Wildlife Refuge.

Most rural residents in the Southwest, especially farmers and ranchers, "go neighboring." Because of their isolation, they develop relationships with neighbors and, rather than hire temporary labor, help each other with seasonal work such as round-ups and branding. However, the Parkers were reclusive, did not associate with neighbors. The locals knew little about them. They were seen in Mountainair only occasionally when they had to go in for staples.

David and Peggy Ray went to live with their grandparents, the Parkers, around 1956, about two years before Ray graduated from high school in 1958.

The students from the outlying areas rode in small shuttle vans or their families' vehicles to reach the crossroads from where the bus picked them up or dropped them off after school. David and Peggy, coming from a short distance, rode David's Cushman motor scooter to meet the bus, and left it nearby during the day. The boys, with typical boy behavior, picked on David. One of the ways they did was by hard-riding his scooter around the boarding area until the bus driver made them stop.

The other students teased David because he seemed shy. "He never looked any of us boys in the eye, kept his eyes down when we talked to him," said Joe. He wouldn't associate with any of the boys. Even on the bus, he sat only with his sister.

Looking back, Joe could not reconcile the cruel, aggressive David Parker Ray he read and heard about with his memories of the acutely self-conscious, inhibited boy. How could the two extreme personalities apply to the same person?

"How could he have changed so drastically in the next few years?" Joe wondered.

Ray hadn't.

Joe had only seen one facet of David's personality. During the time he knew him, David was already into his sadism practices, according to his own diaries that indicated he had begun acting out his fantasies in 1955.

By 1957, Ray had already escalated from his first mildly sadistic sexual practices on one willing victim to criminal sexual sadism, with cruel experiments on unwilling victims, perhaps already resulting in death for some.

Ray listed "BLM Scholle Cave" as the site of all four of his recorded 1957 sadistic adventures. Scholle was once a small community and still has a post office, according to Joe. He knew of no cave on BLM land in the Scholle area, but there might have been some earlier mining nearby that could have produced a little-known cave.

Joe said David Ray had been mechanically inclined even when he was a boy.

Besides the drastic differences in personality—as he knew him to be and how media and authors later described David—Joe was surprised to learn he was said to be an unusually tall man. Joe remembered him as a small or average-sized teenager. David must have gotten a burst of growth in his late teen years as sometimes happens with boys.

Joe said that, at the Mountainair High School reunion he attended in 1999, David Parker Ray was the most popular subject of discussion because of the case's recent publicity. Former school mates were surprised, perhaps pleased, to see media and TV cameras present to report on the small school's reunion, until they realized the media's focus was on the notoriety of one of their former schoolmates.

Ray joined the Army soon after graduating from Mountainair High School, and was sent to Korea. During his few years in the Army, he learned the mechanic trade. Ray lived at various places over the years before he settled in southwestern New Mexico at Elephant Butte. He had begun living there, off and on, by 1984.

Among other things, he had a roadside wrecker service for a while before he was hired as a full-time employee at Elephant Butte Lake State Park five years before his arrest.

On his job application for employment with the State Park, he said he was a repairman in the U.S. Army, drove a concrete truck in Albuquerque, and taught aircraft engine repair in Tulsa, Oklahoma, from 1970 to 1972. He was a mechanic in Tucson; he worked for a railroad, ran a gas station, and was a mechanic in Phoenix. Over the years, he lived in or spent time in several states.

Investigators began looking closely at police records in Phoenix, Tucson, El Paso, Victoria, Texas, and Ciudad Juarez, Mexico. They expanded their investigations to the Mexican border community because of its more than one hundred unsolved rapes and beating deaths of young women.

Some time after Ray had begun living at Elephant Butte full-time, he started working for the Park in 1994, five years before his name became synonymous with cruelty. He had married and divorced several times and had sons, David and Ron, and a daughter, Glenda Jean "Jesse" Ray, born May 2, 1967. Jesse was a name agents regularly heard and saw in their ongoing investigations. She seemed to have direct connections to this case.

Ray had dark blonde hair and moustache, light blue eyes, and stood 6' 4" tall. He weighed 160 pounds at the time of his arrest. He looked older than his fifty-nine years from exposure to weather, heavy smoking and drugs. He was tall and lanky, towering above most of the officers who escorted him in and out of the courthouse and jail. The top of the head of his attorney, Jeff Rein, was level with Ray's shoulder.

Cynthia Lea Hendy, born February 6, 1960, came to Sierra County in 1997 from Snohomish County, Washington, to avoid arrest on theft and drug charges in Seattle, according to her adult son. She also had two daughters, ages eighteen and twelve. Other people had raised her children. She had trouble with the law her entire adult life. In Seattle she had been charged with forgery, theft, drug violations and receiving stolen property.

Hendy had a history of living with abusive men. Her boy friend, John Youngblood, had followed her when she first moved to Elephant Butte. They had a violent relationship until he finally left. She moved in with David Parker Ray at 513 Bass Road less than a year before the case began.

She had green eyes and sparse blonde hair. She stood 5' 4" and weighed 117 pounds at the time of her arrest, at age thirty-nine. She had once been pretty; but hard living and heavy drug use prematurely aged her.

Hendy had been a victim her entire life, said K. C. Rogers. Being dominated by men was all she had ever known.

One of her several local friends told officers that Hendy claimed she participated with Ray in the tortures for the adrenaline rush. It was exciting, Hendy told her friend.

Again and again, it seemed many in T or C and Elephant Butte knew—or should have suspected—what Ray, Hendy and Ray's daughter were doing to women; but people either condoned it or were indifferent. Or worse, they were also involved.

Several of Ray's acquaintances and nearby neighbors told officers, "So what? S and M stuff. Who cares?"

A neighbor who lived behind Ray's property, said, "With the flatland and the lake, sound carries. But I never heard anything unusual."

By coincidence, on both sides of Ray had lived in-laws of law enforcement officers. Lucy—whose son-in-law had been deputy chief of the New Mexico State Police—lived to his south; and for several years, Bonnie Coler and her family lived north of Ray. The Colers had sold their property on the leased lot—a mobile home and a three-car garage—to a therapist and moved before the case broke. Brad Spencer, the Colers' son-in-law, often visited when his wife's family lived there. He said neither he nor his wife's family noticed anything unusual next door. Spencer became a T or C police officer on March 1, 1999. He later became the records clerk for Sierra County Sheriff's Office.

Another neighbor said he and Ray had discussed his cargo trailer a few years earlier. Ray spoke as if he might sell the Toy Box to him later that summer. What was that about? Why would Ray sell it? Was he thinking of moving on? Was he silently laughing while enjoying an insincere conversation with the neighbor? Who knew?

^^^^^^^

Although tall, Ray was never described as a powerful or strong man during the years he lived at Elephant Butte, perhaps ever in his life. Rolf Hechler, now southwest regional manager of New Mexico State Parks, called him "a frail old guy." He believed Ray's "power was the way he used his diabolical mind." In early 2007, Hechler said that David Ray became even frailer as his health began deteriorating in 1998. He took a lot of work leave. About six or eight months before the case broke, Ray had major surgery; a lung or part of one was removed. After undergoing that surgery, perhaps also from the anesthesia, his personality seemed to drastically change. Hechler said Ray began to part his hair in the middle, add pomade or oil to slick it, and combed it straight back. He became careless with his words—speaking more openly disrespectful of women and talking sexually as if he were a brash teenager or young man. During a Park meeting with other employees, Ray bragged about discovering Viagra® and how much he liked it.

His lack of physical strength explains his elaborate pulley systems and weight devices that helped him lift and handle his victims.

Hechler said, "We couldn't understand why Ray gave us so many work hours. He'd voluntarily put in sixty or eighty-hour workweeks. At the end of his workday, he'd go eat and then return, riding with park rangers until two a.m. He was nocturnal. We figured he hung with us because he was a wannabe cop. We had no idea at the time what he was doing, but later thought about it: He was probably casing the area, looking for victims."

Hechler said Ray had once been disciplined for bad behavior. He was given thirty days off without pay because he had ordered an excessive quantity of something the Park could never use. Then the excess disappeared. Later, after the case broke, they found that Ray had taken the extra material home for personal use. Hechler said they also later discovered a lot of other Park equipment and materials at Ray's home. He had not been an easy employee to fire because of his proven skills.

Instead of taking the entire non-working motor out of a piece of machinery, he'd remove only the defective part, repair it and replace it in the motor, giving it and the equipment extended life.

Wilson T. "Rusty" Burgess, now in his eighties, had been a volunteer at the lake for a number of years. First, he had served honorably during World War II as a heroic air rescue pilot, flying tiny Piper Cub planes in the CBI (China, Burma and India) Theater. Lord Louis Mountbatten was among those he transported or rescued. After "Flying the Hump" over the mighty Himalayas, being shot down behind enemy lines and spending eight days crawling through

Japanese patrols and hacking his way out of the jungle, he served with Merrill's Marauders, an elite ground combat unit. He even spent some time in the European Theater. After the war, Burgess became a law enforcement officer. He began as a city policeman in Tupelo, Mississippi. After moving back to New Mexico, he served dual roles as Marshal of Columbus and Deputy Sheriff of Dona Ana County, and then as Deputy Sheriff of De Baca County at Fort Sumner. From there he retired and moved to Elephant Butte.

Park rangers and vacationers respected Burgess, a longtime Park volunteer. Among other duties, he was the designated ramp master, the Lake's authority over the boat launch ramps, bringing order to a difficult task.

Rusty Burgess had known David Ray, who was highly skilled with his hands—especially metal work—for a number of years and liked him. Ray tinkered with old vehicles and got them running. He could go through a pile of discarded junk and make the items useable again, or create new purposes for them. Burgess described Ray as very friendly with everyone, well-spoken and intelligent.

One day, Burgess wanted a larger butane tank at his Elephant Butte home and asked Ray to do the installation and hookup. Ray was creative with the copper pigtail tubing. Burgess, known for his temper, didn't appreciate Ray's creativity and yelled at him, said it looked terrible. Ray explained that he'd made stirrups on the tank so Rusty's grandkids could ride it like a horse. Burgess wasn't impressed. He told Ray that if he wanted to be paid, he'd dang-well better redo it right so it would pass inspection. Ray redid it. In hindsight, Burgess said it was a wonder he hadn't gotten himself killed by his angry outburst at Ray, a guy known to have an unforgiving temper.

David Ray, the scavenger and tinkerer, sold things he found and repaired. One day he asked Rusty Burgess to pay his fee into a flea market so he could peddle his wares. Burgess did. David Ray took a large quantity of things to that flea market, including guns. He claimed he'd gotten many of the guns from his son, David Jr., who was in the military. One of those guns Ray sold was a lever-action 30/30. Other items included a *metate y mano* (bowl and hand-held grinder set shaped from rough native stone, often very old, used by Indians to grind dried corn and grains into flour). Ray said he had picked those up at Fence Lake near Gallup, when he'd lived there.

Burgess bought many of Ray's items.

David Ray had painted a tow trailer for Rusty at his place at 513 Bass Road. He said he saw a lot of traffic there. One day he saw a car with several women pull into the yard.

Rusty Burgess and his wife, Helen, had met Sollie, a wife or live-in partner of Ray's, and thought she seemed like "a nice enough woman." One day they asked him about Sollie because they had not seen her for a while. Ray shrugged and said he had "sent her back." Ray later commented that someone had murdered Sollie in California, and the murderer had urinated all over her body. Rusty later wondered how Ray would have known that unless he had been the one who did it. Rusty did not mention Sollie to case investigators because they never questioned him.

Burgess recommended Ray, because of his handy skills, to Tommy Mutz, then the Park's Region Three manager. Tommy hired David as the Region Three mechanic.

Rusty Burgess said Ray had been very proud of the uniforms issued to him. He needed boots to go with them, so Rusty gave him a size-ten pair of his own. David Ray polished those boots and took great pride in his appearance. Rusty described him as neat, well-groomed, bathed, clean-shaven and hospitable.

He said Ray often took tourists on tours of the lake and Kettle Top. Burgess also said Ray treated his wife, Helen, respectfully. He knew Ray had once gotten into trouble for going into Blue Waters Saloon with his daughter while wearing his uniform, but he didn't think he was disciplined for it. He said David Ray was a valuable employee; he saved the Park a lot of money with his ability to make things from scratch and to repair costly items that otherwise would have been replaced.

Burgess was in the hospital having heart bypass surgery in March 1999 when the case broke. He felt very betrayed, then and still, after learning of Ray's duplicity. "He broke trust with me and my boss [Rolf Hechler]," he said.

According to Rolf Hechler, Ray did not socialize with those he worked with; his social associates were a rough element, many of them friends of his daughter's, locally known as druggies and homosexuals. With her, he frequented places like the Blue Waters and Raymond's. Hechler said many men who worked with Ray were uncomfortable around him. They did not like or trust him, thought he was an agitator, a troublemaker. They knew Ray played mind games. He deliberately set one person against another, and then quietly stood back to see what happened next. An example might be that he'd tell a supervisor the employees weren't taking proper care of their equipment or vehicles. The supervisor reacted by accusing the employees of shoddy or lazy work, and then did unplanned equipment or vehicle inspections. Ray enjoyed practicing remote control.

Manipulating people and causing frictions were among the things Ray did best.

One of the items Ray designed for the Park was a generator converted to a light plant, very useful for illuminating remote accident and crime scenes.

Rusty Burgess said Ray's daughter looked like a man, and he thought she was always "hopped up" on narcotics or liquor. She spent much of her time at Raymond's. Outside of work her father hung around with her and her friends at Raymond's or Blue Waters.

Rolf Hechler described Jesse as strawberry blonde with ruddy complexion, 5' 8" or 5' 9", 135 or 140 pounds. She dressed like a biker and wore chains. She boldly flirted with women, even when men accompanied them.

In 2006 and 2007, the Discovery Channel's "Most Evil" program lists David Parker Ray as one of the nation's most evil. Hechler said, in late March 2007, that he'd watched a TV program about the case; perhaps it was the one on the Discovery Channel. Hechler said Cindy Hendy was interviewed from prison. He cringed when she proudly said she had worked at the Elephant Butte Lake State Park. Hechler explained how it really was: She had been jailed sometime before the case broke, perhaps a year earlier, and was briefly sent to the Lake on a jail work-release program.

In 2000, the New Mexico State Police presented a plaque to then-Park Superintendent Rolf Hechler. On the plaque is inscribed: "In appreciation for the assistance rendered in one of the most bizarre criminal investigations—the Elephant Butte Sexual Torture Case that began March 1999." Hechler explained the reason for the presentation: Elephant Butte Lake State Park "closed operations at their Boating Safety Training Center for several weeks to host the dozens of FBI, state CID, State Police and other investigators. They brought in their own high-tech equipment, added phone lines and set up the incident command center out of this building. We further provided support in the form of lending our heavy equipment and an operator to excavate certain areas of the crime scene. We just let them use our facilities and equipment and got out of their way."

^^^^^^^

Hendy began talking to officers. She said she believed Ray was responsible for countless acts of sexual torture and at least 14 homicides that she knew about from living with Ray for nearly a year.

Investigators had already heard she had said that to friends now willing to quote her. Why were they only now, with Hendy and Ray in custody, giving the news media and police this information, when she had spoken of it to them much earlier?

Hendy said bodies were buried in various places around Elephant Butte and in the desert, and were also dropped into the lake between Ray's property and Kettle Top. Kettle Top is one of several rock formations sticking up out of the water of Elephant Butte Lake. Its rounded shape slopes upward to a small flat top. Kettle Top is not as prominent an abutment as Elephant Butte, from which comes the name of this lake and tiny community, but it is clearly visible from many directions around the lake.

Much of the lake has a shelf that runs out and suddenly ends. Beyond the shelf is a deep drop, causing many accidental drownings of lakeshore vacationers.

At the investigation's peak, the water was 160 feet deep below Kettle Top.

The bottom of the lake has a thick layer of silt that can envelop countless bodies. A State Dive Team member said, of an earlier diving exercise, that he had stuck his arm into the silt up to his armpit and still did not touch *terra firma*. The lake's water is so murky that you cannot see beyond your outstretched hand, he said. A diver can only stay down eight minutes at 160 feet, and it takes him half a day to recover after each dive. He cannot make many such dives over a period of days before his body cannot recover.

In March 2007, Rolf Hechler said the lake loses thirty per cent of its reservoir to silt.

Drownings in Elephant Butte Lake are common, several each season. Many times divers searched its depths for victims. In the past, they even searched the lake for a plane that went in.

In March 2007, Hechler explained about that plane. He said Henry Parks owned the Marina del Sur. He was a pilot and often buzzed his home as a greeting to his family. One day, while his family stood on the balcony watching, he swooped down too close; the wing of his plane hit the water. His plane went down in Cow Camp Cove. At that time, his son, Steve Parks, ran the Park.

No matter how important it was to find bodies to prove Ray was a murderer, at this point, the State Police Search and Recovery Dive Team had not begun to dive in Elephant Butte Lake to search for remains of victims that Ray allegedly dumped there. Divers considered it an impossible task to find bodies below Kettle Top and in many of the deep areas of the lake.

In early 2007, one NMSP diver said he believed many bodies had been dumped in the lake but nothing remains of them now.

Ray had continually outsmarted the law.

^^^^^^^

The third FBI profiler arrived. He viewed the video, listened to the audiocassettes and saw Ray's journals, logs, instructions and illustrations, but chose to not visit the property.

The three profilers said David Parker Ray exhibited traits of a sexual sadist. Victims' physical and psychological suffering provided him sexual excitement and pleasure. Prolonged suffering was his purpose; deaths were his failures. She's no fun when she's dead.

Sexual sadists perform ritualistic sexual behavior and tend to collect and savor souvenirs taken from their victims—like identification cards, hair, clothes, jewelry—even knowing those found in their possessions could implicate them in their crimes.

Serial rapists and killers choose victims at random; there is seldom any personal link between the perpetrator and the victim. That makes those kinds of crimes particularly difficult to solve. However, those criminals do fit certain profiles, and if the profiler is given time and opportunity to study the case, eventually the criminal can be described, helping to lead investigators to the perpetrator.

Most serial rapists and killers live double lives. Their associates—those uninvolved with them—don't suspect that they are capable of doing what they do. Serial criminals are often intelligent and complex people.

Ray was intelligent, and he was certainly complex.

Investigators knew of at least one other woman in T or C besides Hendy who willingly subjected herself to Ray and his cruel perversions. They had found photos of her, bound and gagged, in the Toy Box. "That one couldn't get enough pain," Lou Mallion said, shaking his head in bewilderment.

Officers found Ray had looked at bondage and S and M websites that offered willing sex slaves. Those women didn't interest him; they'd be no fun. Ray wasn't interested in willing women; they and women like Hendy bored him. They were no challenge.

Rogers thought Ray got Cindy Hendy involved with him by showing her it was more fun to help him give pain to others than to receive it.

Rogers gave this scenario as a way he might have convinced her to become involved. At first, Hendy had subjected herself to Ray, and he didn't hurt her too badly so she would stay with him. Then he told her, "You know what I really like? I like doing it to other women." He'd go out and find women willing to participate in S and M, and bring them home. Then one day, he brought home a woman and had Hendy help torture her. Afterwards he told Hendy, "Guess what? She wasn't willing. I kidnapped her. Guess what? You tortured her too so you are a party to it." And Hendy was hooked.

^^^^^^^

When Hendy told investigators about bodies Ray had disposed of in the lake and nearby on the prairie, she mentioned that one of those was a woman named Marie Parker. However, she said it was Dennis Roy Yancy, not Ray, who killed her.

She said she hadn't been present when it happened; David had told her about it.

She gave officers convincing details.

Chapter 16 – Other Victims

Except for a few minor personality clashes of officers from differing agencies, they worked well together. Few had been part of such a large and diverse team or involved in a case of such magnitude, complexity and notoriety.

They believed Ray had murdered multiple times; they needed to find bodies to prove it. They felt foolish saying that they believed there were murders when the primary suspects, Ray and Hendy, were jailed for just kidnapping and sexual abuse. Those are not minor crimes—they had journals, Polaroid photos and artistic drawings to prove that—but officers were certain murders were included with those crimes.

The public was repeatedly asked to call Crime Stoppers with any information about the case. As media coverage ramped up and new information was released, including suspicions of multiple murders, the team became swamped with calls—both tips and queries. They had to install additional telephone lines at their Elephant Butte Lake headquarters, and bring in more operators.

A spokesman told the media that, according to evidence and the continuous incoming calls from all over the United States with new information and new possibilities, this case would be immense and the number of investigators involved would continually grow and expand to other places.

Women called claiming to be victims of Ray. Operators had to sort through the huge quantity of calls to determine which were bogus and which might be legitimate.

Municipal police headquarters from all over the country called to report unsolved murders and missing women. Families and friends called to tell about missing loved ones, the most difficult calls for the officers to handle.

Hundreds of families sought closure, and police departments hoped to close warm and cold cases. All hoped, while also dreading, that this case would give them that closure. So did the case's investigators.

They wanted to nail David Parker Ray with all of his crimes, leaving none unsolved.

This case led them into past missing persons files in various police precincts. There were files on two missing women with particularly interesting links to David Parker Ray: Cynthia Lea Hendy or David's daughter, Jesse Ray.

Officers were sent, a straight shot up I-25, to look at the missing persons files at the Albuquerque Police Department. There, Ernestine Roach, missing persons investigator, and Carla Gandara, violent crimes detective, directed them to two files.

At the time she became missing, Jill Troia was a twenty-two-year-old petite Asian-American living in Albuquerque. She had moved there when she was in the Air Force. Jill's mother, Ann Troia, who lived in Michigan, and Valerie Branham, the woman Jill had briefly lived with in the northeast heights area of Albuquerque in the 1990s, both said Jill was too trusting.

In October 1995, Jill's mother wrote a letter to the Albuquerque Police Department to report her daughter missing. In that letter, Ann Troia said Jill was last seen the night of September 30, 1995, in the company of a woman named Glenda Jean Ray.

Valerie's daughter, Claudia Branham, was a friend of Jill's. Claudia had been out with Jill and her male roommate that night. After a movie, she said, she dropped them off at Jill's apartment. Records showed that later that night, Jill went out again without her roommate. She met some friends at a local Albuquerque club and from there went with one to a restaurant where she and her friend were seen arguing. That friend was Glenda Jean "Jesse" Ray. That was the last known time Jill was seen alive.

There was also a missing persons file on Marie Parker at the Albuquerque Police Department, as well as at the Sierra County Sheriff's Office.

Marie B. Parker, born in 1975, was a young mother of two little girls. She was living in Truth or Consequences when she disappeared on July 5, 1997.

After her disappearance, her children lived with her friend, Julie Lawrence, and later with Marie's mother, Kate, in Albuquerque.

Officers found no arrest records of Marie for prostitution, but her mother told investigators that her daughter had "hooked" in Albuquerque on Central and on the State Fairgrounds.

Marie came from a dysfunctional family and lived a troubled life most of her twenty-two years. The Sierra County Sheriff's deputies were called to Kate Parker's home several times because of domestic problems between Kate and her boy friend, according to Jolene Starr, Sheriff Beyer's executive assistant. Some of Marie's friends said that one of her mother's boy friends had sexually molested her.

Marie was often truant from school when she was growing up in T or C with her mother, and she ran away from home. She was a runaway for five years, and as a teenager, lived with a friend, Julie Lawrence, in Belen, south of Albuquerque. Marie's older brother was in a Nevada prison for murder. Marie had testified against him and his girl friend at their trial.

When she was pregnant with her first child, she returned home to T or C to live with her mother.

Local people who were interviewed said Marie was "heavy into the drug culture of Truth or Consequences." Larry Brock of Center Point, Texas, told investigators that he had wanted to marry her and he gave her a gold ring with a half-carat diamond; but he could not pull her away from her drug life and friends at T or C, he said. Officers learned, when they first investigated her disappearance, that Marie had hocked Brock's engagement ring for $200.

After Marie disappeared, her half-brother, Tom McCauley, told officers looking into her disappearance that she had "dated" Dennis Roy Yancy, but later disliked him.

Yancy was a known associate of Cynthia Hendy, who had recently moved to the area, and of David Parker Ray. Marie also associated with Jesse Ray.

For a while, Marie lived in an apartment at T or C with her brother, Tom. When Marie was evicted, she lived with one of her little girls on the lakeshore in a tent she borrowed from David Ray. In early 2007, Rolf Hechler said Marie had dug a depression in the sand, and draped a tarp above it, for a nesting place. There she and her friends had drugs and booze parties all night and slept all day. One can only surmise how she met her food needs, or where she pottied. The spot where she camped on the shore was not far from Ray's residence on Bass Road. She was living there when she disappeared.

Parker was last seen in the Blue Waters Saloon in Elephant Butte the night of July 5, 1997.

Tom and a friend of his, Kevin Renkin, said she was out with them earlier that evening. She left them saying she would return in a couple hours. She said she was going to the Blue Waters Saloon to meet a couple of her friends. She never returned.

Tom reported her missing the next day after he found her 1993 Geo Metro in the parking lot of the Blue Waters Saloon. Glenda Jean "Jesse" Ray, whose driver's license at that time showed her address as 513 Bass Road, was questioned about Marie's disappearance. Jesse Ray was the last person known to have seen Marie. The Blue Waters Saloon was fairly close to the Ray residence.

Sierra County Sheriff Deputy Lawrence Gaston was an original investigator on that case. He said it had been a friend babysitting Marie's children who first realized she was missing. Gaston said it had begun as a missing persons report, and then was turned over to the New Mexico State Police, assigned to Officer Penny Ryan.

Despite the connections, there had been insufficient evidence to charge anyone with the murder of Marie Parker. Investigators had also found insufficient evidence to charge anyone with the death of Jill Troia, despite connections now intriguing. Besides, without a body, there was no proof either was dead.

In the first week or two of the 1999 David Parker Ray investigation, however, because of his direct and indirect connections to them, suspicions about those two cases were keen. There was now cause to reactivate both of them.

Billy Ray Bowers was yet another among the unsolved files of missing persons or murders that now interested investigators because of Ray connections.

A body had been found in 1989 floating in Elephant Butte Lake wrapped in a blue tarp and roped to two anchors. The corpse had a bullet wound in the back of the head. The body's condition caused identification to take a while. Not long before the Ray case broke, the body was identified as Billy Ray Bowers.

At the time of Bowers' disappearance on September 25, 1988, more than ten years before the Ray case began, he had worked at Canal Motors in Phoenix, Arizona. When he disappeared, David Parker Ray had also worked at Canal Motors in Phoenix. Rolf Hechler said Bowers had been Ray's boss. When he had disappeared, Bowers' coworkers said he and Ray had quarreled about money. One was indebted to the other.

Ray claimed, on his résumé in his employment file at Elephant Butte Lake State Park, that he had worked there as a mechanic from 1982 to 1990. Although David then lived in Phoenix, he had leased property at Elephant Butte, New Mexico, beginning in 1983 and he spent time there. That made a double connection between Bowers and Ray. Some time after the disappearance of Bowers in Phoenix, Ray was living full-time at Elephant Butte.

In hindsight, it seemed strange to rangers that it had been Elephant Butte Lake State Park employee David Parker Ray who helped pull that blue tarp-wrapped body out of the lake.

In early 2007, one of the rangers who had helped retrieve the body in 1989 said he'd heard Ray mumble, "Should have filled it with more rocks;" but for ten years, he hadn't thought much about it. Those words haunt him now.

Two months before the unidentified body, later known to be Bowers', was found, another body in similar circumstance was found in the lake. That body, identified as Janis Pulliam's, was tied to a sand-filled gasoline can. However, FBI supervisory special agent, Doug Beldon, said the investigation of that case determined there was no connection between Pulliam and Bowers or Ray's case. He didn't elaborate.

Now, Hendy had begun telling investigators that David Parker Ray claimed he had killed a man from Arizona named Bowers.

Chapter 17 – Yancy

Because neighbors said Ray often dug in his yard, planting and replanting bushes, investigators ordered a backhoe with a small bucket. It was parked nearby, in anticipation of being used for digging.

Based upon what neighbors said, and evidence and information from the profilers, the primaries on the case had probable cause to write yet another affidavit for a search and seizure warrant. This time, it was not for a surface search inside or outside. It was underground in the yard and it was also in out-of-sight places inside the residence and trailers. Profilers said sexual sadists tend to hide victim trophies inside light fixtures, under floorboards, behind wall paneling and ceiling tile, or they bury them near certain trees, bushes or light poles for markers.

The interviewed victims said their jewelry was missing after their ordeals with Ray and Hendy. Of course, Cindy Vigil, the first known victim who escaped with nothing, was missing everything. Investigators found her clothes in Ray's residence.

During extensive searches throughout the property, various belongings of different women were also found. Trophies.

Mid-morning Wednesday, March 31, several officers and agents entered the enclosed yard of Ray's property and began digging with shovels and prodding the ground with steel rods in specific places marked by FBI agents with small red locator flags.

They found nothing of much significance. A few large dug-up bones proved to not be human.

No human remains were found anywhere at 513 Bass Road.

On the first Saturday of April, FBI agents loaded two trailers and the Toy Box trailer onto transport trucks and took them to the FBI's New Mexico headquarters for further examination. Early into the case, officials brought their own trailers onto the premises to store evidence taken from the scene. Those too, with their contents, were taken to the FBI's lab in Albuquerque.

They removed their barriers blocking Bass Road and the yellow crime-scene tape surrounding seven homes next to Ray's. The tape around his home remained, however, and New Mexico Mounted Patrol troopers continued to guard it.

Two agents from the Albuquerque FBI office returned, again staying at the Black Range Motel.

Long ago, Lao-tzu, founder of Taoism, had said a journey of a thousand miles begins with one step. Agents and officers were about to take an important first step that might lead to a murder conviction in this case. One of many, they hoped.

By coincidence, Dennis Roy Yancy had been staying at the Black Range Motel, just two doors from FBI agents.

On Thursday, April 8, Yancy had approached the husband-and-wife managers of the motel and restaurant wanting employment to pay for rent and meals. He told them he lived in Albuquerque but needed to stay in T or C close to his children, and he was out of money.

He lied, nothing unusual for him. He did not live in Albuquerque. He was a well-known disrespectable resident of Sierra County. His mailing address was a post-office box in Williamsburg, the community next-door to Truth or Consequences.

Born in 1971, he was the son of middle-class parents; his father was a cop and his mother, Anna Norton, was a legal secretary. She later worked at the local HUD office, Hechler said. Even when attending T or C's Hot Springs High School, he was arrested several times, beginning at age sixteen. Charges included burglary and breaking and entering. He began to heavily use alcohol and drugs while still a teenager, and his behavior spiraled out of control. Locals suspected him of a considerable amount of malicious mischief and vandalism, including torturing their pets to death. He had a gang that practiced witchcraft, preying on schoolmates and townspeople. For a period of time, Yancy and his friends terrorized their school and community. He was convicted and served time in the New Mexico Boys' School, the state's reform school for boys in the northeastern part of the state.

After he got out, as a condition of his release, he completed high school and served a tour in the Navy. However, after returning to T or C (if not earlier), he went back to his old troublesome ways. He married a local girl, Christina, and they had a child; but he was still deeply involved with drinking, drugs and hard-core partying. Because of his association with a local homosexual, Yancy was a primary suspect in the weird, sadistic death of that man, a case legally unresolved.

At the Black Range Motel on Thursday, Yancy went into the restaurant and whipped up a batch of biscuits to prove to the managers that he could cook. They needed a breakfast cook; they hired him. The woman said his job would begin at six the next morning.

Friday, April 9, at 7 a.m., arresting officers arrived at the Black Range Motel. In the restaurant, one hour after his new job had begun, officers read Dennis the Miranda warning while his hands were deep in a bowl of biscuit dough. When the officers arrested him, they said it was for the murder, on or about July 5, 1997, of Marie B. Parker.

The managers said they hated to lose him so soon. He made good biscuits.

Officers still had not found Marie's remains, but they believed Yancy killed her. They thought they had enough probable cause to make the arrest. He was charged with murder, kidnapping, conspiracy to commit murder, conspiracy to commit kidnapping, and tampering with evidence. He was held without bond.

District Attorney Ron Lopez said, "The more we are in front of the press, the worse the situation gets regarding finding an impartial jury." He also told the public, "We have sufficient evidence, we can proceed without a body," referring to Marie Parker.

Dennis Roy Yancy was twenty-seven years old. Besides in Sierra County, he had lived off and on in Texas. He worked, sporadically, at a fast-food restaurant and a grocery store.

According to locals who knew him, he was a regular associate of David Parker Ray, Jesse Ray, and also Hendy after she moved to T or C. For a period of time, Marie Parker was Yancy's girl friend. But after she disappeared, her brother, Tom McCauley, had said she no longer liked him. In fact, he said, she was afraid of Yancy because he was "so weird." She tried to avoid being anywhere near him.

Yancy's half-sister, Heather Norton, told officers that she, too, was a friend of Jesse Ray, and she "hung out" with her and her father.

"Everyone who meets Jesse meets her dad," Heather said with strange guile.

David Parker Ray, held at the Sierra County jail in Truth or Consequences, and Cynthia Lea Hendy, held at Dona Ana County in Las Cruces, were still not arraigned for murder.

^^^^^^^

Approaching T or C, the terrain is rolling or dune-like hills and low, sparse vegetation with sandy soil. It is much like that around Las Cruces—a high desert plateau surrounded by distant jagged bare mountains.

Sierra County was named for the mountain range, Sierra de los Caballos—Mountain of the Horses, for a herd of wild horses that Indians discovered there generations earlier.

In 1916, a dam was completed across the Rio Grande above what was then called Hot Springs but is now named Truth or Consequences, creating the Elephant Butte reservoir and lake. Elephant Butte acquired its name from the extinct volcano cinder dome, or butte (rhymes with cute, not butt) rising out of the water, resembling the upper rear-end of an elephant.

The adjacent nine-thousand-acre Caballo Reservoir, also named for Sierra de los Caballos, likewise was created from the Rio Grande; but much later, in the late 1930s. It too was built for irrigation, but more to fulfill New Mexico's water obligations in a 1906 treaty with Mexico.

The Rio Grande runs from north to south, from Colorado through the center of New Mexico—dividing the state into eastern and western halves like two unequal jagged hulls of a walnut—to El Paso, Texas, and into Mexico. Running parallel to the Rio Grande in Sierra County are the San Andres Mountains to the east and the Black Range in the Cibola National Forest to the west, through which runs the Continental Divide. Closer to the Elephant Butte Reservoir are the Fra Cristobal Range and San Mateo Mountains. Closer to the nearby Caballo Reservoir is the Sierra de los Caballos.

T or C was originally named Hot Springs because of the area's natural hot mineral water wells and pools. The small town of Hot Springs was built on top of those springs, around and among the hills and rock outcroppings. The community sits in a tight little valley tucked in by orange and yellow rock formations, framed by the higher mountains.

Except mostly by locals, Hot Springs, New Mexico, was an unknown place in 1950. Besides, there were other places across the U.S.A. called Hot Springs. This little Hot Springs in southwestern New Mexico was pretty much a nonentity.

Ralph Edwards had a nationally-transmitted radio game show, later also televised, called Truth or Consequences. In 1950, he sought a gimmick to celebrate the show's tenth year. One of his staff suggested they search for a town somewhere in the United States willing to change its name to honor the show. Edwards liked the idea, but he said it had to be an honorable town. When he learned little Hot Springs, New Mexico, had beneficial waters, and that the townsfolk warmed to his idea of the name change, he promised their town would become "the greatest health resort in the nation" from his efforts and generated publicity.

Edwards had lofty ideas for the town. He decreed that he and the community would "work hand in hand for the betterment of the nation."

It did not turn out the way Edwards expected. It never became a famous spa, and the remedial hot springs are not plentiful.

In early 1999, despite continued annual treks by Ralph Edwards to T or C, and the oddity of its name, the town of Truth or Consequences remained obscure.

However, nearly fifty years after the name change, beginning March 22, 1999, Truth or Consequences suddenly did become a town nationally, even internationally known—but not as the honorable place Edwards had envisioned.

And for many women, it had not been a healthy place.

Chapter 18 – Confession

Dennis Roy Yancy told arresting officers that he was not guilty.

When he was arraigned in Magistrate Court, his pregnant wife, Christina, sat behind him, silently crying.

She had been married to him since 1977.

On his behalf, Yancy's temporary defense attorney, Steve Sosa, entered a not guilty plea to all charges. Magistrate Judge Thomas Pestak read to Yancy his five counts, including kidnapping and murder. Deputy District Attorney Ron Lopez asked the court to set no bond for this capital crime. If found guilty, Yancy could get life plus forty-six years, in addition to a $45,000 fine.

The court appointed Gary Mitchell of Ruidoso as Yancy's new attorney. Mitchell was a strong opponent of the death penalty and had defended several high-profile defendants. Terry Clark, convicted in the 1986 rape and murder of nine-year-old Dena Lynn Gore of Artesia, New Mexico, was perhaps his highest-profiled case. Mitchell was one of a dozen or more attorneys involved in that case because it lasted many years, but it still brought him fame, at least within New Mexico.

Dena Lynn had been riding her bike to a convenience store a few blocks from home when Clark, a ranch-hand, grabbed her. Clark's brother, who suspected him after he learned the girl was missing, notified police. The child's body was found in a shallow grave on the ranch where Clark worked north of Artesia in southeastern New Mexico.

Clark's attorney had advised him to hurry and plead guilty because then-Governor Toney Anaya, an opponent of the death penalty, was expected to commute all existing death sentences before he left office. That didn't work. Anaya did empty all five death row cells, but that did not help Terry Clark because the court effectively delayed his sentence until after Anaya left office.

Clark's attorneys appealed repeatedly. After fifteen years of trials, hearings and appeals, more than half-a-million taxpayer-dollars, dozens of attorneys and expert witnesses, as many as seven psychological evaluations and mountains of paperwork, Clark was finally put to death by lethal injection by the Corrections Department of New Mexico on November 6, 2001. It only happened then because Clark finally told his attorneys to stop appealing. Even then, despite his repeated orders to end the appeals, his attorneys managed to delay his execution for another year or two.

Immediately following Terry Clark's execution, Corrections Secretary Robert J. Perry made the following statement: "On July 17, 1986, while free on bond during an appeal for kidnapping and sexually assaulting a six-year-old girl in Roswell, Terry Clark drove to Artesia and kidnapped nine-year-old Dena Lynn Gore. [He took] her to a nearby ranch where he sexually penetrated her, then shot her in the head three times. ... While in jail, Terry Clark confessed to a family minister that he had kidnapped the girl, had sex with her, and then shot her when she said, 'You're going to pay for this.'

"Tonight, here at the Penitentiary of New Mexico, personnel and machinery of the New Mexico criminal justice system, the criminal and appellate law code, and the New Mexico Corrections Department have [at last] brought truth to those [Dena's] words."

An additional Corrections Department statement said, "Since New Mexico's last execution in New Mexico in 1960, 7,691 people have been murdered in our state, according to records from the State Office of the Medical Investigator."

The case of Terry Clark—who murdered a child after being found guilty and out on appeal from another brutal child sexual assault—brought a national public outcry.

That case, and other infamous defendants Mitchell represented, brought the attorney notoriety, and a reputation of being a tough state adversary in the courtroom.

Soon after David Ray's preliminary hearing, Mitchell went through various legal motions, including a request for a continuance, on behalf of his client, Dennis Yancy.

^^^^^^^

Police searched old reports for overlooked information on Parker. When she disappeared the night of July 5, 1997, her mother, Kate, was living in T or C. She said she had last seen her daughter earlier that day, before she, Kate, had left town. She said Marie and some of her friends had a party at her house while she was away. When she returned, she found her flowerbeds dug up. At first, she thought it was malicious mischief or disrespectful partiers. Later, Kate believed whoever killed her daughter had buried her in those flowerbeds.

Investigators had dug into the flowerbeds then, but found nothing.

Kate moved with Marie's little girls to Albuquerque. Now, investigators again dug in the area that had once been Kate's flowerbeds, but they again found nothing.

In a surprising development on April 17, 1999, Christina Yancy told newspaper reporters that when she visited her husband, Dennis Roy Yancy, in jail the night he was arrested, he confessed to her that he had killed Marie Parker.

Christina said Roy told her that he, David Ray and Jesse had left the Blue Waters Saloon with Marie to buy drugs for her. However, Yancy told his wife, David Parker Ray ordered him to kill her. He also said David Ray videoed him strangling Marie to death.

He had to do it, Christina told reporters. David made him.

A wife cannot legally testify against her husband. K. C. Rogers thought Mrs. Yancy was stupid, blabbing to the media. But it was fortuitous for investigators.

NMSP Agent Norman Rhoades and Sgt. Rogers interviewed Yancy. When they sat with him, Rogers told him they knew he had killed Marie Parker. He said David and Hendy had ratted on him, and the investigators had the evidence, including a video, proving his guilt.

Yancy immediately broke down and talked non-stop for 45 minutes. He said he wanted to tell them his side of the story, that he was sure David didn't tell it right.

He confessed to the murder while his stunned attorney, Gary Mitchell, sat beside him. Ray gave all kinds of details of the killing. His interview was taped.

"You narc'ed him, didn't you?" Rhoades asked Rogers after the amazing interview.

Rogers grinned. "Sure I did!"

In the taped interview, Roy Yancy said Jesse Ray had gone into the Blue Waters Saloon to pick up Marie. Outside in the parking lot, Jesse held a gun to Marie's head and ordered her and Roy into the truck. Jesse claimed she was taking Marie to meet someone for a drug buy. Jesse ordered Roy to guard his ex-girl friend while she drove them to 513 Bass Road. When they arrived, Jesse Ray took Marie, at gunpoint, into the Toy Box. Yancy admitted that he knew the cruel purpose of the trailer, but he claimed he never entered it while Jesse and David Ray kept Marie in there and sexually tortured her for three days.

Yancy said Jesse and David ordered him to go into the Toy Box on July 8. Inside he saw Marie, naked and bound, on a green cot. David handed him a rope and told him, "You know what you have to do." Yancy said he strangled her while David videoed the murder for a snuff film.

Later, Yancy told officers that he knew where Marie's body was buried. He directed them to a specific location in Sierra County, to a small *arroyo* in the desert north of T or C near I-25. Guiness and Carbon, adept at cadaver-sniffing, went along to assist. They wanted to help dig, but the others declined their offer. Guiness and Carbon were police dogs.

Neither dogs nor officers found anything interesting, just the usual debris washed into *arroyos* during thunderstorms, such as rusted tin cans and old tennis shoes.

Yancy suggested other places for them to look for Parker's remains; and for a while the officers followed his lead on foot and by a State Police helicopter.

No body was found. Was he jerking their strings or did he really have such short or indifferent memory of an event that should have been indelibly marked there forever?

He was a hard one for officers to figure. They found him to be as weird as people who knew him had said.

Yancy later said David had probably moved the body after they buried it.

On Sunday, Christina Yancy visited Roy in Sierra County Detention in T or C. As she passed cells holding other prisoners, one claimed to have a message from David Parker Ray. He whispered to her a message to deliver to her husband: "Rats die in jail."

Monday, officers moved Roy Yancy to the Dona Ana County jail in Las Cruces for his safekeeping. Hendy, also an informant against Ray, had already been moved there away from any possible influence from him.

Roy Yancy later tried to recant his confession, but his own words on videotape, and the quantity of details he gave, nailed him, said Rogers. Mitchell, his attorney, knew he couldn't get him out of the fix he had put himself in; he advised him to plead guilty.

Rogers later said Yancy was convicted of murder and sentenced without a body and not a shred of evidence against him except his taped confession.

That may be the state's only case where a guy was convicted by nothing but his own mouth, said Rogers, with deep personal satisfaction.

^^^^^^^

For centuries, *El Camino Réal* (the Royal Road) was an eighteen-hundred-mile commerce trail from Veracruz, Mexico, to Santa Fe. Coronado and Oñate traveled it in the 1500s. The trail passed through what is now Sierra County and was still used until the railroads came into New Mexico in the 1880s.

Because of no water or shade, the barren *El Jornada del Muerto* (the Trail of Dead Men) was a dangerous ninety-nine-mile section of *El Camino Réal* that passed through a portion of Sierra County. It still is a deadly trek for illegal aliens coming from Mexico.

Investigators had begun to dig in many places in the Sierra County desert. If they found human remains there, would the area become known to future generations as *La Jornada de las Muertas*—the Trail of the Dead Women?

Chapter 19 – The Prelim

On a Friday in early April 1999, FBI Special Agent Patricia E. Rust completed cataloging the contents of the Toy Box and headed home to El Paso for the weekend.

There, she killed herself with her service handgun. Some writers suggested that the suicide was brought on by the case. Her colleagues—police officers and FBI agents who knew her well—dismissed the idea; she was an experienced professional and was accustomed to the worst acts of violence. One coworker suggested that she might have been depressed by problems with a boy friend.

^^^^^^^

That age-old question applied to David Parker Ray: What made him bad? Was it heredity? Chemical imbalance? His environment—his home-life? Was it childhood abuse?

Criminologists say heredity and childhood experience are the two primary factors that produce someone like Ray.

Two FBI profilers from Quantico were still in Sierra County. The investigators were encouraged by Ray's excitement when he learned they would visit him. They believed he would talk more openly to them.

Profilers say that, in order to do an exacting profile, they must assume the entity of the one being profiled, walk in his skin, see through his eyes, think with his sick mind. Police officers were glad that was not in their job description. Working this case gave them enough nightmares without that.

The profilers had spent time looking at the scene—Ray's residence and the Toy Box—before they saw him. They studied his vast quantities of hand-written, typed, and illustrated journals, diaries and posters tacked on the walls. Ray's records indicated many of his victims had died in captivity.

Then the profilers spent several hours with him.

Case investigators hoped he would confess his crimes, including murder.

No confessions were forthcoming from the smiling David Parker Ray, but he happily described in detail many of his "fantasies." In fact, he enjoyed it.

As he continued to be held at Truth or Consequences, he told little truth but investigators hoped to soon lead him to appropriate consequences.

A confession would mean no trial.

David Parker Ray wanted his days in court, as many as possible. It was clear that he looked forward to listening to his victims tell what he had done to them. Reliving his deeds through them gave him pleasure.

Through the profilers' expertise, a chilling profile of Ray emerged, but among the known serial rapists and killers the profilers had studied, Ray's type was rare, nearly unique. His profile fit few.

The date for the combined Ray and Hendy preliminary hearing in District Court was set for Thursday, April 15, 1999. However, Cynthia Hendy would not attend; she waived her appearance. She and her attorney were proposing to cut a deal with the district attorney. The proposal would drastically reduce her charges and lock-up time to a minimum of twelve years and a maximum of fifty-four years in exchange for her testimony. The plea deal was still in the works. Included in it was her exemption from federal charges.

Defendants are legally protected from being prosecuted more than once for the same crime. An exception is if it becomes both a state and a federal case, then a defendant can be prosecuted in both state and federal courts.

On April 15, Ray faced charges with his attorney in the small T or C courtroom packed with people. For the first time, the public and media could view the primary accused, David Parker Ray, and the two victims, and hear first-hand many of the case's sickening details. There some of the audience first learned the identity of the two women, previously known only as "The Albuquerque Woman" or "First Known Victim," and "T or C Woman" or "Second Known Victim."

In the snug courtroom, David Parker Ray faced his two accusers, Cindy Vigil and Angelíca Montaño. Or more to the point, they had to face him again, which would be unpleasant for them. Throughout most of the hearing, Ray wore his smug smile.

While Cindy Vigil was on the stand, the prosecution introduced an important piece of evidence. He handed the metal collar to her, asking if that was what she had worn, the only thing she wore, when she escaped Ray's premises.

The sight of it was too much for her. She screamed at Ray, sitting only feet from her in the cramped courtroom, "You bastard! How could you do that to me?"

The judge cleared the courtroom because of her emotional outburst.

She hyperventilated. The court called emergency medical technicians. Court staff worried about her. She was a valuable witness.

Cindy had asthma. She and her grandmother, always with her in court, had forgotten to bring her inhaler. District Court Clerk Kathy McClean knew she had asthma; she loaned her own inhaler to Cindy until EMTs arrived.

"I know you aren't supposed to loan your meds to other people, but you do what you have to do," McClean later said.

It is unlikely anyone complained about her life-saving assistance.

When court resumed, both of the victims, brought in one at a time to testify, stated under oath that they were whipped, electrocuted, and penetrated with electrical devices that, said Vigil, "… hurt so bad I was screaming. They put tape over my mouth." And she testified that she was "hung from this thing in the ceiling."

She testified that a pulley device, with weights, was attached to her breasts by clips. When she moved, after Ray shocked her with something, the weights on the end of the pulley painfully pulled and stretched her breasts.

She also told the court that Hendy said she and Ray planned to kidnap a ten-year-old girl to use as a sex slave.

Angelíca Montaño testified that she was a captive of Ray and Hendy for five days before they freed her. "I had to play a part to be their friends to still be alive. I didn't think I'd ever see my kids again."

Both women testified that Cynthia Lea Hendy watched and held a handgun on them while Ray abused them.

Art Ortiz, a New Mexico State Police officer, testified about what they found in Ray's Toyota RV after David Parker Ray and Cynthia Lea Hendy were apprehended in it. He said it was later towed to the State Police Crime Lab.

Items he listed in court, found in the RV, included: pieces of rope and chain; metal eyebolts attached to the inside of the RV; a saw and a pair of scissors; a medicine bottle containing a gel substance and a jar of Vaseline; a 12-inch knife; stainless steel tape, six condoms and a roll of duct tape; a battery charger with metal clips attached. In a small trash receptacle were cigarette butts, and used and crumpled adhesive tape with human hairs stuck to it. And in it was a piece of "some kind of plastic, we called it a gag, that had adhesive apparently from tape," he testified. He said the plastic had what appeared to be human teeth marks.

Agent John Briscoe, of the New Mexico State Police's criminal investigation division, testified in chilling unemotional detail about the tools, restraints and other pieces of evidence found in Ray's mobile home. Those included: a device to strap to a person's knees and ankles to spread them wide apart; a pulley system in the ceiling with lead weights attached; rings, clips, and hooks attached to walls, ceilings and tables where chains and other restraints were fastened; a bed with bloody sheets and broken glass; a bloody blanket and an ice pick with blood on it; a roll of duct tape; and Cindy Vigil's clothing. Briscoe testified that there was blood splatter up a wall.

Agent Briscoe said they found on the premises various still photographs of women in bondage, strapped to a table or the chair with the stirrups. When later questioned about these, District Attorney Ron Lopez said they did not know the identities of those women, but they were not the same as the two victims who testified in court. There are other unidentified victims, said Lopez.

Briscoe described what he saw and photographed in an adjacent trailer that Ray called the Toy Box. He said this trailer had a chair with stirrups and various sexual tools. On the walls were signs: "Satan's Den" and "Bondage Room." There were hand-drawn pictures, with how-to instructions, of women being subjected to bondage and sexual torture.

The officer already had the rapt attention of the courtroom. Then he began reading to the court some of Ray's documents found on the premises. One was how to tell the victims what would be done to them.

Another document gave Ray's detailed instructions on how to handle and abuse victims. Briscoe read out loud:

"Psychological and Physical Procedures; Initial Handling of the Captive Personal Fetish.

"Number 1. The new female captive should be gagged and blindfolded with wrists and ankles chained.

"2. Move her into the recreational room; place her body under the suspension chains.

"3. Stand her up under the chains and lock her wrists well above her head.

"4. Place the neck chain around her neck and lock it into place. <u>It Is Permanent.</u>

"5. Clip her leg irons to the floor chain.

"6. Use scissors to slowly remove her dress, blouse or sweater. Cut and remove her bra.

"7. Fondle and abuse her breasts, nipples and other parts of her body.

"8. Keep her blindfolded to increase disorientation, use verbal abuse (dumb bitch, slut, etc.)

"9. Slowly unzip, open and remove the lower clothing. Cut or rip the panties off.

"10. Fondle and abuse her sex organs. Continue the verbal abuse.

"11. Attach the overhead suspension straps to her body, ankles, waist, hips and upper chest.

"12. Remove the leg irons and tighten the ankle straps, pulling her legs upwards until the middle part of her body is horizontal. The ankle straps will force her legs wide apart.

"13. Tighten and adjust the waist, hips and chest straps until the middle of her body is straight. Clip the short fore-chain to the bottom ring on the waist belt so she cannot jerk or lift her body upward.

"14. At this point, the captive is suspended at a convenient height, immobilized and fully exposed. She is uncomfortable, disoriented and probably terrified. Don't cut her any slack. Continue the verbal and physical abuse. Keep her mentally off balance.

"15. Play with her sex organs, rape her vagina and anus. Force large dildos deep into both holes. Use clamps, needles and other devices on her tits and sex organs. Clip and cut lips. Whip her and use electro-shock.

"16. Don't give her time to collect her thoughts. Use her body aggressively during the first hour or two. She will sweat, struggle a lot and exhaust herself. Particularly if the electric shock machine is used extensively.

"17. Intensify her fear. Tell her how she is going to be kept as a sex slave. Describe in detail how she will be continuously raped and tortured. Work on her mind as well as her body.

"18. Keep her body suspended two or three hours. Then lower the gynecological bench, directly beneath her. Lower her body onto the bench, release one arm or one leg at a time and secure it to the bench until she is strapped down. Buckle all the straps on her body until she is totally immobilized, feet in the stirrups and knees forced wide apart. Note: The shock value of disorientation plus continuous verbal and physical abuse during the first few hours of confinement will have a great influence on how docile and subdued the captive will be during the remaining period of captivity. If it is done properly she will be intimidated and much easier to handle."

The courtroom audience sat immobilized, silent. They didn't have time to digest what they had heard before Briscoe read from another document. This one, he said, was advice to guard against ways a captive might try to get free. Investigators had found it tacked on a wall of the Toy Box.

"Remember a woman will do or say anything to get loose. They will: kick, bite, scream, threaten, scratch, yell, run, lie, offer money, beg, offer sex, wait for opportunity. Standard excuses and sob-stories: Menstruating, pregnant, VD, AIDS, sick, kids with babysitter, have to work, sick baby, sick parent, claustrophobia, missed by husband or friend, bad heart, can't miss school. Don't let her get to you. If she was worth taking she's worth keeping. She must be subjected to hypnosis before the woman can be safely released. Never trust a chained captive."

The courtroom audience hardly breathed. They were stunned.

Ray's attorney, Jeff Rein, calmly said some of the charges against his client should be dismissed or changed to less serious counts because the alleged victims' injuries were not sufficient to prove they suffered great bodily harm, and Ray was not accused of holding a gun on the women. He also argued against the charge of aggravated battery because Ray was not on the premises when Hendy allegedly hit the escaping victim with a lamp.

Friday, following one-and-a-half days of courtroom testimony at Ray's preliminary hearing, District Court Judge Neil Mertz ordered that David Parker Ray be bound over for trial in District Court. He was still held on a $1,000,000 cash bond.

D.A. Ron Lopez declined to say whether Hendy would testify against Ray at his trial.

Hendy's attorney, Xavier Acosta, said the plea would be "a true reflection of her involvement with David Ray over the last months. Remember, David's being investigated for years of activity, according to the FBI. Our position has been that she [Hendy] is also a victim in this matter, although she participated in these two acts to which she's pleading."

^^^^^^^

Lopez told the media that the district attorney's office would focus on Dennis Roy Yancy, their suspect now charged with murder.

Chapter 20 – Jesse

In the fourth week of the case, NMSP's spokesman, Lt. Greg Richardson, said the State Police and FBI agents were getting close to making more arrests. Their teams would continue to search for skeletal remains and other evidence in the open areas of Sierra County. He said it was important to the case to find Marie Parker's remains.

They continued to investigate the case involving Jill Troia, last seen with Jesse Ray, said Richardson.

The officers repeatedly told the public that there were more suspects and victims involved with this case.

Most of the FBI evidence recovery teams had returned to their home stations—in Virginia, Texas and Arizona—because nothing remained for them to do in Elephant Butte. Some agents continued to work at the Albuquerque office processing evidence and documents and following leads in many other states.

Jesse Ray had been staying with her brother Ron, thirty-three, in Texas. After her father's arraignment, she returned to Sierra County. She visited her father in jail and—with empty bravado—ordered investigators and media to stay away from her father.

Many witnesses pointed at Jesse Ray as a well-known outlet for drug buys. She seldom worked at conventional jobs; cops believed her primary source of income was drug sales.

Sgt. Rogers located the third known Ray victim, Kelli Van Cleve, in Colorado. FBI Special Agents Carrie Parbs and Larry Haulpt went there to interview her. She was important to the case because she was identified in a video found at Ray's premises, shown naked and captive.

Kelli told officers that Jesse Ray had delivered her to her father, David Ray.

Her memory of what happened to her at Ray's remained sketchy. More came back to her after she read newspapers and saw TV accounts of what happened to two other young women, but she still had a fractured memory.

The audiocassettes, wherein Ray said he would pump amnesia-causing drugs into his victims at the end of their ordeal, would become critically important in Kelli's case, since she had not come forward earlier and her memory remained faulty and erratic three years after her experience.

She said she had been in the Blue Waters Saloon one evening, and Jesse Ray was with her. She remembered leaving the saloon with Jesse, riding on the back of her motorcycle. They didn't travel far before they stopped. She went inside and Jesse and her father went into another room but soon returned. One of them covered her mouth with duct tape and handcuffed her while the other held a knife to her throat.

She said she was strapped to a weight bench in a small trailer that David called the Toy Box. She believed she had been sexually assaulted at least thirty times, but she could only specifically detail six events. (This would become important for the prosecutor.) David told her that he belonged to a satanic cult, and people in that cult had been watching her and wanted her for a sex toy.

Kelli said that after Jesse delivered her into her father's hands, she did not see her again. However, officers and prosecutors believed Jesse was just as guilty as her father in all that happened to Kelli during her four days of captivity.

Like the other two women, Kelli's name and identity were withheld from the public. In published accounts, she was called "Jane Doe Number Three" or "Ray's third victim," although her experience preceded the other two. The court sealed most of the documents pertaining to Kelli, including affidavits and warrants.

^^^^^^^

Monday, April 26, based upon the complaint of this newest victim, officers issued an arrest warrant for Ray's nearly thirty-two-year-old daughter, Glenda Jean "Jesse" Ray.

Case officers, as many as one hundred, had swarmed over 513 Bass Road for weeks, minutely examining it inside and out. Journalists and curious residents kept it under surveillance nearly as long. Investigators had almost demolished it in their searches for hidden evidence. They finally took down the yellow tape and, along with all but a few stray reporters who sometimes wandered about with camera and note pad, at last departed from the place.

To the amazement of the police, Jesse Ray moved back in. She was arrested at her father's 513 Bass Road home on Monday.

Criminal complaints were filed in magistrate court. The district attorney filed identical charges against Glenda Jean Ray and her father concerning Kelli Van Cleve.

Jesse's attorney, Billy Blackburn, said she was innocent, and she would not testify against her dad. He also told the media that there would soon be more arrests.

Certain individuals were already contacting attorneys in the public defender's office to prepare for their own anticipated arrests, he said.

Among the twelve counts against Jesse were kidnapping and criminal sexual penetration.

At her arraignment on April 27, Yontz said, "She procured the victim for her daddy," making her legally liable for what happened to Van Cleve. Jesse Ray was bound over for her involvement and transported directly to Dona Ana County Detention in Las Cruces and held on $1,000,000 bond.

Glenda Jean "Jesse" Ray had grown up in Albuquerque and southeast Texas. Her half-brother, Ron Ray, about eighteen months older, lived in Texas. She had lived with him the past month. After their father's arrest, she returned to Sierra County. Ron said he and Jesse would remain close.

Heather Norton told officers that Jesse had also lived with her brother, Dennis Roy Yancy, in Galveston.

Jesse's seven-year-old daughter lived with the child's grandmother. Unsubstantiated rumor in Sierra County and beyond was that David Ray had fathered the child.

Jesse's friends and acquaintances said she never held a job long. She drove a taxi, worked as a mechanic, and worked at a pizza place in Albuquerque. They also said she had a terrible temper when riled.

Jesse had lived in Albuquerque with a lover, Terri Hafenbrack, for about ten years. Terri said Jesse was a nice person, but she also had an explosive temper. Police records showed Jesse had been involved in several reported incidences of domestic violence, most perpetrated by her against Terri and Terri's friends, including Terri's newer lover.

There was a frustrating irony to this case. In June 1986, nearly thirteen years earlier, when Jesse Ray was about eighteen or nineteen years old, she had contacted the Albuquerque FBI office to report her father's activities. She told agents that her father abducted, tortured and sold women into slavery in Mexico. The FBI looked into Jesse's allegations, in New Mexico and Arizona, but her charges lacked useful details. The FBI conducted only minor investigations, and after a year, closed that case on David Parker Ray.

Law enforcement officers speculated that the FBI was unusually cooperative with the State Police during the 1999 David Parker Ray investigation because they knew "they had dropped the ball" in 1986.

Because Ray lived at Fence Lake in northern New Mexico at the time of Jesse's allegations, the FBI had looked into the disappearance of two Navajo girls from that general area, but found nothing significant.

Police reopened that case after the Ray investigation began in 1999, and officers found Ray's document describing the abduction and torture of Indian sisters that coincided with the dates and areas in that unresolved missing persons file on two Indian girls. Their efforts included a search of Ray's former residence, a trailer at Fence Lake. People who lived there after he did told officers that the trailer had a basement dug beneath it that contained many eyebolts and D-rings.

After her father was arrested in 1999, Jesse recanted her claim about his kidnapping activities. She now claimed she had only told the FBI about her father growing marijuana crops at Fence Lake. She had been mad at him then because he made her do most of the gardening but didn't cut her in on the profits. That was why she had "ratted him out." She insisted her father was not doing white slavery and she never said he was.

Glenda Jean "Jesse" Ray, nearly thirty-two, was arraigned on April 27 in Magistrate Court and charged with twelve counts that could lead to as many as 150 years and a $140,000 fine if found guilty.

On May 12, friends of Jesse Ray gathered outside the courthouse offering her moral support as she was led into the Magistrate Court in orange coveralls, belly chains and leg shackles. One of the women yelled, "I love you, Jesse!"

Jesse was there to appear for her preliminary hearing. FBI supervisory agent, Doug Beldon, told the media that charges, including criminal sexual penetration "against a female defendant are rare."

When someone among the gathered throng outside the courthouse asked Prosecutor Jim Yontz about the chances of Jesse going to trial on such unusual charges, he responded, "If I didn't think I could bring her to trial, I wouldn't have filed charges."

He told them the charges against Jesse pertained to a third (unnamed) victim of Ray's, who had then lived in T or C. He told them that he intended to call Ray's three known victims plus three witnesses—NMSP Sgt. Keith Clayton Rogers, NMSP Agent John Briscoe, and Janet Murphy—to the stand during this third preliminary hearing of the case. Those officers had previously testified at arraignments about evidence, including photos, found at the crime scene.

Sgt. K. C. Rogers, who said he'd been with NMSP for eighteen years, testified that he was called in from Roswell as a supervisor because there was no State Police supervisor available locally. He told the court that the victim was identified from the video found at Ray's residence, partly because she has an unusual swan tattoo on her lower right leg. He testified that the video showed her to be unwilling, and she was strapped to a weight bench in the Toy Box. He had since traced her to Colorado on a lead from her former mother-in-law, Janet Murphy. The police first contacted the victim in late April.

The second witness was Mrs. Murphy. She testified that she had only known Kelli for a month. Kelli and her son had had a whirlwind courtship and marriage. She told the court that the couple married July 16, 1996, and divorced not long after because of Kelli's four-day disappearance. She also said her son and Kelli quarreled about sex.

Kelli had gone for a walk one forenoon and did not return. The Murphy family filed a missing person report the next day, and her son said that if Kelli did not return by the next day, he would divorce her.

She told the court about David Parker Ray returning her daughter-in-law to their home four days later, and that she was dirty and unkempt. Her wedding ring and other jewelry and some of her clothing were missing. She said the girl was drugged and incoherent. Ray had told the Murphys that he found her on the beach, confused and dehydrated. He said he gave her a drink and brought her home. Kelli could only tell them that Jesse Ray had given her a ride to Ray's house on her motorcycle.

Murphy said David Ray "stuck very close to our house" while the family talked to Kelli. Her son, Patrick, told his parents that he didn't want Kelli there, so the Murphys let David Ray take her away with him, she testified.

When questioned by the prosecutor, Mrs. Murphy admitted she had never before seen the victim in a drunken or drugged state. She also said she never again, until after March 1999, discussed the incident of July 1996 with Kelli.

"Sorry we didn't believe her. Sorry we didn't realize what had happened to her," said Judy Murphy on the stand, her voice breaking.

Jesse was bound over for trial in District Court.

Chapter 21 – Pleas & Motions

Defense attorneys—Albert Costales for David Parker Ray and Xavier Acosta for Cynthia Lea Hendy—asked the court to delay their second preliminary hearing for at least twenty days.

Chief District Judge Edmund H. Kase III sealed court paperwork concerning the case. The 7th Judicial District Attorney, Ron Lopez, told investigators to stop speculating or giving details about the evidence.

Cynthia Hendy, through her attorney, was still making overtures toward a plea bargain. She would talk for reduced charges and immunity from federal charges.

She had been shown photos, found at Ray's property, of naked women in bondage. She had identified two, without naming them, as ones she knew Ray had killed. More search warrants were issued. Two were for the Elephant Butte Lake State Park office and garage where David worked. One was for David's personal incoming and outgoing mail—that which was not legal correspondence between him and his attorney—while he was in jail. One was for his post-office box. Another was for film that might have been left at Walgreen's for development by David, Jesse or Hendy.

Because of new leads, officers returned again to 312 Bass Road with warrants to search and remove a few more items.

More than a dozen State Police officers and FBI agents were surprised mid-morning of April 28 when they arrived at Ray's property with another search warrant. They found a couple of people (unnamed to the media) removing items, and loading a flatbed trailer with a generator, welding torch and toolboxes. NMSP Lt. Greg Richardson said the police removed some items from the trailer and let them take what remained. He gave no public explanation.

Ground-penetrating radar (GPR), valued at $50,000, was brought in. All three GPR units in New Mexico belonged to the Los Alamos National Lab. Lt. Richardson said this was the first time GPR was used to help in the search of a State Police crime scene. The radar can scan thirty feet down and "see" objects, and also note, through its operators' interpretations, where the ground had been disturbed.

With the GPR came two operators from Johnson Control. Investigators wanted to also use the device in the yards of Ray's neighbors. Lucy Schmidt, when later interviewed for this book, said she had agreed to the search provided they did not disturb the grave of her little dog, a long-haired Chihuahua, that was near the fence separating Ray's property and hers. They respected her wishes.

April 29, investigators used the backhoe with the small bucket to dig up areas in David Ray's yard. "We [just] found a lot of dirt," said Lt. Richardson.

The public was told that the search of Ray's yard might later include the inside of an underground septic tank. That would be an unpleasant task; they would determine who would do the actual search inside by drawing straws, Richardson said.

Investigators searched for human remains, including Marie Parker's, because they believed she had been killed at 513 Bass Road, as well as for other evidence.

Richardson said some State Police and FBI agents were sent to Fence Lake, a small community south of Gallup in west-central New Mexico where Ray had lived in the mid-1980s. However, he believed no digging had been done there.

In early May, Jesse Ray spent her thirty-second birthday in a jail cell awaiting trial.

The court released a quantity of previously sealed warrants and affidavits on Wednesday, May 13, offering the media and public glimpses into the ugliness of the case. Included among the released records was a long list of what police found in searches of Ray's home and other locations. Officers had previously testified about some of those items in court. Additional items included: identification cards of people not known to have associated with David or Jesse Ray or Cynthia Hendy; anatomy and medical books; and photographs and records indicating Ray's criminal activities had been taking place for years.

The negotiations finally ended; Hendy and the State made a plea deal. She pled guilty to five state charges involving Cindy Vigil and Angelíca Montaño. (She had not lived in T or C or Sierra County in 1996 when Kelli was kidnapped.) With the agreement, her charges were considerably less and her sentence would be lighter than they might have been. With the deal, provided she cooperated in the investigation of Ray and others, she would not be charged with federal indictments. The maximum sentence that Hendy, thirty-nine, could now receive would be fifty-four years in the state pen, instead of more than two hundred years.

Ron Lopez, district attorney, said the deal required Hendy to testify in court against Ray if asked. She might be called to testify as a witness to what happened to two of the victims, Vigil and Montaño. "We haven't yet decided who will testify at the trials," Lopez said. He said she also might be required to testify against the other two defendants, Jesse Ray and Dennis Roy Yancy.

Her attorney, Xavier Acosta of Las Cruces, repeatedly pointed out that Ray was accused of crimes that extended back many years, and Hendy had only been with Ray a relatively short period of time, less than a year. Her exposure to his crimes was limited, he insisted.

District Court records showed she had told officers that Ray claimed involvement in at least fourteen homicides at T or C and had sexually tortured countless women. She said Ray's murders included men as well as women and he had dumped their bodies in *arroyos* and in Elephant Butte Lake not far from where he lived.

Except for Bowers', no bodies connected to Ray had been found.

Ray's attorney publicly countered the remarks by Hendy's attorney by saying she had told officers what they wanted to hear because of the plea bargain.

Although the case investigation now extended to ten states, only Hendy, David Ray, his daughter Jesse, and Roy Yancy had been arrested, and only Yancy was charged with murder.

No trial date was yet set for Jesse or Yancy. All of the defense attorneys wanted their clients' trials held away from Sierra County. "This is not a reflection upon the people of Sierra County," said Billy Blackburn, Jesse's attorney, "but there's been so much publicity and when it's in your home town … people have formed an opinion. I very much doubt we will be able to do it in southern New Mexico. I'd prefer to go north."

Hendy's defense attorney Acosta voiced displeasure over publicly made comments by officials, especially some by Darren White, Secretary of the Department of Public Safety. One of White's comments that Acosta cited, made earlier to local residents and the media, was "the nightmare is behind bars." Acosta said his client's involvement in the crimes had been limited, and those kinds of public comments were misleading and harmed her defense.

[Pending [Hendy's] sixty-day diagnostic evaluation,] Judge Mertz had not finalized Hendy's plea deal, and no sentencing date had yet been set, pending her sixty-day diagnostic evaluation.

Cynthia Lea Hendy would not be sentenced until Thursday, May 11, 2000.

Jesse Ray said she was innocent of all charges. In early July, Billy Blackburn filed a motion for Jesse's trial to be held separately from her father's. There would be too much evidence presented at David Ray's trial that did not pertain to his client, evidence inadmissible for her jurors to hear. He cited, as an example, the audiotapes with the voice of David Ray talking to his victims.

Blackburn also filed a motion to remove District Judge Neil Mertz from presiding over Jesse's hearing and trial. Other defense attorneys and prosecutor James Yontz also filed motions to remove him from presiding over those trials. Yontz complained that Mertz was taking too long to rule on the matter of separate trials for David Ray and Jesse Ray, delaying prosecution. Yontz wanted the trials combined to save time and money.

A July hearing was to determine whether the cases of David Parker Ray and his daughter, Glenda Jean "Jesse" Ray—regarding Kelli Van Cleve—would be joined, or if their trials would be held separately. Then Judge Mertz put that motion on hold.

In late August 1999, the State Supreme Court ruled that Mertz would preside over all of the trials, and left the decision to him whether or not to hold separate trials.

Chapter 22 – Troubled County

Elephant Butte Lake State Park rangers began preparing for the expected Memorial Day crush of incoming tourists. Park personnel told the State Police that they needed their lakeside headquarters returned to them.

NMSP Lt. Greg Richardson told media, "We really appreciate Elephant Butte Lake State Park staff. They provided manpower, loaned their building to us for over a month, treated us great." He said the case was still open and investigation continued. "I don't believe we've heard from all of the victims."

On May 5, 1999, the State Police moved the investigation command post to Las Cruces.

Because of a serious long-term drought, Elephant Butte Lake levels had dropped fifteen to eighteen feet. While this drought was a bad thing for most New Mexicans, it brought more beach to summertime vacationers in Sierra County, which meant more space to accommodate larger lakeside crowds. Although it also meant smaller water surface for boaters, wave-runners, swimmers and fishermen, rangers expected up to 100,000 visitors on the state's largest body of water during the major holiday weekends of Memorial Day, Fourth of July and Labor Day. Rangers had turned away visitors in prior years when the lake level was higher for lack of beach space.

Regardless of the water level, crowding was always a problem on major weekends. That crowding, especially with open-air camps and trailers jammed up to the water's edge, created safety issues for officers and firemen trying reach people in emergencies. They relied upon outside law enforcement assistance, such as their A-Team—a collection of statewide state park employees with experience working at the lake during its busiest seasons—and Sierra County deputies, State Police from outlying districts and volunteers, including Mounted Patrol.

For the most part, the Elephant Butte Lake State Park had a flat budget, dependent upon legislative funding. A legislative bill to move the State Parks Division to the Tourist Department, instead of where it was under Energy, Minerals and Natural Resources, was vetoed by Governor Gary Johnson.

To be more self-supportive, the State Parks Division had recently created a new user fee schedule, unpopular with tourists; but even with that, capital and operating budget was tight.

Memorial Day weekend began at the lake on Friday, May 28. By mid-June, the lake had already claimed three drowning victims. Two of the bodies surfaced, and the New Mexico State Police Search and Recovery Dive Team—which included Agent Rich Libicer, one of the two primaries on the Ray case—recovered the third body.

Elephant Butte did not have a police department, and the T or C police department, headed by Chief David Bryant, had only nine patrolmen—one patrol sergeant and two detectives plus its uniform officers. While perhaps adequate for a community with the static size of T or C, it was very inadequate for the surge of 80,000 to 100,000 tourists on holiday weekends—making the area, temporarily, the state's second largest community.

Like all counties, Sierra depended upon property taxes and sales receipts taxes for income. The additional income generated by sales taxes from tourists did not cover the extra burden of their presence. Sierra County, like other places with temporary income from tourist trade, struggled under budget constraints and already had serious money woes.

With the Ray case, 1999 quickly became a year of financial crisis. Worse, the expenses, caused by this case of international interest, would not end anytime soon. Local newspapers called the case "financially catastrophic" for the county.

On June 8, Sierra County, in the persons of the county manager, Gary Whitehead, and Sheriff Terry Byers, traveled to Santa Fe to present its case to the State Board of Finance, and Governor Gary Johnson, its chairman of the board. The county requested a $50,000 emergency appropriation to help defray some of the costs of the already overburdened county detention facility. Besides the costly housing, transportation and responsibility for the security of the David Parker Ray suspects until their trials, Sierra County also held members of the notorious Los Padillas gang until their trials, because of a Memorial Day weekend murder at the lake. Los Padillas was an Albuquerque drug-ring gang, the most powerful one in New Mexico, and perhaps the godfather of all other gangs in the state.

Manager Whitehead and Sheriff Byers presented to the board their estimated costs for the Ray case—this report is only for a period of six months. Ultimately, because of trial delays and until the case was closed, those costs grew considerably. The serious nature of the case required added security for him, still held in their county jail. The members of Los Padillas also required increased security because the gang had access to money that could be used for bribes and to stage breakouts.

The county's formal presentation asking for financial assistance included these items, comments and cost break-downs quoted below:

1. *Cynthia Hendy—pled her case and is currently held in Grants. Sierra County Sheriff is responsible for transporting her to and from court dates and hearings.*
2. *Roy Yancy—is being held in Las Cruces for security reasons. Sierra County must incur the cost of detention at $75 per day. Court is also responsible for transporting Yancy to and from T or C for hearings and court dates.*
3. *Glenda (Jesse) Ray—is being housed in Las Cruces for security reasons. County must incur the cost for detention at $75 a day and is also responsible for transporting her to and from T or C for hearings and court dates.*
4. *David Parker Ray—is incarcerated in the Sierra County Detention Center. Due to the nature of the crimes he is charged with, Sierra County has increased security at our facility. The media attention has also created some hardship for our employees.*

This case is bizarre and shocking. Sierra County is cooperating with the FBI and State Police with the investigation, taking every precaution to insure no errors occur that would cause dismissal of this important case.

Cost Breakdown:

- *Six months of transports at an average cost of $125 per day: $22,500.*
- *Six months of housing Yancy at $75 per day: $13,500.*
- *Six months of housing Jesse Ray at $75 per day: $13,500.*

Sierra County will continue to pay the cost to house Ray through its regular budget process.

The State Board of Finance granted Sierra County's request presented by the manager and sheriff. The money would be appropriated by legislation.

^^^^^^^

Terry Byers had won the election for sheriff and assumed that position on January 1, 1999. He immediately made changes that were unpopular with some of the community. He changed their uniforms from their traditional brown to black. He demoted the ranking officers—detectives/investigators, sergeants and lieutenant—making everyone under him equals, all uniformed deputies. Kelly Clark and Dave Elston had been investigators and now were deputies again.

Sierra County was no stranger to stress, and March 1999 literally began with a bang.

Pretty Kelly Clark, thirty-eight, a popular deputy, was killed by headshots on March 4 while driving a prisoner to diagnostic evaluation.

Sheriff Terry Byers had assigned Kelly to transport Michael A. Archuleta, twenty-one, to Grants. At that time, the state Department of Corrections facility for diagnostic evaluation intakes, as well as its facility for female inmates, was in Grants.

Originally, the plan was to pick up three more prisoners in Bernalillo on the return trip, after dropping off Archuleta. Because of the additional prisoners, Deputy Rudy Carey had been assigned to make the trip with Clark. At the last minute, Sheriff Byers learned the other prisoners would not be picked up after all, so he pulled Carey off of the assignment because his short-staffed department had no spare personnel. Kelly was both driver and lone security officer on the transport, which is standard in many New Mexico law enforcement departments, regardless whether the officer is male or female.

Archuleta sat in the back seat of the sheriff's unit in his orange uniform, wearing leg-irons, and handcuffs attached to a belly-chain; a partition with a Plexiglass window divided them.

T or C librarian Pat O'Hanlon, who had been a sheriff's dispatcher in 1999, later said that Kelly had left the partition partially open for ventilation out of compassion for her prisoner.

While Kelly drove west on I-40 between Grants and Albuquerque, Archuleta managed to break through several levels of security. He freed his hands, went through the partition and grabbed her .40 Glock handgun. He shot her once in the thigh and twice in the head, execution-style. With the deputy fatally wounded, the patrol car careened out of control, crossed the highway's dividing median and hit an 18-wheeler before it came to a stop.

A Presbyterian minister from Grants witnessed the accident and stopped to offer assistance. Archuleta, still in ankle chains and his orange prisoner jumpsuit, car-jacked that car and driver. He let the minister out of the car a few miles down the highway, and was later apprehended while he stood in a phone booth near Albuquerque.

The death of Kelly Clark, who left behind a young parentless daughter, caused a deep chasm within the community. Many blamed Sheriff Byers for assigning her, a female deputy, to transport a prisoner alone. The three local newspapers, with their opposing viewpoints, widened the rift. Others, including law enforcement officers from across the state, said Byers was given "a bum rap" because single officers, male or female, routinely transport prisoners.

From then until he lost the next election in 2002, Byers' job became more difficult. Before he left his office, he would be embroiled in numerous community and security problems and conflicts.

The budget crunch continued. T or C was short $1.5 million in the fiscal year of 2000/2001, which led to—among other things—the elimination of one T or C police officer and one code-enforcement officer.

To relieve budget problems, in February 2002, City Manager Richard Ramsey and Sheriff Byers proposed that the city police department be closed and T or C contract their law enforcement needs entirely from the Sierra County Sheriff's Department. Under their plan, the sheriff would administer a regional police department that would cover all of Sierra County, including T or C, Elephant Butte and Williamsburg. They said their plan could save $250,000 a year, which would be helpful, considering the county's "recent financial misfortune," referring to the Ray case.

In addition to saving considerable money for the town, it would give the area greater law enforcement protection, said Byers. The Sheriff's Office already handled from thirty per cent to forty per cent of T or C's police calls, "so we should be getting paid and we should be in charge."

However, the sheriff is elected, and the contract would have to be rewritten with each new sheriff's administration, which could change every four years. The proposal was not accepted.

The Sierra County jail continually had serious problems of overcrowding. The inspection by the State Fire Marshal's Office in February 2002 mandated that they reduce their jail population or be shut down. At the time of the inspection, it held more than fifty inmates, including David Parker Ray. They were ordered to reduce their numbers and hire additional staff. If the jail exceeded twenty-eight inmates, they were required to at all times have three full-time staffers.

In May 2002, the city manager, Richard Ramsey, forced T or C Police Chief, David Bryant to resign. Bryant had been chief for four-and-a-half years and had worked for the police department since 1988. A former sheriff's deputy with Sierra County was hired as interim city police chief and later hired as chief. The changes the manager wanted included a crackdown on drugs in T or C and for the city police to work more cooperatively with State Police and the sheriff's office.

Sheriff Byers closed all detention center contracts with the area's communities, causing added friction between the sheriff's office and the T or C Police Department.

In May 2002, the town of T or C filed suit against the sheriff's office because the overcrowded jail put them out of compliance. District Judge Kevin Sweazea delivered an order to the county jail, ordering the T or C police department to book all city prisoners. That did not please the sheriff.

In mid-May 2002, an inmate took a female county employee hostage in the control-room, the room of the records clerk in the small Sierra County Sheriff's Office. The inmate had barricaded the room and handcuffed himself to the woman.

After a standoff, he was fatally shot.

In early May, the U.S. Border Patrol had closed the Las Cruces checkpoint, the one south of T or C, because of highway construction. That left the one north of T or C to handle the majority of federal inspections on I-25. Drug seizures considerably increased at that checkpoint. Still, only busts that net 150 pounds or more of drugs fell under the Federal jurisdiction. The U.S. Attorney's office and the DEA had decided to not handle cases of drugs nabbed at the check-point of less than 150 pounds, leaving local agencies to pick up that responsibility. The State Police declined it. In June 2002, the Sierra County Sheriff's Office announced their refusal to take any more U.S.

Border Patrol drug cases; the sheriff said his department would no longer respond to calls to arrest "small time" drug offenders picked up at the U.S. Border Patrol checkpoint. No local agency wanted that responsibility. Where would that leave those offenders? Free?

In early July 2002, the T or C Police Department said they could no longer support a reserve police officer unit. The acting police chief suspended the reserve unit, saying it was due to lack of insurance and inadequate training for their three reserve officers.

Sheriff Terry Byers lost the election in the primary. On August 14, 2002, when he had only four more months as sheriff, he announced that he would not renew the contract providing law enforcement protection to Williamsburg, the small community alongside T or C. His announcement caused consternation to the community's residents. With or without a contract, the sheriff is required by law to provide protection to all within his county who need it.

An article in the September 29, 2002 issue of the Truth or Consequences *Herald* reported that the "U.S. Border Patrol busts are taxing the local resources for the southwest corridor town of T or C."

Inadequate law enforcement for Sierra County, and its consequences, continued.

Chapter 23 – Trials & Tribulations

The notoriety of the David Parker Ray case did not keep tourists away from Elephant Butte Lake on the long Labor Day weekend. The crowd—on the first weekend of September that included the federal Labor Day holiday on Monday—was the largest in their history. The even larger crowds created a greater inadequacy of park employees and law enforcement officers to handle them.

The trial date for David Parker Ray was initially set for October 4, 1999, but the court expected to change that date. Although Cynthia Hendy had pled guilty to several charges in her agreement, Judge Mertz had not yet signed it.

On June 30, central dispatch contacted Elephant Butte Lake State Park Ranger Terry White advising that an El Paso fisherman had found a gunnysack in the lake containing a suspicious substance. Park Ranger Mike Lanford and Sierra County Deputy David Elston responded to the call, near Chalk Bluffs across from Mitchell Point. More than a month later, the State Crime Lab in Santa Fe confirmed the gunnysack contained human flesh.

For some time, investigators of the Ray case had said the lake was an important place to search for human remains, and they said they intended to send the State Police Search and Recovery Dive Team and a remote-operated vehicle (ROV). The State Police would not say whether or when they intended to search the lake.

In mid-September of 1999, Judge Mertz ruled that David Parker Ray and his daughter, Jesse, would have separate trials. He said there were already one hundred names on a list of possible witnesses to testify.

Blackburn said he was concerned about his client, Jesse, getting a fair trial. He said she wasn't even in New Mexico during the time of the alleged crimes committed in 1999, and he wanted the 1996 and 1999 cases covered by separate trials. He worried the testimony during David Parker Ray's trial would be so emotional that it would harm Jesse's chances for a fair outcome.

In mid-November 1999, the State Police ended a sixteen-month drug sting in T or C, mostly for methamphetamine trafficking. The sting involved twenty officers of various agencies and twenty arrest-warrants containing sixty charges. They announced that they expected to make more arrests.

The law enforcement always seemed over-extended, so many needs taxing limited manpower.

After his initial taped confession, Roy Yancy said he was not guilty of murder. However, he changed his plea to guilty just days before jury selection was to begin for his trial on Monday, December 6, 1999, in District Court in T or C.

Judge Mertz handed down his sentence. Yancy was given fifteen years on each of two counts—second-degree murder and conspiracy to commit murder—plus two years probation. His other charges were dropped. He was also ordered to make restitution to the two young daughters of Marie B. Parker.

Yancy's attorney, Gary Mitchell, pleading for leniency, argued that Yancy helped investigators break that part of the case, closing the long-running missing-persons file on Parker. Mitchell described Yancy as "a likeable young man from a good family."

Defense attorneys are paid to speak well of their clients, but cops aren't. When talking about the case three years later, K. C. Rogers did not speak at all well of Yancy. He said he was totally disgusting.

That's "as good as we can get," said Judge Mertz, referring to Yancy's sentence.

Kate Parker, mother of Marie, and Marie's two young daughters attended Yancy's sentencing, at the children's insistence, said Kate. "We don't think it's fair," she said, voicing her disapproval of the short sentence, which is seldom served in its entirety.

At the end of the millennium, on December 29, 1999, the Truth or Consequences newspaper, *The Herald*, under its banner, "There is NOTHING more powerful than the TRUTH," listed their top ten picks for the past one hundred years for Sierra County.

Listed in the order of their perceived importance to the area, those were: Elephant Butte Dam built in 1916; the town name changed from Hot Springs to Truth or Consequences in 1950; Hillsboro no longer the county seat in 1939; three designated state parks, two in 1964 and one in 1970; municipalities incorporated in 1916, 1949 and 1998; White Sands Missile Range established in 1945; the Gila

Wilderness designated in 1924; Carrie Tingley Hospital for children begun in 1937; the New Mexico Veteran's Center opened in 1984; St. Ann's Hospital begun in 1957; the public library opened in 1933; media mogul Ted Turner bought ranches in Sierra County in 1991 and 1994; Sierra County Fair begun in 1940; the post-mining boom in 1930; and 50 annual T or C fiestas with honored guest Ralph Edwards from 1950 through 1999.

Nowhere was David Parker Ray, who brought international fame to T or C, listed.

^^^^^^^

Cynthia Lea Hendy changed attorneys from Xavier Acosta to Carmen Garza. At a hearing in January 2000, she tried to change her plea from guilty to not guilty. She claimed, through her new attorney, that her former attorney had not explained the consequences of her plea agreement and he had pressured her to accept it. Garza also argued that men had abused Hendy when she was a child, she only had an eighth-grade education, and had a mental disability.

Garza said Hendy had been diagnosed in 1996 with affective disorders and mental retardation, and she was abused in her past marriages and relationships with men. Garza said Hendy's diagnosis found her unable to deal with society. Deputy District Attorney Jim Yontz responded, saying the court-appointed psychiatrist found no evidence that she had mental disorders.

District Attorney Ron Lopez said Acosta had testified that he explained the consequences of her plea and she "knowingly and voluntarily" agreed to it.

Her victim, Cindy Vigil, said it was wrong for Hendy to claim her childhood experience of abuse as an excuse for her own abusive behavior. Vigil said she too had been abused when she was a child, and "I never went around torturing anyone!"

Judge Mertz ruled that Hendy could not change her plea. He also requested a pre-sentence report for her prior to her sentencing.

In early May, the court had tried to reach Angelíca Montaño to have her appear to testify as a witness at Hendy's sentencing in a few days. Angelíca's mother returned the call to the court to advise that her daughter had died on Sunday, May 7. An autopsy later found cause of death to be pneumonia.

Just days before Hendy's sentencing, Yontz announced to the public that one of Ray's victims had died of unknown causes, but her death would not affect Hendy's sentencing. It would also not affect the trial prosecuting Ray in that victim's case, he said. Although Ray's trial in that case was not yet scheduled, it would take place despite her death, Yontz assured the public.

In mid-May 2000, more than a year after the case began, Cynthia Hendy was finally sentenced in the Sierra County Courthouse in T or C. She was given a total of thirty-six years to be served in a New Mexico state penal institution. She received twenty-seven years for her involvement in the kidnapping and sexual torture of Angelíca Montaño, and thirty-six years for her involvement in the kidnapping and sexual torture of Cindy Vigil. As part of her plea agreement, the two sentences were to be served concurrently, and she was exempt from federal charges.

ADA Jim Yontz told the court that Hendy was a knowing and willing accomplice. "The victim was held, drugged, tortured, placed inside a white cargo trailer, strapped into a chair and had a variety of terrible things done to her. I don't know if the Marquis de Sade would have had better tools for torture than the devices found within the cargo trailer."

Hendy's sentencing took place the same day her victim, Angelíca Montaño, was buried.

^^^^^^^

The Seventh Judicial District Court prepared for trials. David Parker Ray would face three separate trials, one for each of his three known victims. The first trial would be for victim Kelli Van Cleve, the second for Angelíca Montaño, and the third for Cynthia Vigil, in the order of their captivity.

A year after the case had begun, the first scheduled trial, to be held in Tierra Amarílla, Rio Arríba County, in northern New Mexico, was to finally begin. This trial, for Kelli Van Cleve's complaint, charged Ray with twelve counts, including kidnapping and criminal sexual penetration.

But again, it was delayed several times for various reasons and processes. Some of the delays were because of defense attorneys' motions to withhold certain pieces of evidence and witnesses' testimony from the jury, then the judge's orders to withhold that information, and then the prosecutors' challenges of those court orders. In the court of law, nothing is simple.

Then David Parker Ray was hospitalized, under an assumed name, in Las Cruces with a heart condition. That caused a week's delay. Sierra County's jail administrator said Ray had already been hospitalized, since his arrect, four times in the past year. He was placed on a heart monitor.

Judge Neil Mertz ruled that the public and news media would be barred from the courtroom during jury selection in nearby Española for Ray's first trial in Tierra Amarílla.

That caused a furor among the media.

Ray's defense attorney, Jeff Rein, approved of the motion, but an attorney representing various news media said the ruling was unconstitutional. That attorney said the trial's delay due to Ray's hospitalization would give him time to take his challenge to the State Supreme Court if Mertz did not rescind his order barring the public.

The State Supreme Court ruled that judges could only exclude news media from jury selection within strict guidelines and only after notice giving media time to oppose the motion to restrict coverage.

Jury selection for the first trial was rescheduled to begin April 4, 2000.

Judge Mertz also reported that testimonies by the FBI's expert witnesses were thrown out because the FBI didn't file their reports in time to give the defense opportunity to prepare challenges to them.

Deputy District Attorney Jim Yontz said their appeal on the judge's rulings might not be answered by the Court of Appeals for several months.

With this first trial on hold, Judge Mertz scheduled the second of Ray's three trials for May 23, a date too that would later be changed. He also scheduled a hearing on the news-media request to allow reporters and the public to attend jury selection for the second trial, after he had ruled to exclude them from the first trial.

Before the second trial began, the first one, in Tierra Amarílla concerning Van Cleve, finally got underway in May with jury selection. Mertz rescinded his earlier decision to exclude the media. They were present.

To select twelve jurors and six alternates, all of whom would hear the case, the defense and prosecution spent twelve court days interviewing more than 125 people. At the end of trial testimony, Judge Mertz would determine which twelve of those eighteen would finally deliberate to determine the defendant's guilt or innocence of the charges.

Mertz had still not ruled on defense motions to exclude certain evidence, including items and photographs, taken from Ray's property.

After the trial began with opening remarks by defense and prosecution, the trial was again delayed because Ray complained of chest pains and was rushed to a nearby medical facility for testing.

Ever since Ray was arrested, he had been held in Sierra County or, when preparations for the first trial began, in Rio Arrîba County. He was also transported five times to hospitals or clinics for health concerns. By this time, his estimated costs—including his two-member defense team, and for Rio Arrîba deputies contracted to provide him security while he was in that county—was already estimated at $100,000. That did not include expenses to transport him by airplane each way between Sierra County and Rio Arrîba County for court sessions.

Only Ray and Jesse were still financial responsibilities of Sierra County because their fates were yet undecided. Jesse's trial was scheduled for July 10 in Gallup.

Justice is not cheap.

After their guilty pleas, Yancy and Hendy had become wards of the state's penal institution, but prior to that, Sierra County had to pick up their costs.

Yancy had been incarcerated for thirty-one weeks at Dona Ana County. Hendy's fourteen-month stay in Las Cruces and her brief visit in Sierra County had cost more than $35,000, plus her defense, security and transportation. Jesse Ray's fourteen months in Las Cruces, before relocating her, had cost $40,000 thus far, plus her attorney fees, security and transportation costs and medical expenses. Her expenses would continue to grow until her trial. Then there would be the District Court prosecution costs including witness fees, mileage, lodging and juror compensation.

^^^^^^^

Tierra Amarîlla is 150 miles due north from Albuquerque and three hundred miles northwest of Truth or Consequences. On Highway 84, it is directly below Chama—home of the Cumbres and

Toltec Scenic Railroad—and twenty-five miles south of the Colorado border.

It is a high mountain village, elevation 7,500 feet and population about six hundred. Mountains, as much as 3,000 feet higher, surround it, as do the Carson and Santa Fe National Forests. A short distance west is the Jicarilla Apache Reservation.

Tierra Amarílla means yellow land or soil; the county's name, Rio Arríba, means upper-river. Tierra Amarílla, like many remote mountainous Hispanic villages in northern New Mexico, seemed unchanged by modern civilization. Farming small plots of land, raising goats and sheep, woodcutting from the nearby forests, hunting and fishing, or migrant work, were the villagers' main sources of subsistence. Some locals were artistic; *santéros* (carvers or painters of saints, or *santos*) and weavers of colorful woolen blankets on hand looms sold their handmade goods to the public. But many of the younger generations drifted away in search of education, a better livelihood and a more modern way of life.

The families of many residents of these mountain villages of northern New Mexico had lived there for generations. They were descendants of early European settlers—who had come as early as the late 1500s and 1600s to the New World from Spain, such as with Oñate's expedition, and trappers and explorers from France, Prussia, Germany and other European countries. Many residents are fair-complexioned and have light-colored eyes, denoting their European ancestry.

Tierra Amarílla, like many of the remote mountain villages, began as a Hispanic settlement, and Spanish remained the primary language spoken at home. That which was still spoken in these isolated areas is closer to the European Castilian dialect than what is spoken elsewhere in New Mexico, which is more influenced by the Mexican neighbor to the south.

In the adobe villages, houses and living conditions were mostly unchanged for a hundred and more years. In the simple adobe homes were still found small beloved hand-carved *santos* (patron saints), passed down within the family for generations, reposing in *nichos* (small indentions cut into adobe walls). Grottos (small private shrines) were often the only decorative accents in yards. Residents passed down and retold *cuentos* (folktales and legends) to their children and grandchildren.

Tierra Amarílla and its Rio Arríba County Courthouse have a small claim to fame, at least within New Mexico. On June 5, 1967, Reyes Tijerina—the self-proclaimed leader of La Raza ("the race")—caused a brief uprising and armed take-over of the Rio Arríba County Courthouse. Two officials were shot, including State Police Officer Nick Saiz, but no one died.

Tijerina served time in the New Mexico State Penitentiary for his attempted armed uprising on behalf, he claimed, of the Mexican-American land-grant descendents who lost their lands following the 1848 Guadalupe-Hidalgo Treaty, when New Mexico became a territory of the United States. Grantees retained rights to their lands with that treaty. Their lands were ultimately lost because they exercised poor judgment. They were taken advantage of by unscrupulous American investors, some of whom were state-level politicians, and they sold their pieces of land for too little. Or in ignorance, or because they could not read and write in English, signed away ownership.

Chapter 24 – Preparations

Criminal sexual penetration (CSP) is the legal term for rape in New Mexico.

By March 30, 1999, David Parker Ray had been charged with a total of twenty-five criminal counts—multiple charges of kidnapping, conspiracy to commit a crime, criminal sexual penetration, criminal sexual battery, criminal sexual contact and aggravated battery. Those charges involved: Cindy Vigil, who was his first publicly known victim but third in chronological order; Angelíca Montaño, who was his second known victim, now deceased; and Kelli Van Cleve, who was his third known victim but the earliest taken of the three, and thus the subject of Ray's first trial.

Long before this trial began, many motions had been filed. The court, in the person of Judge Neil Mertz, granted some of those motions, and some it did not.

The first motion was filed March 31, 1999 to substitute Jeff Rein as Ray's counsel, beginning with his preliminary hearings, in lieu of his first temporary court-appointed attorney. Later, subpoenas had been served to Vigil, Montaño and Van Cleve to appear as witnesses at Ray's preliminary hearings in each of those cases.

On May 7, 1999, the prosecution had filed a motion to enter into evidence an audiocassette tape (exhibit number 78) recorded by the defendant, and also the metal collar and chain that Cindy Vigil was wearing when she escaped from 513 Bass Road. The prosecution filed a motion on May 21, 1999, to release those two exhibits to the custody of NM State Police Agent Wes LaCuesta for trial.

The prosecution had filed a motion on September 24, 1999, to obtain videoed depositions of witnesses Darlene and Donald Breech, the residents at 301 Hot Springs Landing, Elephant Butte. It was to their home that Vigil had run when she escaped from Ray. They later moved from Elephant Butte and out-of-state, which was why their testimonies were taken by deposition, for later use in the trials. But, like that of many other potential witnesses, they were never used in court.

On November 11, 1999, the defense attorneys had filed a motion to hold separate trials pertaining to each of the three victims. Rein believed his client did not have a chance if all three victims were presented to jurors at one trial. For the same reason, prosecutor Yontz wanted one combined trial. He also said one trial would be less costly for the state and more expedient.

Mertz ruled for separate trials.

November 18, 1999, Rein had filed a useless motion to revoke Ray's permission to the FBI to search his property, outbuildings and vehicles, long after they had been searched, and to obtain his medical records. That motion was denied. Rein filed a motion on January 10, 2000, to suppress the nine audiocassettes, recorded by Ray, found on his property. A portion of that motion was denied. Only one audiotape (exhibit number 78) was allowed, and then, just before Ray's first trial, Judge Mertz ruled that it too was inadmissible.

The jurors would hear none of Ray's self-incriminating audiotapes.

On January 14, 2000, Rein filed a motion to prohibit introduction of testimony about the 1986 FBI investigation of David Parker Ray when his daughter had been an informant against him. That ruling was still pending when the trial began.

On February 9, 2000, Rein filed a motion to exclude the testimony of Kelli Van Cleve. That motion was denied. On February 23, 2000, the prosecution wanted the files opened on all three victims at this first trial. That motion was denied; the jury would only be exposed to Kelli's case.

Many witnesses were served subpoenas to appear in court to testify at the trial, but ultimately, few were called to Tierra Amarílla to testify.

While the jury selection process was underway for David Parker Ray's first trial, Judge Mertz scheduled Ray's second trial to begin November 27, 2000, in Estancia, Torrance County, to face charges concerning Angelíca Montaño, the victim who died after the case began.

The scheduling of Ray's third trial, involving Cindy Vigil, was still delayed pending an appeal to the state Supreme Court. The trial concerning her was originally intended to be the first one. The prosecution and the defense both knew Vigil would be the most credible witness against Ray. Rein believed if that trial were first, it would create negative consequences for Ray at his other two trials. He entered motions to delay that trial. He also filed motions to make all of the exhibits found in the Toy Box inadmissible because, unlike the other victims, Cindy had never been inside the white cargo trailer.

^^^^^^^

District Judge Neil Mertz presided at Ray's first trial, held in Tierra Amarílla, Rio Arríba County. District Attorney Ron Lopez and Assistant District Attorney Jim Yontz represented the prosecution. The team of Jeff Rein and Cathy Love defended David Parker Ray.

The jury selection took weeks. In the middle of it, the process was delayed more than a week because Jeff Rein's son shot himself and subsequently died.

By now, with all the delays and the slow process of trying to find enough people to fill the jury seats, and because lurid content of some filed stories made them unpublishable in all but tabloids, the news media lost interest in the case. Only one media representative was in the Rio Arríba County courthouse during jury selection to file AP stories.

Before the trial began, Judge Mertz ruled on some of the evidence he would or would not allow in court. In the judge's presence but away from jurors, prosecutors Yontz and Lopez, and Rein for the defense, spent hours squabbling over every piece of evidence being considered.

Because this trial pertained to Kelli alone, Jeff Rein argued that almost everything found in the cargo trailer in March 1999, and photographs of them, should be inadmissible because there was no proof they had been there in 1996.

Rein made many motions to omit pieces of evidence and testimony critically important to the prosecution of David Parker Ray.

He asked that testimony concerning the FBI's investigation of Ray in 1986 not be allowed. He asked that many items found in Ray's home, including photos of guns, not be allowed because Kelli did not remember them. Rein asked that the bottles of Hot Damn! schnapps containing drugs that were found in Ray's residence and the Toy Box not be allowed because they were consumable; they might not have been there three years earlier. He asked the court to not allow the audiocassette (exhibit number 78) to be played. Rein asked that FBI's expert on violent sex crimes, Special Agent Mary Ellen O'Toole, not be a witness and that the jurors not be told David Parker Ray was a serial sexual sadist; they could make their own conclusions. He also asked that two other FBI expert witnesses not be allowed to testify on DNA and hair analysis.

"A lot of people don't believe hair analysis is a proper science," explained Rein.

^^^^^^^

From the street, the Rio Arríba County Courthouse appears to be two-and-a-half stories—the half-story being the basement floor with only its uppermost portion aboveground to allow for shallow windows. Rather than Territorial style, as were many public buildings built in New Mexico during that era, its architecture is classical. Pale beige with white accents, it sports fancy moldings, three tall columns in front, and tall windows, half of them arched; the front portal also has three tall arches. The Rapp brothers of Trinidad, Colorado, designed this courthouse, the green-domed Chaves County Courthouse in Roswell, and other public buildings around New Mexico, including in Raton, Las Vegas and Santa Fe, between 1890 and 1920.

^^^^^^^

At last, the court swore in the jury.

The trial began Thursday afternoon, June 29, 2000, with Judge Mertz instructing the jury. He preceded his instructions with brief comments about the building. He said the recently renovated Rio Arríba County Courthouse was built in 1917. He called it one of the most elegant courtrooms in the state because of its noble simplicity.

The sounds of vehicles rumbling by drowned out the speakers, especially soft-spoken Jeff Rein, even though they used microphones.

The prosecution and the defense gave their opening statements to the jury.

Jim Yontz, for the state, began by going over the investigation at Elephant Butte. He described the one important seized video—showing the victim, naked and strapped to a narrow table or bench, her arms and legs secured in extreme positions, with duct tape over her mouth and eyes, and the defendant touching her. He described the trailer and its interior.

Rein had previously filed a motion stipulating that it not be called the Toy Box; therefore, during the trial, it was called the white cargo trailer.

Yontz spoke of Kelli Van Cleve, what happened to her and how her new family rejected her when Ray returned her to their home. He said Jesse Ray gave Kelli a ride, which she thought was to a friend's house, and instead was to the home of Jesse's father on Bass Road.

He described the inside of Ray's residence.

He told the jury that Patrick Murphy, now on active duty in the Navy, would testify by taped deposition. He described Kelli's unusual tattoo, called a "tribal swan," and her unique braided hairstyle, both of which could be seen in the video. He said the victim, when she testified, would only specifically recall six different sessions of abuse by Ray because she had been drugged, but she believed there had been at least thirty instances.

Jeff Rein, for the defense, spoke of the call that Kelli Van Cleve received from the New Mexico State Police. He mentioned her tattoos. He said two FBI agents, Carrie Parbs and Larry Haulpt, interviewed Kelli, now living in Colorado. But, he said, she had lived in T or C beginning in June 1994. He spoke of Patrick Murphy and that he had asked Kelli to marry him although his parents had not approved of her. Patrick had warned Kelli against using drugs, and she told him she didn't use them. He said the young couple argued about sex, Kelli left the house and went to several bars. Patrick looked for her; and a female friend of theirs, Cassie, told him she was with a guy.

Rein, trying to confuse the issue, said Kelli had first told acquaintances that she thought someone at a bar had given her drugs. He acknowledged that a collar was put on Kelli and that she was taken to another place, a trailer. He agreed David had dildos and other sexual devices, but possession of those things is not illegal. He said the video showed no sexual penetration, including with dildos. He said Kelli met Patrick the next day (after she was freed) at the courthouse and signed divorce or annulment papers. He mentioned Kelli living with various other men; the State objected, saying Kelli's sexual conduct was not at issue, but Judge Mertz overruled.

Rein concluded for the defense, saying, "This case is not about possession of sexual devices."

New Mexico State Police Sgt. K. C. Rogers and FBI Special Agent Tony Maxwell were scheduled to testify next. During his earlier opening statements, Yontz had introduced Rogers as the command center commander, "the whip, if you will," who assigned, and followed through with, investigators on the case. He said Agent John Briscoe was the crime scene manager for the State Police, and Tony Maxwell was the crime scene manager for the FBI.

After quiet consultations at the judge's bench, the judge dismissed the jury and they were escorted out of the courtroom.

The jury was called back around 5 p.m. that day, June 29, but only for Judge Mertz to briefly explain to them that the defendant, diagnosed with a heart condition months ago, had complained today of chest pains and was taken to a clinic.

Before he dismissed them for the day, he said the court was recessed until at least 1 p.m. the next afternoon.

Kathy McClean, clerk of the Seventh Judicial District, when later speaking of this first trial in Tierra Amarílla, equated it to putting on a Broadway production.

Bringing all of the important witnesses (players) together in court for the pertinent days of the trial (on-stage), expecting all of them to say exactly what they had previously testified to under oath, gathering all of the physical evidence (props) and successfully putting on the trial on schedule was a nerve-wracking event, especially without being able to first hold a dress rehearsal.

It was always uncertain whether a trial would go the way the prosecution, or the defense, expected. It often did not.

Chapter 25 – Trial Begins

Friday, June 30, was another half-day of court. The trial resumed that afternoon without the defendant in the courtroom. The jury also was not yet present.

There was a long discussion between the judge and the defense attorney about Ray's medications, his bottle of oxygen and his need to exercise outside of the building during court breaks.

Because of the various interruptions and delays, the prosecution said they had to submit exhibits and call witnesses out of order. Some of their witnesses had to leave Tierra Amarílla because of other obligations and some could not later return to testify. The prosecution told the court that they wanted to present their key evidence, exhibit number 106, which was the video showing the victim, Kelli Van Cleve, naked and bound.

Judge Mertz said the video's unbroken chain of custody would first have to be established. The prosecution told the court that they would call NMSP Agent John Briscoe out of order to testify about the video's chain of custody.

The jury was called into the courtroom. Peter Bowidowicz was the first witness.

On the stand, he said he was now an Elephant Butte Lake State Park ranger, but on March 22, 1999, he was employed by Sierra County as a field deputy sheriff.

He described receiving the call from central dispatch and going to 513 Bass Road. He was asked to identify certain numbered exhibits as being the lease lot agreements between the State Park and David Ray, pertaining to that address.

He also said the Sheriff's Department asked the State Police to assist on the case, and described securing the scene with crime scene tape, and creating a log. This testimony was important to assure the court and jury that the crime scene was not later compromised. Once the yellow tape was put up, the log was used to record the names and times of all persons entering the scene's area.

Next, the prosecution called FBI Agent Tony Maxwell, who told the court that he had been an FBI special agent for eighteen years, assigned mostly to terrorism and violent crime cases, and had received specialized training. He said he had processed hundreds of crime scenes in his career. State Police called him to assist with the case, he said.

The FBI had been called on March 24 and they arrived at Elephant Butte the morning of March 26. Upon their arrival, the State Police "took us to the property and showed us the layout. The property was about 60 feet wide and 125 feet or more deep. There was a mobile home at the back [of the property], several storage buildings, a sail boat, a motor boat and a Dodge pickup."

Maxwell was asked to stand beside a property drawing on an easel in the courtroom and describe the layout. "It's an open property with a front gate," he said, and pointed to and named each item: the mobile home and its attachments, which was the primary dwelling, a small white storage shed in back, a small red storage shed in back; a motorboat, a sailboat, a white cargo trailer, and the Dodge pickup. He pointed to a fixed awning-type carport on front of the residence, to the garage on its south side and the location of the rear glass sliding doors.

He told the court the FBI evidence recovery team set up a mobile management post in front of the property, but he spent much of his time at the main command post beside the lake.

He said thirty FBI agents were assigned to the case and other law enforcement agencies were also involved. There were three teams, eight people each, assigned to process evidence in different areas of the property. He was the teams' leader. He described the "very specific searches" and processing of the crime scene, the gathering of necessary resources and supplies, and how the investigators logged and protected the discovered evidence.

Maxwell said search warrants were obtained, and he described the search patterns used by the processing teams. The evidence recovery team and all others who entered the crime scene were required to wear Tibex coveralls to avoid contaminating the scene. Only those assigned to the task, or who had legitimate reasons for being there, could enter the scene while it was processed, and their comings and goings were observed and logged.

In compliance with the search warrants, on March 27 the teams systematically began to search the home and the cargo trailer. Those areas were the largest tasks, and ultimately the most important, and took the longest to complete. The other team began with the Dodge truck, and as they completed it, they moved on to other assigned areas that included the garage, the storage buildings and boats.

Maxwell testified that the New Mexico Mounted Patrol provided security—"the custody and control" of the property and an extended area, every night beginning about 6 p.m. when the crime scene teams left. He noted that members of the state's Special Investigations Division (SID) also protected the scene at night.

He testified that on March 30, FBI Agent Ken Switzer "collected" the video, exhibit 106, inside and at the rear of the cargo trailer near the door, under a camera tripod; and he and some others viewed it that same day.

"Evidence collection is very specific," Maxwell said, when questioned by defense attorney Jeff Rein.

Maxwell testified in detail, as far as he was personally involved, as to the chain of custody of the video.

A photo, showing where the tape was found, was introduced, but objected to by Rein, who said the photograph also showed other objects that would be prejudicial to the jury. The judge overruled and the photograph was entered as evidence.

The judge recessed the court and dismissed the jury on Friday afternoon, providing for a long Fourth of July weekend, until 1 p.m. Wednesday, July 5, 2000.

Chapter 26 – The Video

On Wednesday afternoon, July 5, the defendant was in the courtroom, connected to an oxygen tank, when court resumed.

The first witness called that afternoon was State Police Agent John Briscoe, for the limited purpose of testifying to the chain of custody of the videotape. He would be later recalled for other testimony.

Briscoe said he was an officer with the State Police for almost twelve years, and he had been with criminal investigations since January 1, 1995, about four years.

Besides working regular local crime scenes, he said he was sometimes assigned to work with the state's major crime scene processing team.

He testified that he was assigned to the case with K. C. Rogers, and instructed to go to Elephant Butte.

"Who was the first law enforcement person to enter the white cargo trailer?" asked Yontz.

"I was."

"Was there a search warrant authorizing you to enter?"

"Yes sir."

Yontz directed Briscoe's questioning to the specific videotape.

"Who seized this particular video?"

"Agent Ken Switzer."

Testifying about the video, Briscoe said other videos were found in the cargo trailer, but many were still unopened and unused.

Rein spent considerable time at the bench complaining. "This is a key piece of evidence … because of the length of time [between its discovery and today], we don't know where it's been … there's been a multitude of people who have handled this tape …no explanation of who handled it or when."

During Rein's whispered conference at the bench, he said the original video had even been "sent to Washington D.C. There's no explanation of who handled it, or how. It is incumbent upon the State to be more thorough in their proper chain of custody …"

In that whispered bench conference, Yontz argued that there was no need for a person-to-person chain of custody record because there had been sworn testimony as to the video's authenticity.

After several such conferences, Judge Mertz overruled Rein's objections.

According to questions by the defense and John Briscoe's testimony on the stand, the original video was handled many times by many people, many copies were made from the original, and the chain of custody was not well documented. Because the judge had already ruled against his objections, the defense bypassed several opportunities, while questioning Briscoe—who sounded unconfident on the stand—to discredit the video. Still, Rein managed to register his opinion.

When Briscoe said the tape had spent a period of time in the trunk of his car, Rein asked him if he had a lock box in his trunk.

"No sir."

Rein asked, "You say you are the crime scene property manager?"

"Yes sir."

"And you don't have a lock box in the trunk of your car?"

"No sir."

After Briscoe testified that he and Lou Mallion had made a video of the interior of the cargo trailer, he was dismissed from the stand.

The prosecution next called State Police Sgt. Keith Clayton Rogers, who said he had been a criminal investigations supervisor for the state for a little over two years. He spoke with a confident voice and manner.

Rogers said he had held the rank of sergeant for almost three years when he was assigned as supervisor to this case's investigation, in charge of the command center. "Their regular supervisor [for that NMSP district] was out-of-state," he explained.

"We held briefings with the agents, briefings every morning and every evening of every day." He described his various duties as commander of the command center located near the lake at Elephant Butte, which included manning telephones.

He said agencies involved in the case were the "New Mexico State Police, Special Investigations Division of the Department of Public Safety, the Federal Bureau of Investigations, and the New Mexico Mounted Patrol who are our civilians ..."

Rogers continued, "Also, [we used] the Parks and Recreation in a minimal amount because we were using their facility."

Rogers was asked to describe the contents of the video. He said he had viewed it, the same day it was discovered, with two FBI agents and Briscoe.

"The video appeared to be of three different settings ... one showed the defendant, Mr. Ray, in the video adjusting equipment inside the utility trailer on the property. Another portion appeared to be of the ceiling area. Another portion showed Mr. Ray and a young woman. The woman was strapped to a table, her feet in what appeared to be stirrups, her arms strapped high above her head. Ray was touching and fondling her, and she reacted to his touch. Her face was duct-taped, at one point the tape came loose and Ray re-stuck the tape to her face."

Rogers described the woman as a "white female, blonde, with a tattoo on the outside of her lower right leg, her hair appeared to be in braids—cornrow or Bo Derek braids. Her legs were spread out wide apart so only a portion of the tattoo could be seen." That tattoo, her hair and being a white female were the only identifying features they had to find her, he added.

"Did you try to locate this woman?" asked Yontz.

Rogers said he and FBI Agent Larry Haulpt had worked on that. From gathered local intelligence, they learned of a young woman, named Kelli, who fit that description.

He described using the computer program, Rapid Start System, to cross-reference her, trying to find a match for the woman seen in the video. He said he thought it was the words "white female" and the name "Kelli" that directed them to a lead called in by Janet "Judy" Murphy.

Murphy, who now lived in Phoenix, had called the command center after she heard about the David Parker Ray case. When Rogers called Murphy after finding the reference in the computer program, he learned that the unique description of the tattoo and the braided blonde hair of the woman seen in the video matched that of Murphy's daughter-in-law.

Murphy had called the command center to report an incident that happened three years earlier involving her then-daughter-in-law, Kelli. She called to advise that she had only recently begun to believe that Kelli had been Ray's victim.

From Murphy, Rogers acquired the full name, address and phone number of Kelli Van Cleve. He called Kelli on April 15.

"When you contact somebody about an investigation, say a witness, are you careful in that sort of contact?" asked Yontz.

"When you first contact someone, especially a potential victim, you have to be careful what kind of information you give them so they cannot use it, give it back to you."

"What kind of questions did you ask?"

"Had you ever lived in Truth or Consequences? Did you know David Ray? That sort of thing."

Rogers testified further about the chain of custody of the video before it was viewed in court. After Rogers was dismissed from the stand, the video was played.

To guard the privacy of the victim as much as possible, Judge Mertz—and earlier also the State Supreme Court—ruled that the video would be played for the court and jury only, not for audience or media. The video had no sound, and the video camera and screen were positioned to limit that view. The judge came from behind the bench and sat with the jury to watch it.

The tape was fast-forwarded past a blank portion of the video. It first showed the ceiling of the trailer while the defendant, Ray, adjusted the camera.

The brief recording was of a naked Anglo woman, with silver tape over her mouth and eyes, her arms tightly secured above and behind her head and her secured legs bent and spread wide apart. The defendant stood beside the woman and stroked her body, and the woman responded in a negative way to his touch. The tape on her mouth came loose, and the defendant was seen refastening it. The defendant unfastened her arms and she crossed them over her chest. Then the tape ended.

Following the viewing of that brief video, it was admitted as evidence.

The State asked to present the videoed deposition of Patrick Murphy. The defense objected, saying Murphy should have testified in court in person. The judge overruled.

On the video, Patrick Murphy began by saying he was a U.S. Navy Ensign-5 stationed in San Diego. At the time of the taped deposition, he said, he had been in the Navy almost seven years.

He had met Kelli at a local pub in Elephant Butte, and they dated for three months before they married and briefly lived together with his parents in Elephant Butte. He described Kelli and the tattoo on her leg, and said she seldom drank and did not use drugs. He said they often argued about sex because it was painful for her. He said that, after an argument, she spent the night on their couch, left the house the next morning and did not return. He looked for her that day, then spent the night, drunk, on the beach. He described what she had been wearing when he had last seen her the night before she disappeared, white shorts and a white t-shirt, and her braided hair style. The next day he reported her missing to the police as a preliminary to filing an annulment. He said Ray returned Kelli to his parents' house three days later, and testified how dirty she looked and smelled. As long as he had known her, she had kept herself very clean, took many baths. He said he had called her a "clean-nik."

Her appearance that day was shocking. When he saw her, he said, he was furious. She was not wearing shoes, she was still in the same clothing, was missing all of her jewelry, and she was incoherent as if she were under the influence of a narcotic.

Kelli told him and his parents that she could only remember waking up in the truck with David Ray, and nothing else.

He and his family would not allow her to stay; they wouldn't even let her go into the house for her belongings. She left with Ray.

While she had been missing, a friend of theirs—Cassie—who was herself interested in Patrick, had told him that Kelli was with another guy. He admitted he was jealous and believed Kelli had been out partying. After the annulment of their marriage, he returned to duty in San Diego and Cassie went with him.

Court was recessed until the next morning.

The next morning, July 6, after some discussion between the defense and the State about another witness, the first witness called was Janet "Judy" Murphy, mother of Patrick. She said she and her husband moved to T or C in 1995. She testified that she had never seen Kelli drink to excess. The testimony she gave was similar to that of her son, except that the defense asked her why she had not wanted her son to marry Kelli. Her reasons included her belief that Kelli did not love Patrick and she only married him for security. She said she had believed Kelli had lived off of others prior to their marriage.

Todd Thompson was next called to the stand. He said he previously lived in T or C, was acquainted with Kelli, and that she never used drugs and seldom drank liquor. He said he saw her the afternoon of July 25, 1996, at a bar, Raymond's, and she seemed upset. From there, both of them went with some other people to the Blue Waters Saloon. Kelli was not intoxicated when he last saw her that night.

John Schum, an FBI agent for twenty-two years, testified next, but only as to the chain of custody of the video. When he said he provided advice to investigators at the crime scene, the defense objected to that comment, saying they had no opportunity to interview him prior to his appearance in the courtroom. Prosecution argued that they'd had plenty of time, months in fact, to question him.

Next FBI Agent Ken Switzer briefly testified as to the chain of custody of the video.

After lunch, the court called Kelli Van Cleve, subsequently remarried and now named Garrett, to testify.

Chapter 27 – About Kelli

Kelli Van Cleve Garrett, now twenty-six years old, said she lived in T or C with a friend, and was employed by a home healthcare agency, when she met Patrick Murphy. She said she had actually known him perhaps one-and-a-half years, but they dated for three months before their marriage, which only lasted two weeks. She quarreled with Patrick over sex—a woman problem, she called it. Sex hurt, she said.

She left the Murphy home morning of July 25, 1996, walking to the nearby home of a friend.

"Where did you go?" asked Yontz.

"To Becky's."

"Walking?"

"Yes."

"What were you wearing when you left the house?"

"White shorts and a white t-shirt."

When prompted, she described what she did and where she went the rest of that day and evening. Those places included friends' homes and pubs—Rocky's Lounge, Raymond's, and then the Blue Waters Saloon in Elephant Butte.

"Did you drink anything when you were at Rocky's?"

"No."

"Did you drink anything while you were at Raymond's?"

"No."

"Why not?"

"I was the designated driver."

"Did you drink anything while you were at Blue Waters?"

"Yes. One beer." She said that was the only drink she had the entire evening.

She said Jesse Ray and other friends were with her most of the time she was in the bars. She played pool and stayed at Blue Waters from about 8 p.m. or 9 p.m. until around 11 p.m.

"Then what happened?" asked Yontz.

"Jesse offered me a ride home."

"Did she take you home?"

"No."

"Why not?"

"She said she was too drunk. I said, then take me to a friend's house."

Jesse claimed she first needed to go home and drink coffee to sober up. She took her by motorcycle to the home of her father, David Ray, on Bass Road, about one mile away. Kelli said that was the first time she had ever been inside that residence. While she sat on a couch, David and Jesse left the room briefly, and then both returned. One of them held a knife against her throat. She could not remember which one of them did what.

She said they put handcuffs and a dog collar on her, and she was taken outside to a nearby trailer where she was tied down on what she described as a modified weight bench. She never saw or heard Jesse again, only David Ray.

She said Ray repeatedly tried, but could not fully insert large dildos into her. She could only specifically remember six sessions when David Parker Ray had come into the trailer to molest her. When he was not with her, she was left alone, naked and bound, on the narrow bench in the trailer. She did not remember being fed or given a drink of water, and recalled being allowed only once—still shackled—to use a nearby portable toilet. She said she was kept immobilized on the bench in the trailer for three days. She believed David Ray tried to force dildos into her at least thirty times, but she could only give details about six times. She said she cried to David Ray to stop, but he would not.

"He told me he was a member of a Satanic group that wanted me for a sex toy. He said I'd be of no use to them when he couldn't put them in."

She remembered being taken, later, to the Murphy home by David Ray, and when the family would not let her go inside the house, that Ray took her to the home of an acquaintance, David Connelly, and left her with him.

She said she has had memories ever since, but thought they were nightmares. "I guess I didn't want to remember."

She testified about receiving a phone call from law enforcement. Prior to that she had been unaware of the investigation going on in Elephant Butte.

Later, a police officer and an FBI agent went to her home in Craig, Colorado, to question her.

Rein asked if the officers had briefed her on what she had probably experienced; she said no. It was only after they finished questioning her that they showed her photographs taken from a video and asked her to identify the depicted woman, herself, and the man, David Ray. While they were with her in Colorado, she said, the officers took photos of the tattoo on her leg for identity purposes.

When questioned on the stand, she testified that she had never seen the video. She had pain and vaginal bleeding for three or four days after Ray took her to the Murphy house that day in July 1996.

When Rein asked how she knew David Ray was the one hurting her, since her eyes were taped, she said she knew his voice when he spoke. She also knew only he was in the trailer with her because sometimes the tape on her eyes came loose and she could peek under it. She saw him, and sometimes had glimpses of the dildos and other things sitting nearby on a cabinet and hanging on the walls of the trailer.

Kelli's voice and demeanor remained calm throughout the questioning until she was shown, and asked to identify, the photos of herself taken from the video. Her voice broke. "That's me," she said, crying.

She was shown another photo and asked to identify the person in it. "David Ray."

"Is he in the courtroom? Where is he?"

She pointed, saying, "Over there in the striped shirt, with oxygen."

She cried softly through the remainder of the questioning until the court's break.

Since her experience, she said, she no longer goes anywhere alone, is afraid to sleep, afraid of people, and does not like sex. And, she said, "If I am alone, I have a pistol sitting beside me. I'm scared." And she said, "I'm not the same person anymore. I used to be outgoing, and I'm not anymore."

"My husband now, we fight all the time about sex. I don't like sex anymore; I don't want anybody touching me. I don't think he's ever seen me naked."

It was after the officers showed her, in Colorado, the photos from the video that she fully realized what she had experienced "wasn't a dream. It was reality."

She knew she needed counseling and went to Dave Spencer for professional help.

The witness asked for a break; and the judge recessed court until after lunch, when Kelli's questioning continued.

Rein often objected during Kelli's testimony, and when he cross-examined her, he tried to discredit what she said. He made a point of her scanty memory, of her relationships with other men, and of her behavior the day she left the Murphy home with David Ray and disappeared.

Rein also mentioned that a later boy friend of Kelli's had drowned in her presence, implying that event caused her emotional trauma leading to her testimony against David Ray. The state objected to the relevance of that line of questioning, saying the drowning had nothing to do with this case. Rein argued that it was an element of Kelli's mental anguish; Judge Mertz overruled the state's objection.

Kelli acknowledged that her fiancé, Jim, had died the day he proposed to her.

She was excused from the stand at 3:20 p.m.; the court recessed for fifteen minutes.

When the jury was brought back into the courtroom, the State called FBI Agent Larry Haulpt, stationed in Las Cruces, to the stand.

He said he assisted with the investigation at Elephant Butte. He testified about what he knew of the chain of custody of the video, and then the court was dismissed for the day.

Chapter 28 – Testimony

The old courtroom, which had neither fresh air ventilation nor air conditioning, was hot and unbearably stuffy.

On Friday, July 7, several portable air conditioners were brought in for the comfort of the jurors, but they were noisy, making testimony difficult to hear. Despite microphones, more than once someone asked the speaker to repeat testimony.

That morning, prosecution recalled State Police Agent John Briscoe to the stand to testify about various exhibits to be presented. But before he was called in, the judge, prosecutors and defense attorneys spent time in chambers discussing which exhibits would be or would not be allowed.

Briscoe, with his youthful face, took the stand. He said he was the manager of the crime scene at Elephant Butte. He explained the processing of the crime scene and the collection and management of the evidence. He was asked to look at and identify approximately twenty-four photos taken of the interior of the white cargo trailer. After they were admitted as evidence, Briscoe was asked to describe each photo, and confirm they showed the same views and objects he had seen when he first saw the crime scene.

The photos began with views of the back door of the trailer, and the view inside the trailer from the doorway.

The third photo showed inside the trailer looking left. Briscoe explained that under the stovetop was a hidden cabinet. "The door drops down ... What it is ... kind of like a cot, with straps and chains, where if a person raised up, her face would be right underneath the other shelf. And the door could be closed" with her lying inside.

The defense objected to Briscoe's description, but was overruled.

Next was a photo showing the view to the right, towards the rear of the trailer, that included the large stainless steel medicine cabinet and its contents. Briscoe identified the photo and described what was shown in it.

A ceiling view showed "pulleys, straps, chains and padlocks, right above where the chair was."

The photo of the middle of the trailer included "drawings of females in bondage, written instructions and reminders of how to handle a victim, sexual devices, and more straps and stuff hanging on the wall."

While the defense did not object to Briscoe's spoken reference to "the chair" (which probably was not in the trailer when Kelli was there in 1996), Rein frequently objected to certain photos being admitted as evidence, and to Briscoe's explanations of what they depicted, but the judge overruled.

The prosecution asked him to read out loud what was printed on exhibit number 61, which Briscoe called the "Remember List." He began by saying the word "Remember" was at the top, written in large red letters. It was the same document he had read at Ray's preliminary hearing, but heard for the first time by these jurors. It began: "Remember: A woman will do or say anything to get loose..." And ended with: "If she was worth taking she is worth keeping. She must be subjected to hypnosis before the woman can be safely released. Never trust a chained captive."

Prosecution asked him to identify exhibit number 122 and read it out loud. Briscoe called it the "Don't Forget List." He said written at the top in red letters was: "Don't Forget the Unexpected." He read what was listed: "Neck chain, handcuffs, leg-irons, hood or gag, wrist or ankle tape, bondage bar, phone, radio mike, door deadbolt, alarm system, keys."

Items 61 and 122 were entered as evidence.

Briscoe said the photo, exhibit number 32, showed a black robe, bars with hooks, weights hanging on the wall. Next photos showed the portable toilet, the television monitor, tripod with camcorder, things hanging on the walls—including dildos, restraints, straps, wrist clamps and whips, and items on a shelf—including a box of gloves and an inhaler. He was asked to read to the court what was written on the pictured item in one photo, and he did with obvious discomfort: Vaginal stretcher 1-3/8" to 2-5/8".

Briscoe said exhibit number 60, which he called a document, was found on the left wall of the white cargo trailer. After it was entered into evidence, Yontz asked him to read it. Briscoe first read its title: "Psychological and Physical Procedures. Initial Handling of a

Captive, Personal Fetish." It listed eighteen items, which he read aloud to the court, beginning with: "One: The new female captive should be gagged and blindfolded with wrists and ankles chained. Two: Move her into the recreational room. Place her body under the suspension chains." It was the same document he had read at Ray's preliminary hearing.

Briscoe read all eighteen items, ending with what he said was written in capital letters at the bottom. "Note: The shock value of disorientation, plus continuous verbal and physical abuse during the first few hours of confinement will have a great influence on how docile and subdued the captive will be during the remaining period of captivity. If it is done properly, she will be intimidated and much easier to handle."

Briscoe testified about the two-dozen photos, and said he had photographed all but one.

After all photos were accepted into evidence, Jeff Rein cross-examined the officer. He asked how he knew the same cargo trailer shown in the photographs was there in 1996. Briscoe said he believed it was the same trailer because he could see it in the Kelli Van Cleve video, which he had viewed more than once. Rein asked him the same question about depicted items in many of the photographs. Briscoe admitted that he did not know if some of those items in the photos had been there in 1996.

Rein argued that it was only speculation that the same white cargo trailer and its contents, including the video equipment, were there in 1996. His objections to the photos being accepted as evidence were overruled.

Photos of the modified chair found in the trailer in March 1999 had been denied as evidence because it was probably not yet used in 1996. What Kelli was strapped onto—by her description and as seen in the video—was a modified weight bench.

When Briscoe was excused, Rein asked for a bench conference. He complained that Kelli and an FBI agent—allowed to remain in the courtroom after their testimonies—sat next to the aisle where the jury passed as they came and went from the small courtroom. He argued that their close proximity might influence the jury. The district attorney said the witnesses had a right to sit where they could see the exhibits. The objection was overruled.

The next exhibit, the modified weight bench, was brought into the courtroom. The judge told the jurors that it was exhibited only for the purpose of testimony about it, but would not be entered into evidence.

Agent Trent Pederson, a special agent with the FBI for three years, testified about the bench. Prior to being an agent, he had been a licensed attorney in California and Utah. He said he had been assigned to the evidence response team in Elephant Butte. He arrived at the scene the afternoon of March 26, and taped off his assigned areas. Those were the white storage trailer and the red storage shed with the white top, both of which were in the back yard of the defendant's property. He had found the modified weight bench, now in the courtroom, in front of the red shed. He testified that the bench seen in a photo, exhibit number 108, was the same one that he had found. He described the modifications to the bench that included D-rings and wheels added to it. When questioned, said he did not know when the modifications had been made.

The defense asked if he could say that same bench had been there in 1996. Pederson said he could not, but it looked exactly like the weight bench seen in the video with Kelli strapped to it, and as Kelli had described it.

After lunch, the prosecution wanted to present David Spencer as an expert witness. The defense objected, asking that he not be allowed to testify because he was not an expert. Arguments about whether or not to allow Spencer's testimony took up considerable time. At last, Judge Mertz agreed to conduct a Daubert hearing of Spencer, and dismissed the jury from the courtroom.

The purpose of a Daubert hearing is to determine in court whether a witness is qualified for the label of, and to testify as, an expert witness.

Spencer, a psychotherapist, was the counselor Kelli saw in Colorado.

The jury was dismissed until Tuesday morning. Before they left the courthouse, they sent the judge a note complaining about their lunch location. They wanted to eat their meals elsewhere.

David Allen Spencer took the stand and testified about his qualifications that included his professional training—a Master's degree in clinical social work, his experiences and the types of cases he handled. Spencer also told the judge why Kelli had sought his help. She was feeling distressed, had problems sleeping and eating, struggled with anger and difficulties in her marriage. He said he questioned her about her earlier life and gave her tests, which showed thirty different categories in which she had problems. He said the test was commonly used to establish whether or not someone had been raped or sexually abused. He told the court that Kelli had told him, in her first session with him, that she had been kidnapped and tortured for three days. As a result, her behavior had changed. She now isolated herself from other people, she didn't trust people, took unusual security measures at home, and felt she had received many betrayals in her life. She had trouble opening up to anyone, she had immediately blocked her experiences from her memory, and suffered from feeling that she had no control over her own life.

Spencer testified that, after he had consulted with Dr. Martha Young, he diagnosed her with post-traumatic-stress disorder and depression.

Although he had never before testified in a criminal trial, he said he had testified twelve times as an expert witness.

After Spencer was dismissed from the stand, the State asked the court to accept Spencer as an expert witness.

The defense argued that he was not a doctor, he could only assume someone was telling him the truth, and he was not qualified to give an opinion and should not be allowed to testify before the jury. The State and the defense continued to argue. Finally, the judge found that David Spencer, by his education, training and experience, could render an expert opinion in this case.

On Friday afternoon, July 7, at 3:53 p.m., Judge Mertz dismissed the court for the day and said it would not resume again until July 11.

When court was back in session on Tuesday, July 11, the jury was called in and psychotherapist David Spencer was sworn in to testify.

Spencer said he first saw Kelli in his office in September 1999 because she had difficulty eating, sleeping, had marital difficulties—including arguments over sexual contact, and was distressed. He spoke of the test he had given Kelli, and about her family history and employment record. He said she drank little alcohol. He described what Kelli had recalled to him of her experience in late July 1996, that Jesse took her to David Ray's house, her memory of being strapped down onto a table against her will, and of David Ray subjecting her to sexual abuse. She told him how she reacted, since then, to depicted sexual abuse on television, and about her dreams and feeling unsafe when she was alone, and her efforts in trying to have trusting relationships. He spoke of studying case histories of other people who, after trauma, had amnesia or repressed memories.

Spencer was dismissed from the stand.

After the jury reviewed the exhibits, the State rested its case, declaring the presentations were completed.

The judge said that he could not grant the jury's request for an alternative place to eat.

Chapter 29 – Trial's End

After the jury was dismissed, the prosecution and the defense argued about the choices of verdicts.

The defense argued that the State did not prove a basis for the kidnapping charge, that great bodily harm to the victim had not been proven, that she received no permanent impairment. Rein said there was no evidence that Kelli had been unsafe. He also argued that there had been no evidence of a firearm being used in her case and he complained about the conspiracy issue. He argued that Kelli had not established six counts of criminal sexual penetration in the first degree. He agreed only to charges of kidnapping in the second degree, one count of conspiracy and one count of CSP.

The prosecution responded to the defense's objections to each of the charges, and then Judge Mertz spoke of his findings as to each of the defense's motions.

After the jury returned to the courtroom that afternoon, the judge told them the prosecution had concluded their presentations, and the defense also "rested." That meant the defense team would present no defense other than that already given. Before Judge Mertz dismissed the jury, he asked them to return at nine the next morning to hear his instructions before they began deliberation.

The defense waived Ray's right to be present in the courtroom during those instructions.

After the jury left the courtroom, the defense and the State continued to wrangle over the various counts charged. The court was finally dismissed at nine that night.

Court reconvened Wednesday morning, July 12. Jeff Rein said the credibility of the victim had always been an issue, and was still an issue. The judge told the prosecution and the defense that each of them had one hour to present their closing arguments. Rein said he needed more time for his closing; he asked for one hour and fifteen minutes.

Before the jury was called in, the judge told the spectators to behave themselves.

After the jury was seated, Judge Mertz told the jury that the presentation of evidence was concluded and he would now begin instructing them about the applicable rules of this case.

The judge went over, and explained the elements of, each of the counts. He also told them to make no conclusions because the defendant did not testify on his own behalf, nor should they concern themselves with the consequences of the verdicts they reached.

The prosecutors for the State began their closing summation. Yontz went over counts and definitions, including: kidnapping, conspiracy to commit kidnapping, great mental anguish—first and second degree, and conspiracy to commit criminal sexual penetration.

He also touched on each piece of testimony and evidence that had been presented to them: the testimonies of Deputy Sheriff Bowidowicz and Agent Tony Maxwell; what was seen on the videotape; the Rapid Start System that helped them locate Kelli; Patrick Murphy's testimony and his search for her, including on the beach; his describing the return of Kelli on Sunday by David Ray; the testimony of Todd Thompson, saying that Kelli had left Blue Waters with Jesse; the chain of evidence establishing the facts of the case; Kelli's testimony about what the defendant had done to her, and the six distinct sessions with Ray that she described; how Kelli was taken home and her family's rejection of her; the phone call Kelli received from the State Police, and officers later showing her the photographs taken from the video; the testimonies of David Spencer and Agent Briscoe; Ray's documents found in the white cargo trailer that were read to the court; the torture chamber; the videotape.

The prosecution concluded by asking the jury to find David Parker Ray guilty of all charges.

The judge recessed the court for lunch.

After lunch, when the jury had returned to the courtroom, the defense council presented their closing summation.

Rein discounted many of the photos taken in March 1999, saying items shown in them were probably not there in 1996. Kelli was not open or honest with her therapist. She already had sex problems before her experience with David Ray; she quarreled about sex while she was married to Patrick. He said that two years after the incident with David Ray, Kelli continued to be friendly with Jesse. "This case is about the credibility of Kelli, and you cannot base a conviction of the defendant upon her testimony."

The prosecution objected. Yontz told the judge that the defense was laying guilt on the wrong person; the defense was victimizing the victim. The judge overruled the objection.

The prosecutor gave his final summary. Yontz spoke of the victim shown in the videotape with her eyes and mouth taped. He said the defense was trying to put Kelli on trial. He spoke of all of the soundproofing in the cargo trailer seen in the photographs. The depicted evidence could not be disputed, including Kelli shown in the video. Yontz said that Kelli had been raped and tortured for three days, and she clearly described six different sessions that she remembered, and the great mental anguish that she suffered.

Judge Mertz told the jury that they were to select a foreman to speak for them, and he announced which of the originally selected eighteen would deliberate and which were alternate jurors.

The designated jury began their deliberation at 2:15 p.m. on July 12, 2000. Within forty-five minutes, the jury asked that a television, VCR and the videotape be sent in to them so they could review the tape.

Thursday, July 13, after the jurors had spent more than eight hours in deliberation, they were brought back into the courtroom. The jury foreman, Mr. Sanchez, informed the judge that they could not reach a unanimous verdict.

Members of the jury disagreed on all counts.

Judge Mertz asked Mr. Sanchez whether continued deliberations would bring them to agreement. He said no. The judge polled the jury and they agreed that there would be no unanimous verdict. The judge went over the verdicts of each of the counts, beginning with the six charges of criminal sexual penetration, either in the first or second degree; to all they could not agree. Mr. Sanchez informed the judge that the result was also the same for all of the other counts.

Judge Mertz declared a mistrial.

District Attorney Ron Lopez immediately prepared an order for another trial, to retry David Parker Ray on the same charges. The State only had six months to prepare for it. The court recessed at 5:30 p.m.

Kelli Van Cleve Garrett burst into tears. She was devastated by the outcome of the trial and said she did not think she could go through another one.

Outside of the courthouse, visibly frustrated District Attorney Ron Lopez said he could not understand the verdict. Jurors were not given all of the information in this trial, but he had hoped they had enough to put the pieces together. Having three separate trials, separating the experiences of the three known victims, hampered the State's ability to present their case. He added that Ray carefully chose his victims; he picked women he believed would be easy targets to discredit on the witness stand if he were ever caught.

Lopez should have also mentioned the hypnotic drugs that Ray gave his victims before he released them.

Defense Attorney Jeff Rein had done well the job the court assigned him, that of providing his client with the best defense he could. He had successfully raised doubt in the minds of at least two jurors.

Two young Hispanic women (ages twenty-three and twenty-one) told the media outside the courthouse that they had voted for acquittal. They found Kelli and her testimony not credible.

"I wasn't convinced ... I know a lot of people enjoy rough sex," one said.

The other said, "I think David Parker Ray did kidnap and torture other women, but I don't think he ever killed anyone." An inexplicable comment from the juror, since this trial was not about murder; it was about Ray kidnapping and torturing a woman.

This case opened in March 1999. This first jury trial—that began a year later with selection of jurors in late March 2000, and was delayed many times, and finally began again on June 29, 2000, and, after portions of three weeks in the courtroom—came to an end late in the day of July 13, 2000, without resolution.

The principals of the case—the defendant, the judge and district court clerk, the attorneys, all of the witnesses and the evidence—departed Tierra Amarílla, Rio Arríba County, for their long journeys home.

When David Parker Ray departed Tierra Amarílla the next day, a reporter asked him, who should have been delighted with the outcome of the trial, to say something. He tersely said, "No comment."

An armed pilot, accompanied by a Sierra County deputy, flew Ray back to Sierra County, where he was to remain in jail awaiting his next trial.

Chapter 30 – More Delays

District Attorney Ron Lopez announced that Ray's next scheduled trial would be the retrial. However, he noted that if Ray's trial concerning Montaño was not held before January 31, 2001, that case's prosecution "would be in jeopardy." Lopez's term as D. A. would soon end, and Assistant District Attorney Jim Yontz was expected to lead the prosecution team for the next trial.

Motions had begun months earlier, pertaining to the other two scheduled trials, that would also ultimately affect the retrial.

David Parker Ray had been charged on February 17, 1999, with ten criminal counts pertaining to the now-deceased Angelíca Montaño: kidnapping, conspiracy to commit a crime, criminal sexual penetration, aggravated battery and criminal sexual contact.

Witnesses were summoned. Those sixteen people were put on notice that they might be called to testify. A motion was made on May 15, 2000, that the primary testimony of Montaño, who had died eight days earlier on May 7, would be entered into evidence by pre-taped deposition. On June 6, 2000, notice was posted that the jury trial pertaining to her would begin in Estancia, Torrance County—in central New Mexico—on November 27, 2000. Later, that setting was vacated to schedule at that same place and time, instead, the retrial concerning Kelli.

Jeff Rein, Kathy Love and Sara Singhas—David Parker Ray's court-assigned team of public defenders—withdrew their services on September 21. Ray needed a new defense attorney. On October 3, Lee McMillian of Albuquerque was given that assignment.

The second trial, to retry Ray on the same charges concerning Kelli, began in Estancia on November 27 with jury selection.

Then, in the middle of that jury selection procedure, on the morning of November 30, 2000, Judge Neil Mertz died in his shower.

Neil Mertz, a resident of Socorro, was fifty-five years old when he died of a massive heart attack. He had been the District Judge of

Division III, Seventh Judicial District of Sierra, Catron, Socorro and Torrance counties, since March 1996.

The trial was postponed until another judge was selected.

The two remaining judges of the Seventh Judicial District were Thomas G. Fitch and Edmund Kase III. Either of them could appoint a judge for the district to replace Mertz.

When each one appointed someone to preside over the Ray case, the prosecution or the defense attorney struck him down. Kase tried to appoint Fitch; Yontz struck him. Kase tried to appoint himself; Lee McMillian struck him.

A panel, selected by Chief Justice Gene Franchini of the State Supreme Court, was to select replacement candidates for presentation to the governor to fill the position of the third district judgeship for the Seventh Judicial District. District Attorney Ron Lopez, who soon would no longer hold that office, was on the list. If he were appointed judge, he would have to disqualify himself from presiding over the Ray case.

Governor Gary Johnson would make the final selection.

Gov. Johnson was a Republican, but he turned out to be unlike any Republican the State—and perhaps the country—had ever seen, at least as respects his stand on wanting to legalize marijuana, perhaps even harder drugs, to reduce jail and penal institution crowding. Because of his nationally-publicized controversy while governor, he embarrassed many New Mexicans of both Republican and Democrat persuasions, including many in law enforcement and the judicial system.

Darren White, Secretary of the Department of Public Safety, resigned his position as the state's "top cop" in 2000 to protest the governor's position on drugs. As White's replacement, Gov. Johnson had selected Nick Bakas, a retired captain of the Albuquerque Police Department.

Now, when selecting the third judge for the Seventh Judicial District, who would also preside over the important upcoming Ray trials, Johnson wanted a Republican judge who would not let David Parker Ray plea-bargain out of a tough sentence.

In late February 2001, the panel and the governor together selected Kevin Swaezea, thirty-seven, as the Seventh Judicial District Court judge to replace Mertz. Soon thereafter, Gov. Gary Johnson also appointed him to preside over the David Parker Ray trial, although this new judge had no prior experience with criminal trials.

A preliminary hearing was set in Estancia for March 23, 2001.

The prosecution desperately wanted the judge to allow this jury to hear at least one of the audiotapes of Ray telling his victims what would be done to them. Ray had played a particular tape for both Cindy Vigil and Angelíca Montaño after he kidnapped them. However, Kelli had no memory of hearing it, or of certain things described in it being done to her while she was in Ray's captivity. Before the first trial, the defense's Jeff Rein protested that those parts were not applicable to Kelli Van Cleve's case.

Judge Neil Mertz had ruled that audiotape was inadmissible at the first trial at Tierra Amarílla. Those jurors never heard it, and that trial ended without a verdict.

The prosecution believed there would surely be a guilty verdict this time if this jury could hear Ray describing the things he would do to his victim, the same things Kelli remembered and described under oath as happening to her.

Together, Jim Yontz and his co-prosecutor, Claire Harwell, took a copy of the audiotape and wiped out the parts to which the defense had previously objected. The tape was reduced in length by almost half. Judge Sweazea listened to it in his chambers and agreed that it would be played for the jurors during the retrial. During legal proceedings, this would be referred to as the redacted tape.

This was an important victory for the prosecution.

Selection of the jury for the retrial—that had begun November 27, 2000—resumed on April 2, 2001, more than a year after the first trial's jury selection had begun.

This time, in the small centrally-located town of Estancia in Torrance County, with cattle ranching as a primary industry, the juror pool contained a broader variety of people in age, background and education. Although the prosecution took great care in choosing jurors, the selection of twelve jurors and three alternates took only five days.

Another sticky point, to be settled before the trial began, was the defense's choice of a thirty-five-year-old witness, a self-declared "dominatrix" or "diva" from Albuquerque. McMillian had chosen her as a witness because she would describe in detail sadism and masochism, bondage and domination, as if they were ordinary alternative sex practices.

When he introduced the woman to the judge in a private hearing without jurors, McMillian admitted, "We have taken a step into the twilight zone."

The "diva" said the fear fantasy was a large and exciting part of the victim's pleasure, and "victim" was an appropriate word to use during sex games. The defense hoped she would make David Parker Ray seem like a regular guy who just liked kinky sex with willing partners.

Judge Swaezea was offended by the woman's detailed descriptions of the type of sex acts that those kinds of people practiced. After listening to her for a while, he ruled that she could be a witness for the defense—but only identifying Ray's various devices as sex toys—provided she did not advocate her alternative life-style.

Chapter 31 – Retrial

The first day of testimony in the second jury trial for David Parker Ray regarding Kelli Van Cleve Garrett began April 9, 2001, in Estancia.

Judge Kevin R. Sweazea, district judge, Division III, presided, with the State's lead plaintiff attorney, Jim Yontz, heading the prosecution team, and Lee McMillian defending David Ray.

Before the jury was called in, McMillian took considerable time protesting the judge's decisions. The judge had allowed the redacted audiotape. McMillian argued that Ray had said at the beginning of the recording that it was made for entertainment purposes only; the witness, Kelli, had no memory of hearing it when she had been with Ray; and the nature of the tape "is extremely inflammatory." He said the prejudice it would cause outweighed any reason to play it for the jury.

Yontz argued against the judge's decision to allow testimony by the defense's key witness, the self-proclaimed "diva;" McMillian wanted her to testify about the consensual use of the "sex toys" found on Ray's property.

Yontz suggested that "if Mr. Ray wants to tell us [about the devices], put him on the stand." Yontz was toying with McMillian; he knew the last thing the defense wanted was to put David Parker Ray on the stand. Yontz also argued that the proposed witness "knows nothing about the contact with the victim and what went on in the cargo trailer."

Next, McMillian argued against reference to the drugs found on Ray's property in the bottles of Hot Damn! schnapps. "Ms. Van Cleve never indicated she was given alcohol," he said; she only mentioned being given a drink of water. And she "never indicated that she took pills." He asked that the triptyline and the 40 milliliters of amitriptyline found in the bottle of schnapps, and photographs of the Hot Damn! bottles, not be allowed as evidence.

Yontz said that the motions, on March 6 and March 28, 2000, provided the defense with the procedures and charts that identified the drug found in two bottles and the pills found in a pen by investigators. He said there was relevance tying everything together—Ray's own comments about using drugs on his victims and why, and what was done to the victim and why she remembered so little after she was released from captivity. Yontz also wanted an agent to testify about the drugs and their effects, and about their easy availability in Mexico. Especially about Kelli's poor memory, said Yontz, "the drug is relevant to this case."

McMillian continued to argue about the admissibility of the drug evidence and lack of proof that drugs had been used on Kelli. He also argued as to the expert status of the druggist to be called as a witness.

Judge Sweazea decided to allow drug testimony and evidence.

The jury was brought into the courtroom; the judge addressed and instructed them.

Yontz gave his opening remarks. He said Ray had given Kelli sodium pentothal and barbital, which he called "brain-washing techniques." Trying to elicit sympathy for Kelli, he told the jury that she'd had a bad marriage and a terrible experience in 1996; then she suffered through testimony at a trial that ended with a not-guilty verdict in 2000.

McMillian gave his opening remarks for the defense, and commented that the sexual choices of S and M, and bondage and domination, "are not that unusual in our society." He also said some of Kelli's marriage troubles were about sex. He spoke of Kelli's barhopping the day she left the Murphy home and her claimed experience at Ray's house—"an odd fact she doesn't [much] mention for three years." She didn't talk about it until the FBI visited her in Colorado, and her story "changed with the telling." McMillian added, "Evidence will show you this is not a person held against her will, she could have escaped if she wanted." And, he said, the videotape would show "it could be a fantasy among consenting adults." He suggested that she had been a willing participant until the investigation of the case began and the video with her was found; then, because of shame and embarrassment, she denied she had been willing.

The first witness called was Peter Bowidowicz, a Sierra County deputy, on March 22, 1999. He testified about his arrival at 513 Bass Road in Elephant Butte that day, and confirmed the photo showing David Parker Ray's front gate and sign, admitted as exhibit number one. His testimony primarily was to show that the crime scene remained uncompromised. He described the property, including its dimensions, the fence line and Ray's neighbors on three sides.

Byron Wilson, ranger with New Mexico State Parks, testified next. He spoke of the State Park's lease of the property at 513 Bass Road to David Parker Ray. He said he had inspected the property on several occasions looking for violations such as non-allowed storage of machinery and equipment. This lease was due for renewal in 1999.

Kelli Van Cleve Garrett testified as the third witness. She spoke of her troubled, brief marriage to Patrick Murphy. She said she had a tilted uterus, making sex painful, which upset her because she could not have a normal marriage. She left the Murphy house because she was upset; "I was not angry at Patrick."

She said Cassandra—"Cassie"—had braided her blonde hair in cornrow braids, and she described where she went that afternoon, including to Cassie's. Kelli went there to ask her to leave Patrick alone and quit trying to take him away from her. Kelli testified about the rest of her day, the bars she visited and what happened to her after Jesse Ray took her, by motorcycle, to the home of David Ray. Soon after arriving, she said, they handcuffed her and wrapped her mouth and eyes with duct tape, stripped her and took her to another, smaller trailer where they secured her on a narrow table, with her legs apart and her hands tied above her head. She compared the circumference of one of the dildos Ray tried to insert as that of a can of Copenhagen (chewing tobacco). She said Ray had tried to insert dildos at least thirty times, and "it hurt every time. It was the worst pain I have ever felt."

Yontz asked her to describe each of the incidents that she could remember when Ray had molested her. She said she licked the tape until it came loose; from under the tape over her eyes she could see David in the trailer, but not Jesse. With the loose tape, when she was able to talk to him, she begged him to stop, to let her go home. She said she expected him to kill her, and she wished he would to end the experience.

After the lunch break, Claire Harwell resumed the examination for the state. Kelli said she had no sense of time because of the tape over her mouth and eyes; and she believed the trailer had no windows. "He would quit and then try again. The next time, he didn't leave, but stayed in the trailer. He would then try again. When he would leave the trailer, he would lock the door behind him. He left and came back again. He continued to try" to insert the dildos.

"How many times did this happen?"

"Quite a few."

Sometimes the tape was loose and she could peek under it; other times, Ray took the tape off, and for a while her eyes had difficulty adjusting to the light. When Harwell asked her, she described what she saw in the trailer.

Kelli said Ray told her he was in a Satanic sex worship group. Because the dildos didn't work, he said, they would have to let her go; she would be of no use to the group. Ray refused to tell her who else was in the group.

She said she had left the Murphy home on a Thursday and was returned on Sunday. Harwell asked Kelli to describe the last episode in the trailer that she could remember. She last remembered the phone ringing and David leaving the trailer.

Next, Harwell asked Kelli to tell the jury who was shown in the video.

"I'm on the bench and David is there." She said she recognized herself because of the tattoo on her leg. The video was taken in Ray's trailer, she recognized it, and she was not a willing participant.

"At no time did I want any sexual activity," she said. Harwell asked her to describe how she had told David she did not want to be involved. "I told him no. I tried to reason with him. I said I wanted to go home to my husband."

"Did you struggle with him?"

"I could not move."

"Did you want to punish Patrick?"

"No!"

Harwell asked, and Kelli described, how she was taken home, how she felt, what happened at the Murphy house.

Then Harwell asked her about her sketchy memory. "I couldn't remember anything. Then I started having memories. They seemed like they were not real. Now it is just … it is real."

"How are the memories?"

"Like snapshots. The sound of duct tape makes me cringe. I watch a movie and something in the movie will trigger something. The sound of tape reminds me of him. I hate him."

"Describe how you first started remembering this."

"The first out-loud memory … my sister was talking about her husband being restrained. I said, 'That was done to me'."

"What was another memory?"

"A cop showed up; he was an FBI agent. He said I was a witness to a kidnapping and they would contact me later. I had no idea what they were talking about. At that time I still had no memory. K. C. Rogers called. He said David Ray had been caught doing this to other girls."

"Doing what?"

"Raping them, basically. No details."

McMillian objected. He approached the bench to object to the reference to other rape victims. The judge instructed the jury to disregard the witness' last remark.

Kelli said police interviewed her at her home; and afterwards, they showed her a photo. When she had seen it, she threw the photo at them. She knew, at sight of that photo, that it was not a nightmare; it was real.

Kelli described how she had been changed since her abduction, her fears, lack of trust, and her need to see a counselor for two years. "I do not talk about this to people because it is very embarrassing. I do not want people to think less of me. I didn't do this; he did. [But I feel] I am the one in prison."

She said she has had to speak of this many times but "I've never had to speak of this in front of the media."

McMillian examined Kelli for the defense, and immediately attacked her for her last comment. Kelli acknowledged that this was her third time to testify in a courtroom against David Ray.

(The media were present in the courtroom in Tierra Amarilla, after Judge Mertz had ruled to allow them, and she had testified at preliminary hearings when they were present, but because of stress, she might have not have been aware of them.)

He questioned her about her earlier life in T or C, her friends—including her friendship with Jesse, her relationships, her marriage to Patrick that had begun as a joke. She said Judge Mertz had married them in the courthouse. The defense asked her about her tilted uterus, and whether it had been repaired. Kelli said no. He asked her to describe her day and evening prior to going to Ray's. In response to a question, she said she believed she had been alert during her entire ordeal at Ray's; but afterward, it had been blocked from her memory.

McMillian asked if she sought advice about the divorce. He asked if she had willingly gotten back into Ray's truck at the Murphys'. And asked if David hadn't released her in a safe place after they left there.

"He left me in a safe place the second time," Kelli responded pointedly.

McMillian questioned her about having no memory of a kidnapping until the FBI and police contacted her. He pointed out that her memory of those events seemed to continually expand. As an example, until her court testimony, she had never mentioned hearing the key in the lock when Ray had left the trailer and locked the door.

Kelli said she remembered it during the trial, when giving it as an example of knowing how many times Ray had come and gone, but no one had previously asked her specifically about it.

When asked, Kelli said she had no memory of being drugged or given alcohol while she was with David. Yet, said McMillian, she claimed to be incoherent after she was released.

McMillian asked if she and her attorneys went over their plan of attack before she testified. Kelli said she had talked of "putting him away so I can get on with my life."

He asked if she would have told the Murphys if it [her experience with Ray] had been consensual.

"Probably," said Kelli.

"Did you have consensual sex with Mr. Ray?"

"No, I did not!"

"Did your feelings of what happened make you crazy sometimes?"

"Yes it did."

"Were you told [by your attorneys] what answers you should give?"

"I was told what the questions would be, but not what to say."

Kellie Van Cleve Garrett was finally dismissed from the stand late that afternoon.

After recess, when the jury had returned to the courtroom, FBI Special Agent Anthony Maxwell was called to the stand. He gave the history of his career and his experience with forensic evidence. The state asked the court to consider him an expert witness.

"A crime scene may be small like a closet, or large like Oklahoma, or extended like a kidnapping case. Crime scenes occur anywhere," said Maxwell. He cited his personal experience working large crime scene investigations. He said about a thousand FBI agents are involved with evidence response. He described procedures and evidence discovery. Yontz walked him through various photographs to identify for exhibits, and to explain and describe a diagram of the residence.

He said he did not immediately bring in the FBI evidence recovery team because he had made an agreement with the State Police, but ultimately thirty investigators assisted with the case.

The questioning turned to the modified weight bench found outside the red and white shed behind the residence. Responding to a question by Yontz, Maxwell said, "It was specially constructed with rings. It resembled another item found at the crime scene." And he spoke as to the relationship of the two, the dimensions, length and width.

McMillian argued that the bench found at the scene could not be positively identified as the same one seen in the video with Kelli. However, those photos were admitted into evidence.

On cross-examination, he asked Maxwell about the "padding on the contraption," and the leg and arm supports. Maxwell replied that, from his own observation, it was similar to the one in the photo.

After questions and testimony as to the chain of custody of this exhibit, the judge dismissed Maxwell as a witness and then dismissed the court at 5:20 p.m. April 9th.

Chapter 32 – Retrial Continues

On April 10, discussions in the courtroom began before the jury was called in.

Yontz brought up the knife, badge and Hot Damn! schnapps found inside the bedroom at 513 Bass Road, that was being considered for court evidence. He mentioned the 1993 audiotape in which Ray said he used drugs, including sodium pentothal, and their effects on his victims. Yontz said these drugs are used as a date-rape drug, and he mentioned how Kelli said she felt after David Ray had released her. "He uses the drugs to affect their memory. We know he used it in 1999 … on Vigil."

Claire Harwell, also for the prosecution, said the drug is "something that is not in a medicine cabinet at home."

McMillian for the defense said it is a prescription drug, and there had only been 40 milliliters in the [almost empty] bottle. From prior Van Cleve testimony, she first thought she had been drugged while she was in the Blue Waters bar; she was unable to identify the knife found at the scene as the one David or Jesse threatened her with; and she said she had consumed nothing, no food or drink, while at Bass Road.

He said he would move for a mistrial if the knife or the Hot Damn! was introduced.

The jury was called into the courtroom.

FBI Agent Trent Pederson was called to the stand. He was the team leader of the search for evidence of the red storage shed. He described what he called a modified press bench, found outside the shed, that had "a number of modifications [including] D-rings around its entire surface."

The next witness was New Mexico State Police Agent John Briscoe, who gave a history of his police experience and said he now had a specialized responsibility, that of belonging to the state's crime scene major processing unit. He described what happened after he arrived at the Ray property: the search warrants, the security of the scene, and official photographs and videos taken of the scene, inside and outside. The video taken of the crime scene was shown and Briscoe explained each view.

McMillian said Briscoe was at the scene "in 1999, but he did not know what the place looked like in 1996."

Briscoe said the door into the white cargo trailer was locked; he called a locksmith to open it for investigators. He systematically described to the court the interior of the trailer and the objects seen in the photographs. Following objections from the defense that were overruled by the judge, he read aloud Ray's various documents found inside the trailer and tacked on the walls, including the "Don't Forget List" and "Procedures to use with Captives."

McMillian questioned the chain of custody of the exhibits and evidence.

Briscoe was then directed to the investigation inside Ray's residence, and he testified about the layout and referred to diagrams and many photo exhibits.

McMillian asked to approach the bench; he complained about a knife which Kelli could not identify, and a schnapps bottle seen in photos.

The jury next viewed the videotape, which took up the rest of the morning.

After lunch, before the jury was in the courtroom, Yontz brought up the subject of photographs of syringes found at Bass Road. The defense objected, but Yontz said, "This is a method of administering drugs."

When the judge questioned their relevance, Claire Harwell said, "The drugs are mentioned on the tape." The judge overruled the defense's objection.

The next exhibits were an original and the redacted audiotape. Agent Briscoe testified to the authenticity of the original audiotape, which he listened to during the lunch break. After defense objections, it was entered into evidence. Next exhibit shown to Briscoe, number 132, was a photo of syringes, which was also entered into evidence after defense objections.

Briscoe said all members of the team took videos as they proceeded to gather evidence.

The video of the crime scene was accepted as an exhibit.

Briscoe was asked to describe in detail the 513 Bass Road property as he saw it in 1999. McMillian repeatedly asked him if he could testify that each item he described was also there or was exactly the same in 1996. In most cases, Briscoe said he could not.

The jury was brought into the courtroom with Briscoe still on the stand. The prosecution went over various exhibits with him, with the defense regularly objecting to them and questioning the officer whether he knew if those items were there in 1996. Briscoe was again asked to describe the inside of the cargo trailer.

McMillian asked Briscoe if he knew whether the cargo trailer was the same and in the same position in 1996. Finally, the officer was dismissed from the stand but told to remain available in case he was recalled.

NMSP Sgt. K. C. Rogers was the seventh witness called to the stand, and after giving his career history with the State Police, said when he was called to the scene on Bass Road he was stationed in Roswell and went directly to Truth or Consequences. He was briefed and learned what kind of assistance was needed. He said he was given a specific role, that of supervisor in charge of the entire operation, and "we established a command post." He described it, and the "agencies involved with the investigation, with as many as seventy to one-hundred people investigating at one point." He said he was given the primary responsibility, which included an even flow of information, and he led the daily briefings. "I did pretty much everything."

While describing the command post, he explained the Rapid Start System. Every piece of information was taped and fed into the computer system—to whom it was assigned, and follow-up information. The Rapid Start was a valuable tool, including for reviewing found evidence.

Yontz asked him about the videotape.

"It raised more questions. We felt this was a woman we would be able to identify because of her identifying marks and hair style. It was the hair and the tattoo that assisted us in identifying the woman," said Rogers.

The defense went to the bench to object to the officer's wording that implied this was not the only victim.

The defense also objected when Rogers spoke of his conversation with Mrs. Murphy about her former daughter-in-law, but that was overruled. Rogers said he acquired the name of Kelli Van Cleve from Mrs. Murphy. He described how he located and talked to Kelli, saying, "We gave her no information about the case." He added, "We felt she was a victim of Mr. Ray's, based on what she told us and viewing the video." He explained that in the video, she "had worn it [her hair] in cornrows and the tattoo of an Indian swan [was seen]."

Defense objected, saying Kelli had not told Mrs. Murphy that she was raped or tortured, and Mrs. Murphy had also testified that Kelli hadn't told her anything like that.

Rogers responded with, "Certainly it did not seem [on the video that] she was there on her free will. We had a tremendous amount of evidence," and he added that he was "not surprised about hearing that Kelli hadn't told Mrs. Murphy about her experience."

The judge adjourned the court, saying they had to deal with an issue.

Court resumed at 3:13 p.m. without the jury. Yontz explained, regarding the inconsistency of testimony, that Judy Murphy made the assumptions on her own after seeing the news about the other women being raped and tortured. She thought perhaps her daughter-in-law might have experienced the same because of her disappearance and being returned, three days later, to her house by David Ray. Kelli did not contact Mrs. Murphy in 1999; Judy Murphy contacted the NMSP.

The jury was called back into the courtroom and K. C. Rogers was dismissed from the stand.

Witness number eight, NMSP Officer Wes LaCuesta, was called. He cited his police experience and said he was called to the scene in 1999. His involvement with the case was as a supervisor. He was shown exhibit number 62, a metal collar and chain and, when asked, said he had no personal knowledge that those were on the property in 1996.

Next to testify was mechanic Todd Thompson, who knew and socialized with Kelli in 1996. He said she drank little, "kept her wits about her," and he was one of those with her the night she disappeared. He described that particular Thursday evening with Kelli while he was present, where they went, who else was present before he left and she later disappeared. He said he saw her again the next Sunday morning. "She wasn't herself. She took pride in how she looked [but] she looked like she had been sleeping in her clothes, looked nervous. I asked her where she had been and she couldn't tell me." When asked about her emotional status, he said, "She was shaking. She wasn't her normal, talkative self."

After her disappearance, Thompson said, she had lived with him for three weeks. "She couldn't remember what had happened to her when I asked."

Following the recess, Yontz said exhibit number 291 had been admitted into evidence and would be played for the jury. He said Officer Briscoe had identified the exhibit, which had been found in the stereo at Ray's home.

The redacted audiotape recording of David Ray's voice was played in the courtroom. It began with the date it was made, July 23, 1993, and the statement "If necessary, this tape will be upgraded. You are here against your will.

"You can be sure about being raped, thoroughly and repeatedly. You will be trained and used as a sex slave … You have no choice in the matter. You were taken by force and will be used by force … [My choice is those] having a fine body … [I prefer] early to mid-teens, easy to train. [You'll be] kept in a hidden slave room [that is] soundproofed. You are just a pretty piece of meat. … [About your experience here, you will just have to] deal with it after being turned loose. Your value to us is that you have an attractive, useable body, new and fresh … [You'll be kept with] knees and legs pushed wide apart …[and subjected to] oral sex and games. You will have a crash course in sex education … I get off on mind games. You will be drugged up with sodium pentothal and barbital. … [I use] brainwashing. You won't remember anything. … [You will be] turned loose on some country road.

"No one will look for you here. … [There'll be] no knights in shining armor. Concerning escape, this environment is more secure than a prison. [We have a] hidden playroom with steel walls, steel door … [We have] electronic surveillance… [We're] not concerned about you escaping. You'll be fed and watered on a regular basis but you will be feeling weak and hungry all the time. You'll be trained and used as a sex slave, can't say no, naked all the time. You'll have to lie there and take it. No options. You are a potential threat to us [so you will be] trained, taught the rules and punishment. The rules will become law. Punishment includes the whip and electro-shock. After the first day there will be no slack. I am your master and the lady your mistress. We are into dungeon games. Show proper respect. Respond to commands. Here you are a slave. We'll be practicing a lot. The same with your mistress. Concerning oral sex, if you bite, you will be punished. A slave must obey every command. Punishment may be hard or brutal. About talking, you cannot speak. Concerning the rules for the latrine: if you make a mess, you will be punished. Learn the rules and you will not be punished … [You'll be] in bondage or on the gynecological table. We prefer a slave that has already been trained. You definitely need to be docile … after the newness wears off. You'll spend three to four hours in the playroom. I'm sure you realize you are on thin ice. … Playroom is equipped with surgical instruments. To be completely safe, you have to be completely docile. You are expendable. We have no qualms about slicing your throat.

"I'm telling it like it is. I cannot get off with a girl unless I hurt her first. [The playroom has] soundproofing. There is a time and place for screaming. There are times you will be stressed. Your training has already been initiated. [My victims are] human toys … there will be an adjustment period… don't struggle or resist.

"There are things I have to know about your body, physical or medical conditions, childbirth, sexual preferences. The proper way to answer the questionnaire is strapped down on the gyno table with electrical clamps on nipples. Think about what you are saying. Each time you screw up, it will be a little bit worse. Start each answer with 'Master.' You will be raped several times during the day. I cannot predict change in procedures. Be smart and be a survivor. End of tape: July 23, 1993."

Testimony and evidence ended for the day at 5 p.m.

Chapter 33 – Two Murphys

After the jury filed into the courtroom on April 11, 2001, witness number 10, Patrick Murphy, was called to the stand to testify. In the previous trial at Tierra Amarílla, he testified by taped deposition, but he was present at Estancia.

He cited his military service. He said he never knew of, or suspected, Kelli of taking illegal drugs. He was the one to bring up the idea of getting married; he was just teasing because they were trying to get Cassandra to leave him alone.

He testified that their "marriage started out great," but "there were problems with sexual relations. Intercourse was painful for Kelli. It was not a highly desired thing for her. As a male, I was insensitive. She had medical problems. Those caused arguments.

"Kelli was angry about the whole situation."

He said he saw Kelli leave for a walk; he was not concerned at the time, but eventually did become concerned. "It became later in the evening and she was still gone." He said he "went to the VFW to sulk and drink beer with some friends." When Kelli did not return home that night, he went back out after midnight to find her and went to "local establishments." He went to the lake, consumed more alcohol, and after he did not find her, passed out on the beach.

He described her being returned by Ray to his parents' house. "When Kelli got to the house I was very angry. She was weak, beyond fatigue, disoriented, babbling. She had the same clothes on as when she left. She was not clean this time. She had a pungent odor about her. She was babbling incoherently, kept repeating stuff. I asked her what happened and she said she didn't know. She was out of it."

Patrick identified Ray in the courtroom as the man who had brought Kelli to his parents' house, then dressed in a uniform. "His whole demeanor was shady. He stood only six or eight feet from all that was being said. He did not present himself as an authority figure. Ray said he had made a sweep of the lake and found Kelli."

The defense objected, saying his comments sounded like hearsay.

Patrick continued his testimony. "Ray said he had picked Kelli up at the lake and gave her some iced tea. She did not appear [to me] that she had been at the lake; she did not have any sand on her."

Responding to questions about his and the family's reactions, he said, "I was very angry and she could not explain anything. The marriage was annulled and Becky Smith brought her to the house to pick up her clothing."

The defense, questioning him about his relationship with Kelli, asked if they had intercourse before their marriage.

"Yes."

"Before you got married, did she have the same physical problem as after you got married?"

"Yes."

"Did she cry?"

"No. She wanted to clock me a few times. Like, get the hell off."

The defense asked Patrick about planning their fake marriage. He said, "The joke was going to be on Cassandra. She was pursuing me. It was a joke. But I was thinking it would be kind of nice."

The defense asked him why Kelli's use of drugs was such an important issue with him. "I would lose my [military] security clearance. It is a very serious matter."

He said while Kelli was missing, Cassandra called him, saying she had information about her, and what she told him made him angry with Kelli. "I felt the marriage was over." He said Cassandra helped him "do the do-it-yourself divorce."

The defense brought him back to the day Kelli was returned to the house. "I judge a person by their uniform when I'm wearing a uniform. I thought it was a scam when he [David] drove up."

"When Kelli got there, you didn't cut her any slack."

"My decision was pretty much made. I thought Ray was bringing her back because they had been together."

"Did she appear to be afraid of David?"

"Can't say she was, can't say she wasn't."

"Did you see her get out of the vehicle and get back in?"

"I didn't see her get out but I saw her get in. Saw her go back through the gate. Four-and-a-half years, not the hangover, have affected my perception. Kelli was crying and sitting on the porch."

"Did it look like Kelli was afraid to get in the truck with Ray?"

"Didn't have a gut feeling about Kelli being afraid. Didn't care if she left. ... I handled it like a jerk."

The jury was dismissed and attorneys and the judge consulted. The prosecution objected to the questioning about sexual matters and specific instances of conduct. The judge said he did not view the questioning as character evidence. Harwell said the important issue was to protect the victim's privacy. The defense objections included reference to an existing injury, and Harwell said she would not include sexual dysfunction in her comments.

Yontz said the issue was first-degree kidnapping, criminal sexual penetration and great mental anguish, and complained that McMillian was "trying to impeach her testimony with specific instances of conduct."

Harwell agreed to mention mental anguish but not bodily harm. The judge said the defense could inquire about the victim's physical condition without getting personal.

Yontz added, "As long as he doesn't get into sexual conduct."

The judge said, "Those questions beg a response about sexual activity," and he read the legal definition of great mental anguish, which is characterized by extreme change in behavior.

The jury was called back into the room at 11 a.m.

The defense continued his cross-examination of Patrick, questioning whether his home was a safe place as regards to his parents' behavior towards Kelli in not providing her medical care when she seemed to need it.

Patrick bristled at the attack on his parents. "My parents are responsible and respectable. My parents' home is a safe place."

Yontz cross-examined him on redirect. "When Kelli got to your parents' home, she looked drugged, out of it? What medical care did your parents provide for her that day?"

"She was disoriented." Yontz pushed him to answer the question and Patrick admitted, "She wasn't allowed to stay there."

When Yontz tried to ask him about the couple's sex practices, the defense objected and they approached the bench. Yontz said he was simply bringing up the subject of "the alternate sex practices the defense had been inferring all day." The jury was dismissed.

After the jury was called back into the courtroom, Judge Sweazea told them that the next witness scheduled to testify, Janet "Judy"

Murphy, was unavailable. Therefore, a court clerk named Hoon would read the woman's prior sworn testimony to the court.

According to the read testimony, when Judy Murphy was questioned whether her attitude toward Kelli had changed, she answered, "Yes."

She described Kelli being returned by David Parker Ray. "His vehicle pulled up, he was in a state vehicle, Kelli came through our double gate; she appeared disoriented. She was not focused. She was kind of, gave us the impression that she was on drugs."

And Judy Murphy said, "I have seen people on drugs. She just … wasn't Kelli. When you talked to her, she was kind of wandering off. She was kind of looking around. Kelli's really a clean person. This was an unusual state to see her in. Kelli was always changing clothes. Kelli was a very, very clean person."

Murphy described Kelli sitting on the edge of the porch's cement flooring. "We thanked Ray for bringing her. Ray stayed right close. He said she was a good kid, said she was dehydrated and he gave her some tea."

Judy Murphy was questioned about her displeasure over her son's marriage to Kelli and her attitude towards her. Murphy said she had met Becky and Jesse and was not happy with Kelli for bringing those kinds of friends to her house. "Cassandra was the one who braided Kelli's hair. It was an all-day project to spite Patrick about not wanting Kelli's friends around. Patrick agreed with me [about Kelli's friends]."

When Kelli disappeared, "Patrick was upset and went to a friend's house; Cassandra followed him. I didn't really know Cassandra. I was more concerned with how Patrick was feeling." Cassandra spent quite a bit of time with Patrick during this crisis. She told him that she knew where Kelli had been.

Hoon completed her reading from the transcript by saying that Janet "Judy" Murphy was dismissed from the stand.

The jury was dismissed for lunch.

Chapter 34 – The Diva

Court resumed, without the jury, after lunch. Michelle Aycheson, the self-proclaimed "diva," was called to the stand, prior to her testimony for the defense as an expert witness on the subject of sadism and masochism, and bondage and domination. Without the jury present, the court conducted a Daubert hearing to determine if the woman was qualified to be an expert witness.

The defense told the court that Aycheson had listened to the unedited tape and the redacted one, similar to the one already played for the jury yesterday. McMillian said she would be asked where such tapes are available, where they can be traded by people who enjoyed that type of thing.

Harwell objected. "What do other people and other tapes have to do with this case? This prejudices the State."

McMillian said Aycheson's qualifications proved she was an expert.

Aycheson said she had explored the subject for fifteen years and had been in the public eye for nine years. "I travel to national events filled with classes. I have mentors who are experts in the sadomasochism field." She gave her history with S and M, including: a seminar in 1994, a gender play in Fort Lauderdale, classes she taught in S and M, which she called safe, sane and consensual. She said she practiced as a professional dominatrix. She explained the fear fantasy and fetish practices that included kidnapping and raping, and the "sexual charge" of role-playing, fulfilling fantasy. She spoke of using Saran wrap and duct tape and breathing tubes.

McMillian asked her if, when she had listened to the tapes, she could distinguish what type they were, whether fantasy or threatening.

Aycheson said, "It is very focused. I have been requested to make tapes like that. The first line told me it was for entertainment."

When the defense asked for her "personal knowledge of this kind of stuff," she answered, "There's a magazine on newsstands in Albuquerque."

"How many articles in the magazine tell about acquiring such material?"

"Several. At one location, I found six magazines. These had videotapes available." At a conference in Chicago, she said, she found at least two vendors who had audiotapes.

When asked about her contacts, she said, "That would be a long list. Right now, I could travel to the East Coast and stay with someone each eight-hour drive. The community is unto its own."

When questioned by the judge, McMillian explained that Aycheson had seen the chair and gyno table; that was the purpose of her testimony.

The judge again emphasized his question, asking what the defense had in mind with her testimony, such as identifying certain things. "What I have heard so far only goes to consent."

McMillian handed Aycheson exhibit number 102 and asked her to identify it. She said, "It is a homemade dildo or penetration device. Its label says 'vaginal stretcher'." He asked her to identify what fetish that related to, and to speak of her familiarity with sexual fetishes.

She spoke of the practice called fisting, and described what that was, and said she had given and received instruction on it. She said she went to a conference in Austin, Texas, and had attended seminars and studied it in private.

The judge said the witness was going on about fetishes and devices and asked how that was relevant to the case. McMillian responded with, "None of these people [jury] know any of this stuff. Very few of the items [found on Ray's premises] have been identified. There's no foundation these objects were present [in 1996]. There is only an inference."

Harwell commented, "He has previously offered all of this. This is nothing new."

Judge Sweazea said, "We've heard the same remarks. I was interested in knowing what these items were used for."

Yontz complained, "We have no indication from the defense what these items were used for, and his [Ray's] involvement in S and M."

McMillian responded with, "The tape is evidence. In the tape, he states he is into dungeon games, S and M."

The judge said, "This is what I want to avoid... detailed and lengthy testimony about fetishes confusing the jurors." But he added, "The cargo trailer is presented as a torture chamber and the defendant is entitled to present it as otherwise."

Harwell objected, saying the witness could only testify to what she could identify.

McMillian said, "All these things are in evidence and the jury should know what they are." The counsel approached the bench and told the judge that all of this is "substantially new to everyone and it would be helpful to the jury to know what these items are."

"I thought this [Daubert] hearing was going to be only to identify the items," Judge Sweazea remarked.

McMillian said, "All the document exhibits are consistent with the fear fantasy;" the witness' research on the sites and where they are available are also pertinent.

"Aycheson cannot say that, because these things exist, it was consensual," said Harwell.

McMillian responded, "It's a harmless practice. BDSM [bondage, domination, sadism and masochism] is where homosexuality was thirty to forty years ago."

The judge questioned, "The witness testifying that Mr. Ray is a practicing ..."

"She can. They discussed his participation in many of these fetishes." Aycheson had visited with David Parker Ray and discussed this with him.

Claire Harwell objected. "This is a ruse to get Ray to testify without getting on the witness stand."

Yontz said the witness had not used any scientific testing or scientific terms. Harwell added that "we can go to the Internet and" get this same kind of information.

The judge again asked the relevance of the line of the witness questioning. He said it should stick with the instruments being introduced.

Yontz pointed out that "No one has identified these items as instruments of torture." He said it related to the view that Kelli had when she was in restraints, and the reason for the photo showing the medicine cabinet.

McMillian said, "Those are unknown objects. The jury has a right to know what those items are."

Yontz commented that there had been no evidence that the rape and capture of the victim were fantasies and "Aycheson cannot say this [case] is consistent" with a fantasy.

The arguments on the subject of the admissibility of Aycheson as a witness continued, including her ability to identify Ray's use of a device labeled "nipple pincher."

Sweazea acknowledged, "I am comfortable to say Aycheson has more information than the jurors and I have."

Harwell said she would still hesitate to qualify her as an expert.

The judge continued, "It appears that Aycheson has the knowledge. But I will not permit testimony on fetishes unless there is information on the practice of them."

Yontz pressed on. "Aycheson cannot testify until David Parker Ray does, concerning contingency." Yontz proposed testimony from his own expert witness on criminal sexual sadism. "She [the State's proposed witness] would be coming in from Washington, D.C., so there would be a two-day delay."

Michelle Aycheson was dismissed from the stand; but the discussion among counsel and the judge continued.

McMillian enumerated Aycheson's qualifications as an expert witness. Finally the judge said, "The counsel has reached a stipulation with Ms. Aycheson to identify the items in the trailer but no consent or fetishes will be mentioned."

The court recessed at 3:10 p.m.

A judge in a criminal trial must remain totally neutral to assure that the defendant has a fair and impartial trial and given every lawful opportunity to defend himself. If Ray were found guilty, Judge Sweazea wanted no loophole left open that would allow him and his attorney to later appeal his sentence.

Chapter 35 – Testimony Continues

April 12 began with the judge opening the floor to counsel; the defense and State attorneys discussed various exhibits. They also discussed the media's rights to access of certain information.

Claire Harwell said, "For the record, the media is present."

The jury filed into the courtroom and Yontz called his eleventh witness, Jerome Madrid, who was the state park's field operations supervisor and, for a while, Ray's supervisor. He identified David Parker Ray and his signature on a form and then was dismissed from the stand.

The judge swore in the next witness, Larry Haulpt, FBI special agent assigned to the Las Cruces office. Haulpt cited his experience, how he became involved with the case, and his assistance in gathering evidence at the crime scene. He spoke of meeting Kelli at her residence in Colorado.

Claire Harwell conducted the questioning for the State.

"Did you tell her why you were there?"

"No. We explained we were there to talk to her about the days she was missing, that we were conducting an investigation. We asked her what her involvement was. She seemed nervous, tense, but quite cooperative during the interview" that lasted about two hours. "She seemed to have an emotional wall put up around her. She did well until she described the details of what happened to her. … She would withdraw into herself. Her eyes would become glassy. It was not so much the wording but the emotion in her face. She did not use much eye contact. She was consistent and spontaneous. I looked for a change in spontaneity and there was none. … There were some things she could not remember but some things she did. We wanted to know if she had heard anything in the media. This was very important. She was asked this at the onset. We were careful to not ask her leading questions."

Haulpt testified that they showed her the still photograph after the interview. He explained what a leading question is, why they are careful about not asking leading questions because the information would later be scrutinized. He said a female officer, "Carrie Parbes, conducted the interview with me present."

He continued, "We showed her the still to find out if she would be able to identify herself—Exhibit 115. After the interview, I handed her the photo. It was a compelling moment, the look of anger and disgust. She threw it. After she threw the photo, she picked it up again and started identifying the items in the photo. When the memories had come back, she thought she was going crazy. And now [with the photo] it was being confirmed that this did happen to her."

McMillian cross-examined, asking if he had received training in conducting interviews.

"I have not received training in interviewing, but I have conducted many and seen many people in pain."

Haulpt studied the transcript of the interview of Kelli in Colorado. Responding to McMillian's question of whether Kelli was then able to describe any act of penetration, he said, "There was penetration with objects." Defense asked if she was able to remember that Ray pinched her nipples. "She did recall that happened. It made her scream." And "She was able to remember Jesse being involved."

He reiterated that Kelli remembered Ray pinched her, and she remembered he also used a device—as well as his fingers—with which she stated that he penetrated her at least thirty times.

The defense objected and asked if she had given a specific description of any single act of penetration. "No she didn't. [On the transcript] she remembers the number of times that she mentioned." Defense asked if she had not described a particular act. "That's correct. She did not describe a particular act."

Brenda Herschizer was next sworn in as a witness. "Kelli is my sister. We grew up together. When she moved to Colorado, we have become close again." The prosecution asked if she had any knowledge of Kelli being taken captive, and Brenda answered, "Yes."

He asked her to describe Kelli's reaction during an incident when they saw someone in shackles. "Kelli was ghostly white and started rubbing her wrists."

"Tell us about when someone was using duct tape."

"When my husband ripped the duct tape, she held her stomach and went ghostly white and left the room. Her response is different than normal. If we go anywhere at night, we go get her. She has a weapon within easy reach. Her husband works graveyard [shifts]. She does not like to be alone."

Harwell asked how Kelli protects herself at home. "She has a violent reaction when she is startled. She keeps her dog with her all the time." She went on to say, "Her husband is a big man and Kelli likes him to stand by her when people walk behind her. She did not have these fears when she was growing up."

The defense cross-examined Brenda. When questioned, she said the incident with the duct tape, her seeing Kelli's reaction to the sound of it ripping, occurred after she moved to Colorado. Defense asked Brenda if her sister had violent boyfriends.

"Yes."

When asked if she had been aware, in 1996, of Kelli's experience with Ray, she said she was not. She became aware of her personality changes after her sister moved to Colorado.

The judge dismissed the jury for thirty minutes. When they returned, he advised them, "The defense is going through some records that were not available until today." He then excused the jury for lunch until 1 p.m.

The prosecution asked the court to dismiss the defense's witness, Michelle Aycheson, from the courtroom before testimony by counselor David Spencer. Yontz approached the bench.

"If she is an expert witness, she is entitled to listen to the testimony," said the judge.

"What about her other testimony ... as far as identifying the objects? [Hearing Spencer] may influence what she says," said Yontz.

"Her testimony is essential ... and she will stay," ruled Sweazea.

The jury entered the courtroom and Harwell called the State's fourteenth witness, David Spencer. He cited his qualifications, certifications and thirty-one years' experience as a social worker.

Harwell asked him, "What kind of psychotherapist are you?" Spencer cited his qualifications.

"Do you treat victims of trauma?"

"At least two or three in my caseload."

Harwell stated, "Mr. Spencer is an expert." Defense did not object.

Harwell led Spencer, through questioning, to speak of his knowledge concerning Kelli, her experience in 1996, and her resulting effects, including post-traumatic-stress disorder. He said she was "exhibiting this stress two years before she came to see me. It has impacted all of her life."

"Are Kelli's symptoms consistent with rape victims?"

"They are consistent with that."

"Do you think Kelli has suffered emotional damage that requires treatment and is characterized with extreme changes?"

"Yes."

McMillian cross-examined Spencer. "Kelli did not tell you about her first marriage?"

"She did tell me."

Defense asked him if he knew about Kelli's prior relationship. "Kelli told me about it."

"What about her series of short and tense relationships with men?"

"Kelli recalls the relationships," and he added that Kelli had told him of the relationship with Murphy and her problems with sex "and intimacy with life partners. She was aware of those things but not aware she had severe sexual difficulties. I was aware of the tilted uterus, but not aware of Kelli not wanting Murphy to touch her."

Responding to specific questioning, Spencer said he was "aware of Kelli's brief experience with marijuana and learning of sex and drugs with a family member."

The defense spoke of Kelli's financial difficulties, and her difficulties in relationships. McMillian suggested that she "continued with that chain of events." He expressed his doubt that the abduction took place.

Spencer said he did not agree with McMillian. He explained what he knew of memory gains and false memories.

McMillian spoke of "the nature of human memory, the controversy of the false memory syndrome."

"We don't know that it's so controversial anymore."

McMillian questioned Spencer extensively about therapeutic tools and techniques, Kelli's various trauma reactions, and he threw in some hypothetical situations for him to also address.

After court recess, and the jury returned to the courtroom, Harwell proceeded with her redirect cross-examination. Harwell struggled to find a way to ask a certain question without incurring defense objection on leading a witness. At last she was successful.

Spencer said, "It is very common, especially for adult women, to be affected by the loss of control and fear of losing control again. When someone accosts them, they feel used, horrible, dirty, guilty. Like they should have been able to prevent it."

"Like people thinking less of her?"

"Yes. It is a common response."

"What about false memory?"

"That is not an accepted diagnosis."

Harwell asked, and Spencer responded to, many questions about false memory, a subject first brought up by the defense.

Harwell asked him about Kelli's susceptibility to suggestion.

"She is pretty strong in her opinions and determinations. She's not quick to change her mind. She may be considered bull-headed. I don't think she is very suggestible."

McMillian cross-examined him. "Are you versed in false memory studies?"

"No."

"Are you careful about how an interview is conducted and what is asked?" McMillian indicated that would bear upon a patient's consensual memory. Defense said Kelli was present at the law enforcement interviews, and with lawyers and victim advocates.

"I was not present," said Spencer.

Claire Harwell asked Spencer whether Kelli's gaps of memory are "about disassociation or memory loss?"

"Disassociation."

Judge Sweazea dismissed David Spencer from the stand. He told the jury that the State rested its case presentation, but "there are issues that need to be discussed." He excused the jury for the Easter weekend, telling them to return on Monday and to not discuss the case with anyone.

After the jury left, the judge and counselors discussed motions, criminal counts and their wordings, the number of times the State proved that Ray sexually abused Kelli, the element of the use of a firearm, removal of the word "murder" in testimony, and the instruction to the jury about use of a deadly weapon.

Yontz said, "Ray is capable of causing death or bodily harm. He used restraints, chains. There's no need for a step down; they are all felonies."

Sweazea agreed that they are applicable to each of the criminal sexual penetration counts. He asked for the State's contention.

Yontz cited Ray's "using large items to penetrate a person's body, the whole series of surgical instruments hanging on the wall."

McMillian said the burden of proof was required as to criminal sexual penetration.

The judge brought up counts of criminal sexual contact. Claire Harwell said those should not be merged with the CSP; "there are different facts."

At 4:23 p.m., April 12, Judge Sweazea dismissed the court until Monday morning, April 16, at 9 a.m. for a three-day Easter weekend. On Monday, the defense was scheduled to present its evidence and witnesses, including the "diva."

Chapter 36 – Defense Closes

Monday morning, April 16, the State team, led by ADA Jim Yontz and assisted by Claire Harwell, was in the courtroom, along with the defendant, David Parker Ray, and his counsel, Lee McMillian.

Before the jury was called in, the attorneys and the judge haggled over various motions, points and counts. The controversy included the number of proved criminal sexual penetrations and instances of criminal sexual contact. The defense claimed there was no proof that Ray was armed during the offenses. The State said there were surgical instruments in the trailer, and Kelli had been initially threatened with a knife.

Finally, the judge asked the defense if it was ready to proceed; McMillian said, "Yes."

The jury entered the courtroom. The judge addressed the jury, telling them that, before court was in session, the defense attorney had assisted a juror who had a flat tire. The counsel had waited with the juror until help arrived, and then he left. This on-the-record statement was to negate any claims of impropriety.

The judge announced that the defense was ready to proceed with its case.

Defense Attorney McMillian stood and said, "The defense rests."

Without saying so to the jury, that meant he would not, after all, put the "diva" on the witness stand in front of them, nor would he present any other witness. Just as Jeff Rein had defended Ray in Tierra Amarílla, many of McMillian's defense strategies had been done, and would continue to be done, outside of the presence of jurors.

The jury was excused from the courtroom.

The attorneys and the judge again argued over various motions, points and counts. The defense argued over first-degree kidnapping because he claimed that Ray had released Kelli in a safe place. And Yontz argued that great bodily harm was not the issue.

They argued over the conspiracy counts. Yontz said, "The daughter allowed this to happen." And Harwell added, "Ray's daughter knew what the trailer was for, she knew what was in there." Defense argued that there was only enough evidence for one conspiracy count, and he claimed that Kelli testified to only four distinct acts of abuse by Ray. Yontz offered the analogy of a bank robbery co-conspirator, one who is a party to the crime: he plans it, or stands guard outside, or drives the getaway car.

The judge said there was evidence of four separate occasions and, therefore, four separate co-conspiracy counts. Defense conceded there were four occasions. Harwell said Kelli heard the key in the lock six times. The judge, after checking his notes, agreed, saying his notes showed six times. He denied the defense's motion to reduce the number of those counts.

They discussed the audiotape.

McMillian complained, "The State rested, and now they are trying to submit more evidence." And he said the audiotape would "have a prejudicial effect and prohibitive value. We don't know if it was used ... There is no indication that it is part of this case."

Sweazea said, "I can admit it if I find it necessary," and it was submitted as evidence, exhibit number 60.

The defense objected to the redaction, but the judge said he would accept it as it was.

Next, defense argued that the videotape did not show the victim was unwilling. He said, "There was physiological evidence of arousal, and lack of resistance."

After the haggling ended, the jury was called back into the courtroom. Judge Sweazea told them, "You've heard all the evidence in this case."

Of course, the jury had actually heard only a small portion of the available evidence. They had just heard all they were going to be allowed to hear.

Judge Sweazea began instructing them in the law and their duties. He said, "Do not draw any inference of guilt because the defendant did not take the witness stand." He spoke of the various elements of the case including, as regarded the kidnapping charge, that the defendant had voluntarily released the victim in a safe place. He spoke of the conspiracy charge, what it meant and how it related to this case: whether "the defendant and another person agreed together to commit kidnapping." He spoke of the four possible verdicts and, the varying degrees, of which they could choose only one for each of the criminal sexual penetration charges. He added that the State must prove to them that the CSP was unlawful, which included the element of personal safety of Kelli, and whether the defendant acted intentionally. He spoke of the definitions of great mental anguish, physical force and physical violence. Each guilty verdict for criminal sexual contact meant that the sexual contact was not consensual.

He instructed them to not be concerned with the consequence of the verdict, and he said their verdict must be unanimous. Their sole duty was to ascertain the truth in the case.

The prosecution team began with their closing statements.

Claire Harwell addressed the jury. She began by making analogies about circles: the circle of wedding bands. "This was a horrible incident for Kelli Garrett. She preferred to think herself crazy than to think about what happened to her. When he grew tired of her, he just left, over and over again. She did not know the passage of time or passage of days. She had duct tape over her eyes.

"David doesn't look scary today. He's frail and thin. Remember who he really is." She spoke of the audiotape, and then played it for them.

After playing the tape, she resumed her closing arguments. Speaking of Kelli and Patrick, she said, "The relationship was new and fragile." And she said, "Cassandra was pursuing Patrick. Kelli returned after being gone for three days, and she could not explain what happened." She spoke of Kelli's loss of confidence, after being abducted and raped and then returned to a suspicious husband. She asked them to recall what Patrick had said during testimony, that he thought there was something shady about David. He was in uniform when he returned Kelli, but he had not been at work. Patrick saw no signs that Kelli had been on the beach, and she looked drugged.

"The circle of friends, Kelli's friends. She had thought Jesse Ray was a friend, yet Jesse and her father held a knife at her throat and held her against her will." Harwell continued with the circle analogy. "A steel collar, the mark of a slave, around her neck where she cannot move. When Kelli is unchained, all she moves are her arms. Why does she not try to fight?" Harwell posed the question in an incredible voice. She asked the jurors to close the circle by finding the defendant, David Parker Ray, guilty.

She then played the videotape for the jury.

Afterwards, Harwell spoke of the kidnapping of Kelli. "David and Jesse worked together to commit these crimes. Jesse said she just needed to stop for coffee. She knew what was going to take place. They deceived her [Kelli]. It is clear they both knew that sexual offense was intended. One of the issues is whether or not David Ray took her to a safe place [afterwards]. Taking someone who is drugged, incoherent ... David did not share any of this information when he released her."

Harwell went on, "The conspiracy charges. The key part is to prove that they acted in concert." Concerning kidnapping in the first degree, she said David knew what to expect; he was waiting for a victim. She spoke of the CSP or rape charge; the definition included insertion of an object into the vagina. She was restrained and threatened with a knife. "It has been five years since this happened and Kelli is still bothered by this event."

She told them to recall Spencer's testimony. Kelli had no reason to minimize her symptoms to her therapist and he knew she suffered great mental anguish. She was affected with personal injuries and mental health problems. "Kelli was not in that trailer voluntarily."

She again referred to the conspiracy charge, which meant "helping someone commit a crime. It was perpetrated by Jesse. We know he wanted it to happen because of what happened, how it was conceived and how it was carried out. Ray encouraged his daughter to make it happen. In the audiotape, it does not talk about 'I', it talks about 'we'."

Harwell added, "When evaluating CSP, there are elements of physical force and physical violence. Kelli was unable to move for three days. And we know there was a knife to make her compliant from the beginning.

"Concerning conspiracy, how did we know David was going to rape her? When Jesse got to the house, they went to the back room and came back out together with a knife. Jesse knows what her father is all about. And the audiotape talks about raping and kidnapping."

The defense approached the bench. "There is no testimony that Jesse lived there in 1996," protested McMillian.

Harwell continued, "In the videotape, the jury has seen the defendant touching Kelli Garrett while she was restrained. He was assisted in this. His daughter brought her there. Why did David do this to Kelli? It must be associated with David's desires. It is still painful for

Kelli to talk about this. He took advantage of her vulnerability, which caused sexual arousal for him. He was acting intentionally; he intended to commit a crime. The knife and the handcuffs in the trailer speak to his intent, as does the audiotape. There is no doubt as to his intent. First-degree CSP must show great mental anguish. Kelli is still intensely fearful of people. You have seen critical pieces of evidence: The audiotape, the soundproof ceiling. He lays out the plan on the audiotape. He returned her while he was dressed in a uniform. The woman in the video is sobbing. She has lost muscle tone because she has been bound for three days."

She again played the videotape for the jury. She pointed to the video camera and the soundproofing that he referred to in the audiotape. "Watch her throat and her face. ... She is trying desperately to make a sound; you can see by her throat that she is weeping. Kelli wanted to be with Patrick. Patrick wanted a normal sex life," and she spoke of the fight they had. "Kelli was not able to enjoy normal relations with her husband; why would she consent to what David Ray did to her? Remember, Cassandra and Jesse were left alone with Kelli's beer [when she left the Blue Waters bar for a while]. Ray stated in his audiotape that he would drug his victims. Still, Kelli has shown an astonishing memory. She was able to conclude the width of the dildo by the 'feel' of it."

Harwell referred the jurors to two exhibits, photos depicting dildos, and pointed out the accuracy of Kelli's testimony.

"Remember David's statement in the audiotape? 'No knight in shining armor will help you.' He was wrong." She reminded the jury of how combined agencies did find Kelli, and the meticulous way they went about locating her.

After a brief recess, the defense delivered its closing argument. McMillian told the jurors, "Look not only at some of the evidence but at all of it. I want to point out some things for you." He spoke of the testimonies of officers and agents Bowidowicz, Wilson, Maxwell and Pederson. He said they saw the property in 1999 and could not swear that all they saw was also there in 1996. He mentioned the thirty-seven photos identified by Briscoe. "Was all that there in 1996?" He spoke of the position of the trailer and said, "You can see the neighbor's house." He mentioned the carport and awnings; were they there in 1996? "Exhibit number 33, showing chains and chair. None of those were identified by the victim." He systematically went over many of the photos with the jury, including one showing the "gurney structure," what he called the shelves inside the cabinet that had eye-bolts. "That has not been identified by Van Cleve." And he spoke of the "fetish items, erotica. Was it all there in 1996? Your verdict must not be based on speculation. ... even Van Cleve will not tell you she saw this stuff."

He went on, "K. C. Rogers and LaCuesta identified a neck ring, but it does not resemble what was put on her neck. Kelli described what was put on her as leather." And he criticized Agent Haulpt's testimony. "No notes, no tape recorder. Haulpt said he conducted thousands of interviews. Can we count on the accuracy of his observations after the time lapse?" He spoke of the fighting with Cassandra; "What does this contribute to the case?" McMillian asked. Patrick didn't know Kelli to take drugs, but he knew her friends did, even before they were married; and he spoke of "their fight about sex."

He added, "Now Patrick feels bad because he surrendered his wife to the boogy man. But at the time, he believed Kelli was cheating on him. Cassandra made him think she was. He formed an opinion. The State would like you to think he was wrong. We know Patrick was a jealous husband. We know how a young, jealous husband would react."

He pointed out how Kelli got back into Ray's truck and rode off with him. If she truly had any inkling, any gut-feeling, she didn't act on it. Kelli came back and signed the divorce papers, and then went to live with Connolly for several months.

He spoke of the testimony by Kelli's sister. "She had no history with Kelli for ten years, until after Christmas of 1999. The sister is unfamiliar with Kelli's history. Then she speaks of two incidents: when the brother-in-law was restrained, and the duct tape. First she [Kelli] claimed to have no memory of that time, then her memory is amazingly clear."

About the duct tape, he said, "If you have it on you and then it's taken off after three days, it will leave a mark." He implied that should have been noticed by people who saw her after she was taken to the Murphy house, but apparently wasn't.

About Spencer, he said, "He is a licensed counselor and social worker. Spencer's function is not investigative; he does treatment based on what he is told." Referring to Spencer's progress reports on Kelli, he said, "Kelli had other sources of trauma: the drowning of a boy friend, the rejection, the abusive relationships. Those alone would trigger her symptoms noted by Spencer. Either independent, or combined with what happened at Ray's house, could trigger false memory syndrome. Spencer has no knowledge of this syndrome."

McMillian continued, "About Ms. Garrett, we must make some observations that are not particularly charitable. And there are some inconsistencies—her employment record; her history in T or C. She became homeless [after the Murphys rejected her]. She moved in with a bartender and lived with him several months. Then she met a nice young man who drowned ten feet away from her. We know this has to be hard. Abuse. Abandonment. Rejection. Those pose questions. She was in and out of jobs, relationships, and housing was a dire problem for her in southern New Mexico. Then there is Kelli's memory. She doesn't know and she doesn't remember until the FBI arrive and show her the picture. Can anyone be expected to say this was voluntary? The news, the FBI, the embarrassment of her husband being there."

He spoke of the audiotape. "Does this raise reasonable doubt? The audiotape has some pretty ugly stuff, and the State would have you believe everything is true except for the first thing that is on it: 'This tape is for adults only, for entertainment purposes.' And mentioned on it were things that did not happen. Mind games; the whole tape is mind games."

McMillian continued, "About the drugs, there's no evidence. About the syringes, about having your throat cut, there's no evidence. The dead-bolts, the closed circuit TV systems, the whip, the electroshock machine; there's no evidence they were there in 1996."

He systematically went over the contents of the audiotape. "The contents of the obnoxious tape, listen to it with an eye and an ear." He spoke of motive, intent, preparation, sound-proofing, of the evidence recovery team and what he called their questionable methods of preserving the evidence. On the tape the voice spoke of turning her loose, and she was turned loose. The tape spoke of "electrical clamps on the nipples; that didn't happen to Kelli."

"Look at the video, the details and the sense of it. Look at the evidence critically. Watch the gentle manner in which Ray touches Kelli. Look at her muscles. This is not torture."

And, following up on his earlier remark when he had said there was physiological evidence [on the video] that she was sexually aroused, he now said, referring to the video, "The vulva is engorged."

(Even if the video was clear enough to show that kind of detail, that swelling was more likely caused by days of sexual abuse. During an early interview for this book, K. C. Rogers had said David was angry that his victim's clit was too small for him to get a hold of to pierce. He strung her up and whipped her between the legs with a Sam Browne belt until he could.)

"There are no marks on this woman's body," said McMillian, referring to the video. "Can you tell honestly if she is crying?" he asked.

About the videotape, he said, "There are alternative explanations. Some are things we do not want to deal with in our lives."

He pointed out that, on the video, Kelli "is moving her arms, she's stretching."

(Ray had released her arms after he had them suspended and tightly secured by overhead straps for more than three days.)

He continued, "There is an opportunity to escape if she wants." And he made reference to the different type of collar that Kelli identified.

He said there was no evidence that she was drugged. He told the jurors to express neither prejudice nor sympathy in their decision. He reminded them to consider the credibility of the witnesses. In light of all of the evidence, consider truthfulness, he said. "Kelli cried on the stand. She was angry, indignant. And then I got her on cross-examination. Kelli was relaxing, smiling, laughing. That is not indicative of a person who was really harmed."

He added, "You have to take all evidence into account. You have to decide whether David released Kelli in a safe place. When that didn't work [because the Murphys wouldn't accept her], he took her somewhere else. There's no evidence of drugs or injury. She did not seek medical help. There was no kidnapping or conspiracy or intent to commit sexual penetration. You have to put intent in there to all of these crimes.

"This determines the course of Kelli's life, whether she faces it as a victim or as a person who is getting help."

He ended his closing with this plea: "Do what is right. Find him not guilty."

Chapter 37- State Closes

In a criminal trial, the State is allowed to make the final summation.

Yontz began by attacking the defense's closing arguments.

"McMillian said it didn't happen. It did happen." Yontz quoted from one of the exhibits to jurors. " 'If she's worth taking, she's worth keeping.' It did happen." In reference to the defense's criticism of the way the crime scene was kept secured by Deputy Bowidowicz and the other officers, Yontz reminded them of the guards, logs and other security measures. He reminded them of the testimony by Ranger Wilson, who had inspected the property in 1993, 1994 and 1999 and there were no changes, no moved trailers, no additional trailers. The property was the same in 1996 as it was in 1999. He reminded them of the care the FBI takes when working crime scenes and recovering evidence, and of the agent's testimony and evidence given concerning the black bench on which Kelli was tied, and the significance of the bench shown on the videotape, which had played an important role.

"Kelli was able to see certain things" in the trailer that confirmed what was said on the audiotape, he said. "She was naked and chained up. Stringent bondage. She was drugged." He referred to the details on the audiotape that McMillian said didn't happen. "She does not remember what happened." He reminded them of the collar around her neck, the statement "it is permanent" said on the tape, the steel doors, the television video, the illustrated poster tacked on the wall of the trailer.

Yontz again reminded them what was said on the audiotape. "If you are told to hold your leg out to place a chain on it, you must respond with 'Yes, Mistress'." She had to get consent to use the bathroom. He reminded them of the dildos and their sizes, the chains, the surgical instruments. Those were things Ray described on the audiotape when he made it in 1993, things found in the cargo trailer in 1999; they were there in 1996.

He spoke of Ray's motive. "I can't get off until I hurt a girl first," he quoted from the audiotape. He reminded them that the prepared questionnaire mentioned on the tape that was made in 1993 was found in the cargo trailer in 1999. It was there in 1996; David tells us it was all there, said Yontz.

About the testimony of Todd Thompson, "The facts and details he gave, he saw Kelli the next day and what he said is consistent with what everyone else said." He said Patrick Murphy's testimony was also consistent with others'. Yontz reminded jurors of what the audiotape said: The drugs will not allow you to remember.

About when Ray returned Kelli to the Murphys, he commented, "Why did David appear in uniform? He wanted it to look official." And he said, "If you really think someone is dehydrated, you get medical assistance. Remember how close he stayed to her; he wanted to hear what she said. Kelli [could only] walk six or eight feet and then sat down. She had no choice but to leave with him. Remember Patrick's description and Judy's testimony about how she looked?" And he added that she was "wearing the same thing for four days. She smelled like she hadn't had a bath for a while. Her clothes were disheveled. Is there any evidence she was anywhere else except with David?"

Yontz spoke of the integrity of the testimony, and reminded them about Kelli's problems after 1996 and Spencer's testimony. He mentioned Kelli's troubled life, the investigation that led officers to find her in Craig, Colorado, and that the Murphys didn't know what had happened to her. He also spoke of the important legal element of whether Kelli was left in a safe place, and of the conspiracy charge that meant another person, Ray's daughter, participated—aided and abetted.

Yontz told a story about fox hunting in England. Hunters drag something, a red herring, to obliterate the true scent of the fox. The defense wants you to follow the red herring.

"Leave prejudice and bias at the door. Look at Ray's plan, motive, opportunity. Remember exhibit number 60: Psychological Procedures, Initial Handling of Captives. 'Fondle and abuse her nipples and upper portion of the body. Intensify her fear. ... Captives will be constantly raped and tortured.' Remember what it said about the shock value. There is nothing more torturous than being held totally nude and restrained and someone touching you. Why was she held for three days? He couldn't get the dildos in; his friends would be angry at him."

Yontz completed his final closing arguments to the jury.

Judge Sweazea addressed the jury and announced which of them were designated as the jurors and who were alternates.

The jurors were excused to begin their deliberations at 4:15 p.m. on April 16, 2001.

At 9:30 that same evening, the jurors returned to the courtroom with the verdict.

Chapter 38 – Verdict

On the night of April 16, 2001, the judge asked, "Ladies and gentlemen of the jury, have you reached a verdict?"

"Yes, we have." The foreman handed the printed verdict to the judge.

Judge Kevin Sweazea addressed David Parker Ray. "At this time, I will read the verdicts."

"Count one, kidnapping: Verdict guilty.

"As to the special interrogatory, did you find beyond a reasonable doubt that the defendant voluntarily freed Kelli Van Cleve Garrett in a safe place? Yes."

Kidnapping is first degree unless the jury finds that the defendant voluntarily released his victim in a safe place, which would make it kidnapping in the second degree.

"Count two, conspiracy to commit kidnapping: Verdict guilty.

"Count three, assault with the intent to commit criminal sexual penetration: Verdict guilty.

"Count four, criminal sexual penetration in the first degree: Verdict guilty.

"Count five, criminal sexual penetration in the first degree: Verdict guilty.

"Count six, criminal sexual penetration in the first degree: Verdict guilty.

"Count seven, criminal sexual penetration in the first degree: Verdict guilty.

"Count eight, criminal sexual penetration in the first degree: Verdict guilty.

"Count nine, criminal sexual penetration in the first degree: Verdict guilty.

"Count ten, criminal sexual penetration: Verdict guilty.

"Count eleven, criminal sexual contact: Verdict guilty.

"Count twelve, conspiracy to commit criminal sexual contact: Verdict guilty."

Judge Sweazea asked the foreman and each individual juror if that was his or her verdict. Each responded, "Yes."

He dismissed the jury, instructing them to not talk to anyone about the case, and told them to return the following day for details and debriefing.

He ordered David Parker Ray to be transferred to Los Lunas to begin his sixty-day evaluation prior to sentencing.

Court was adjourned.

^^^^^^^

Two more criminal complaints against David Parker Ray were still pending, those of his other known victims, Angelíca Montaño and Cindy Vigil.

Ray's victim taken in mid-February 1999, Angelíca Montaño, had died of pneumonia in May 2000, before that case went to court. For that one, Ray had been charged with ten criminal counts: kidnapping, conspiracy to commit a crime, multiple counts of criminal sexual penetration, aggravated battery and criminal sexual contact.

Various dates and places had been set for that trial. On November 9, 2000, it was scheduled to begin August 7, 2001, at the Lincoln County Courthouse. Ten days later, it was rescheduled for Torrance County District Court in Estancia to begin November 27, 2000. That one was postponed until spring 2001, and then vacated and replaced by the retrial about Kelli Van Cleve Garrett that ended in guilty verdicts on April 16, 2001.

The filing date for closing the Montaño case had been March 2, 2000.

The case of Cindy Vigil—who first brought the activities of David Parker Ray to light—had been repeatedly delayed because of various motions before the New Mexico Supreme Court. Vigil had been taken March 20, 1999, held and tortured for three days, and escaped March 22, 1999. She was the only one of the three known victims who escaped before she experienced the Toy Box.

One of the defense's successful motions, on March 27, 2000, for continuance on that trial, cited Ray's poor health.

The law enforcement investigators and the district attorney's office had believed from the beginning that of Ray's three known victims, Vigil would be by far the most credible witness against him.

This was what the defense also thought; and, therefore, they worked hard, and successfully, to delay that trial. On May 15, 2000, the State gave notice of its intent to introduce for this trial Angelíca Montaño's testimony, which had been taped before her death.

Both the defense and the State made motions to suppress the testimony of various witnesses for this trial. Some of the State's potential witnesses included jail inmates.

Ray's trial pertaining to Cindy Vigil was finally scheduled for late June 2001 in Estancia's Torrance County Courthouse.

In addition to Ray's trials concerning those two victims, also pending was the trial of his daughter, Glenda Jean "Jesse" Ray, for her involvement with the Kelli Van Cleve case. Jesse's court-appointed attorney was Billy Ray Blackburn of Albuquerque. She had been charged with kidnapping, conspiracy to commit a crime, assault with intent to commit a violent felony and six counts of criminal sexual penetration. If convicted of all charges, she could be sentenced to a century in state corrections.

Jesse Ray also could face additional trials, including her involvement with the kidnapping, sexual abuse and murder of Marie B. Parker.

Chapter 39 – About Cindy

On Monday, June 25, 2001, the second trial (not counting the one that ended in a mistrial) of David Parker Ray—billed in the media as the most sadistic criminal in New Mexico—began in Estancia. This one concerned the complaint of Cindy Vigil and the State of New Mexico.

It was Cindy's escape that finally brought Ray's forty-five-year spree of serial sexual sadism to an end.

After instructions by Judge Sweazea and opening remarks by Prosecutor James Yontz and Defense Attorney Kevin McMillian, Cindy Vigil spent most of the day on the stand telling in detail what Ray did to her. She graphically told the jurors which items he used and techniques of torture he practiced on her.

To questioning by both the State and the defense, she said she had been working as a prostitute on Central Avenue in Albuquerque when David Ray and Cynthia Hendy forcibly grabbed her and transported her to their property in Elephant Butte.

Most of her highly emotional testimony was painful to hear. "I wanted to die," she said. "I didn't want to live."

On Tuesday, the court listened to police and other investigators detail how they secured the crime scene and gathered evidence. FBI's chief of quality assurance, Richard Gurrieri, explained to them how Cindy Vigil's DNA was taken from sex devices and pieces of broken glass in the residence on Bass Road. Ray's attorney, McMillian, argued that DNA testing was inconclusive.

The trial came to an abrupt end on Monday, July 2, one week after it had begun, when David Ray pleaded guilty to kidnapping, criminal sexual penetration in the second degree and conspiracy to commit kidnapping.

ADA James Yontz consulted with Ray's two known living victims, Cindy Vigil and Kelli Van Cleve Garrett, before accepting his plea. They were both in favor of it. They wanted to end their nearly three years of public testimony that caused them to repeatedly relive their experiences. They were emotionally drained and wanted to get on with their lives.

As he shuffled out of the Torrance County courthouse, handcuffed and shackled, a gaunt David Parker Ray told the media that he had plea-bargained to get his daughter released from jail.

Chapter 40 – The Plea

In early July 2001, Ray had entertained a plea agreement with the district attorney's office. He agreed to plead guilty, provided the scheduled trial for his daughter, Jesse, was dropped and she was set free, and his charges were reduced.

Attorney General Patricia Madrid and Seventh Judicial District Attorney Clint Wellborn announced to the media that the State and David Parker Ray had entered into a plea agreement. Ray agreed to waive any direct appeals for the trials already held, he would plead guilty to reduced charges concerning Vigil, and he also agreed to plead guilty to federal charges of white slavery for a maximum of twenty years added to his sentence.

In line with her father's plea bargain, Jesse Ray pleaded no contest to the kidnapping charge, and the remaining charges against her were dismissed. On count one, kidnapping, she was sentenced to the state prison for nine years; but that sentence was credited for time already served while pending her trial and, in lieu of the remaining time, she was sentenced to five years of supervised probation—until September 17, 2006.

Jesse was set free on September 17, 2001.

David Parker Ray's guilty pleas saved the State considerable additional legal expense.

He pleaded guilty only to first-degree kidnapping, conspiracy to commit kidnapping and second-degree sexual penetration of Cindy Vigil. The criminal complaints against him pertaining to Montaño were dropped.

^^^^^^^

David Ray had little else to do, besides thinking, while sitting in his cell.

He gave his situation serious thought and changed his mind about pleading guilty.

Chapter 41 – O'Toole

Court resumed on September 20, 2001.

Present were counsel for the State, Jim Yontz; defense counsel, McMillian; and the defendant, David Parker Ray.

Judge Kevin Sweazea told them he had three legal matters for them.

The first was the defendant's motion to withdraw his guilty plea.

McMillian claimed that the drugs Ray was taking affected his capacity and ability to make proper decisions when he pled guilty. He also claimed that his poor health and exhaustion rendered him incapable. Defense quoted from entries in the *Physician's Desk Reference* about the medications he was taking and their possible side-effects.

Yontz said Ray was responsive during the course of the trial. The State observed him writing notes, speaking with his sister and acting alert and capable.

The judge said Ray's medications were prescribed doses and he observed him visiting with the audience. During the plea, Ray was questioned extensively and was "quick with the response," said Sweazea. "Immediately after his plea, he was interviewed by the media and he expressed his desire to help his daughter. I believe he was thinking clearly."

Judge Sweazea denied the defendant's motion to withdraw his plea.

Next on the court's agenda, the prosecution called an expert witness to the stand to testify.

She identified herself.

"Mary Ellen O'Toole, supervisory special agent with the Federal Bureau of Investigation in the Washington, D. C. National Center for Analysis of Violent Crimes." She said she worked specifically with the Violent Crimes Unit.

She said she had been a violent criminal behavior specialist for twenty years, and before that, a senior criminal investigator with the San Diego district attorney's office. She had a Bachelor degree in criminal behavior, Master's in counseling and a PhD in public administration, plus seventeen years of training in behavioral sciences. She trained law enforcement people, psychologists and psychiatrists all over the world in criminal behavior, and lectured on criminal sexual sadism.

She also played an active role in certain crime scene investigations, "primarily to extend our basis of knowledge and that of the behavior of the offenders." She said she had interviewed convicted serial killers and murderers, and interviewed six sexual criminals.

"Are you familiar with the term, sexual sadism?" asked Jim Yontz.

"Yes sir."

"What is it?"

"Paraphylic behavior is a type of sexual dysfunctional behavior. It ranges from mild to extreme. I have written papers on this topic. Sexual sadism is little explored and is not known well. There is a criminal and non-criminal aspect to aberrant sexual behavior. As the behavior becomes more aberrant, it becomes criminal. The extent of sexual sadism is not known, but criminal sexual sadism is rare. It is the extreme behavior that law enforcement is interested in, that becomes criminal sexual sadism."

She added, "Criminal sexual sadism is not well understood by law enforcement or the psychiatric community."

O'Toole said FBI Agent John Schum of the Albuquerque office called her into the case. She did an on-site visit and participated in the investigation because of the extent of the crimes involved.

She came, along with her partner, to New Mexico the day after she received the call. They do not usually go to the scene, but because this was such a unique crime and because of its seriousness, they sent the FBI behavioral scientists, she said. They became involved because the case concerned sexual sadistic behavior, as well as the extent of the crimes.

She initially met with NMSP officers at the Elephant Butte command center. They reviewed all of the case information, were briefed on the interviews and defendants' behaviors.

"We look at presence of behavior and the absence of behavior when evaluating a crime scene. We looked at what was made available and included an on-site visit to the residence. Based upon the extent of my experience, it immediately appeared to me that the behavior was consistent with a criminal sexual sadist."

"What is a criminal sexual sadist?"

"Criminal sexual sadism involves someone who is not consenting. Non-criminal parties are consenting and they talk about it.

Criminal sexual sadism is non-consensual and the acts may be lethal or fatal.

"Criminal sexual sadism is of law enforcement interest; sexual sadism is not. Criminal is the acting-out behavior that involves the use of people who do not consent. Non-criminal sexual sadism is with partners who say it is okay to include me in this behavior. Sexual sadism is sexual arousal to another individual's response to physical or emotional pain. It is the person's response to [receiving] certain pain or behavior; [therefore] the victim has to be alive. Paraphylic behavior known as sexual sadism can involve acts where people say you can go up to this level but not beyond. Criminal sexual behavior is where the parties did not consent to the behaviors imposed on the victim at the extreme range, and those can be lethal or fatal."

Yontz asked for her impression when she initially looked inside the white cargo trailer.

"We went into it at the very beginning. I saw different kinds of collateral evidence. There was a large supply of dildos, a large variety of handmade instruments. There were customized instruments. Seeing the instruments and the different kinds of sexual paraphernalia in the trailer, and because of how they were made and how they were electrically used, [it was evident they] could cause injury to someone.

"The trailer was extremely impressive in terms of sexual sadism. Criminal sexual sadism is extremely rare. We are familiar with this because we have studied these cases. We have more case studies than any other organization in the world. To build this kind of trailer, it took an extensive amount of time, money and talent. You could tell there was an enormous amount of effort expended to build and maintain this trailer."

Yontz asked, "Did the trailer indicate sexual sadism or was it over the line into criminal sexual sadism?"

"In my opinion, based on the initial evidence seen inside the trailer, the paraphernalia and the lethality of the instruments indicated that kind of behavior. It was sexual sadism at the extreme end of the continuum, which would be classified as criminal sexual sadism."

Yontz asked, "Has your initial opinion changed?"

"My initial evaluation of the evidence has never changed; in fact it never faltered from the beginning."

"You say you've interviewed criminal sexual sadists?"

"Yes."

"How many incarcerated criminals have you interviewed?"

"In my entire twenty-five-year career, one hundred. Within the law enforcement community, criminal sexual sadism is considered a rare behavior. We cannot explain why it is so rare. Sexual sadism is not so rare, but they don't come to the attention of law enforcement. People who cross over the line and begin using non-consenting partners usually come to the attention of law enforcement fairly quickly. We don't know the reason why people opt to cross over the line."

Yontz asked, "Can the behavior reverse itself?"

"There is no evidence that this type of behavior can reverse itself."

O'Toole continued, "We work closely with the mental health community. Criminal sexual sadism is a learned behavior; it is learned early on and evidences itself in the early teens. Paraphylic behavior is very strong. As it progresses, it is heavily steeped in violent sexual fantasy. If it is fueled, it can become lethal. If the person who is engaged in that behavior makes that conscious choice to cross over the line, the American Psychiatric Association opines that the only way to prevent the behavior is through apprehension; it is not something that will stop on its own. Criminal sexual sadism has a coexistence with other personality disorders, one of which is psychopathy, which is a genetic disorder. When the two are together, they are not treatable. There is no known treatment that will undo what causes that behavior."

Under his cross-examination, McMillian first attacked O'Toole's credibility. Then he asked, "Have you seen other facilities like the white trailer?"

"I have been in facilities where there are sexual paraphernalia, but not to the extent I saw in the white trailer."

"Have you seen facilities used by professional dominatrix?"

"No."

"So you don't know if the things in the trailer are consensual or not."

"We, the FBI, have seen facilities used by professional dominatrix, but we deal with criminal sexual sadism."

"You don't know whether there is any difference between dominatrix and criminal, do you?"

"We do know the difference between facilities used by consenting sexual behaviors and those of non-consenting sexual behaviors. I have a reasonably good idea of the difference between the two. Experientially, I know the difference between consenting and non-consenting behavior."

"How much experience do you have interviewing consenting people?"

"I have interviewed probably five or six consenting sexual sadism people."

"That is not a statistically significant number is it?"

"No."

"And you would say that your unit knows more about criminal sexual sadism than anyone in the whole world?"

"Yes, in criminal sexual sadism, that would be my testimony."

"It is not a therapeutic term recognized by anyone but the FBI?"

"It is recognized by the American Psychiatric Association. The criminal part simply reflects that it is a criminal matter."

"It is not a therapeutic term?"

"It is used by mental health folks as well as law enforcement."

"Who?"

"For example, in UCLA they use that term to describe when it is criminal behavior versus when it is sexual sadism between consenting adults. It is not strictly a law enforcement term."

"The difference in your mind is the issue of consent, right?"

"Our opinion is the same as that of non-law enforcement people. But with the progression of sexual sadism, there is also an escalation of the violence used on the victims."

"So the straight answer is yes. The difference is consent."

"The difference is also the increasing lethality, with more and more violence."

"No one would consent to be killed."

"The intent of the sexual sadist is not to kill. But I am aware of one case where they did consent to being killed. A sexual sadist wants a living victim."

"It would still be against the law to kill someone even if they consented to be killed, right?"

"Yes."

"For our purposes today, the difference between a criminal sadist and a sexual sadist is that someone has been charged, correct?"

"Not at all. The difference between a sexual sadist and criminal sexual sadist is that the criminal sadist has taken someone who does not want to engage in that behavior and forces them. At times, by default or by design, the person dies."

"So it is solely a law enforcement concept, isn't it?"

"No. Someone may seek mental health assistance, especially when they use non-consenting partners. Sometimes they seek mental health professionals at some point in their evolution of sexual sadism to criminal sexual sadism."

"So if someone came to Ray's trailer and consented to what happened in there, it would not be criminal?"

"If they consent to what is happening, it is not criminal."

"The difference is consent?"

"No."

The defense and O'Toole continued to argue the point that consent is not the only difference between the two types of sexual sadism.

"Based upon simply seeing the trailer alone, with no other information, I would consider that criminal acts are a strong possibility [even before] looking at the instruments and the shelves that were pulled out to hold bodies, the writings on the wall, the recordings."

McMillian questioned O'Toole about the FBI's Violent Crimes Unit to which she belonged.

"There are twenty-two criminal analysts in the unit."

"Everyone knows the same stuff?"

"Based upon our experience, and the opinion of the American Psychiatric Association, we say at the severe end of sexual sadism, apprehension is the only way to stop the activities."

"Isn't it treatable?"

"If they are acting out on non-consenting partners, if this is a lifetime activity, I do not think these people are treatable."

"So you do not think Mr. Ray is treatable either."

"The behavior is all I can go on; I am not a psychiatrist. I am here to explain what the behavior is and the impact of the behavior. I have an opinion of what I saw, but I do not have an opinion about whether Mr. Ray is treatable."

Yontz, questioning O'Toole on redirect, showed her the drawings and records found in the white cargo trailer.

He showed her a drawing "of a woman suspended from the ceiling being whipped. Is this drawing and similar drawings consistent with criminal sexual sadism?"

"Yes it is."

He showed her another drawing, that of a rocket-shaped device. "The object shown at the base of this [under the victim], did you find an object like that at the residence?"

"Yes, a similar object was recovered."

Yontz continued to show her Ray's drawings found in the cargo trailer and asked her if similar objects or devices were displayed in the residence or cargo trailer. To each, she answered yes and that it had been categorized as a sexual sadism item, or that records indicated they were used on victims.

After Yontz asked her to identify more photograph exhibits and questioned her about them, she said, "We considered all of the drawings and records that we found at the site. We look at the totality of what we find, of an entire situation ..."

Chapter 42 – Sentencing

The victims and their families asked to address the court, said Assistant District Attorney Jim Yontz. Judge Sweazea agreed, but ordered the media to not photograph any of them.

First Kelli Van Cleve Garrett spoke. "I'm glad this day is finally here for justice to be served for David Parker Ray. I don't want him to die. I want him to live long and suffer long as he thinks about his putrid life. And then I want him to burn in hell. If there is any shred of humanity in him, he needs to tell all the things he has done to others so they can begin to heal. His crimes are ones that even prisoners cannot stomach; he will find no friends in prison. He'll have to watch his back.

"By his perverted inhumane acts to me, Cindy and Angie, he has changed our lives. But I am a survivor, not a victim. I have suffered, my family has suffered, my friends have suffered, but that has made me stronger. He's not normal. He's a sick pervert. His punishment should be people controlling him and torturing him and abusing him to satisfy their own obscene fantasies just like he did to us. God will never forgive him. I will never forgive him. I dream about all the evil and painful things I would do to him if I could, but I must be satisfied that he will lose his freedom and that he will die without ever being free. It's not enough but it will have to do.

"I thank all of those who helped me survive: the prosecutors, the FBI, the State Police, my friends, my family. There are hundreds of people who worked to bring David Parker Ray to justice. I just wish he would live out the full sentence that he is going to get."

Next Loretta Romero spoke. "My daughter was Angelíca Montaño. She was one of the victims. I'm sorry I'm not prepared, I didn't write anything. This comes from my heart and for my daughter. Angelíca was traumatized by the experience. Angela had a good heart, she was always happy. When this happened, she lost all respect, she lost her smile, she lost everything. I'm here today for her. I hope justice is done for my daughter as well as her two little boys.

I feel Mr. Ray has destroyed many lives, my daughter's life and my two grandsons' lives. We are not a big family; that was all the family we had. I feel sorry for these [other] families for they feel the same way I do. I am human, I have things I could say but I will show respect to the court. I feel sorry for him. We may forgive him but we can never forget for the rest of our lives."

Bertha Vigil, Cindy Vigil's grandmother, faced David Parker Ray, looked him in the eye, and spoke directly to him. Her voice began firm and strong and then shook with deep anger. "Mr. Parker, I want you to listen to what I have to say to you. You are a horrid excuse for a human being. Anyone who did what you did to my granddaughter should not be called a human being. Put yourself in my position. How would you like someone to do that to your daughter? I hope that you will have to live with this for the rest of your rotten life. Cindy will have to live with it. Every night she has nightmares of what you did to her. Because of that, she's not the only one who suffered; her little boy, my great-grandson, suffers too. He wakes up in the night crying. The doctor said it is because of the nightmares Cindy had when she carried him."

(Some time after Cindy's experience, she went through drug detoxification, developed a serious relationship and had a child.)

Her grandmother continued, "So you did not just ruin Cindy's life, you ruined the whole family's lives; we all have to live with this. Every day I pray that you will suffer. I am so glad you will be put away so that you will not hurt anyone else. Satan has a place for you. People like you do not have a conscience."

Bertha Vigil added, "I hope that other mothers will thank Cindy for having the courage to get away from you people so that you can be caught before you do any more harm to other little girls. I hope you burn in hell forever!"

Cindy Vigil, the last of the victims and their families to address the court, spoke. She was so overcome by emotion that her tearful words were difficult to understand. Unlike her grandmother, she did not—could not—seem able to face David Parker Ray. She spoke to the judge. "No sentence is harsh enough to equal the agony I have been through every minute of my life ever since this happened to me. I have not only scars on the outside, but I also bear internal scars that will never heal. My life, my family's lives, and the lives of all his other victims will never be the same as a result of the horrific acts committed. Every chance of my ever feeling safe and secure has been torn from me. I have a hard time accepting affection, even a simple hug, without the overwhelming fear I get, from being tied down and helpless, that overtakes me. I cannot be alone in the dark, cannot go outside in public by myself. I constantly fear being abducted again. That will probably haunt me forever. I ask for the maximum punishment you can give. I want him to live inside those four walls of prison for the rest of his life. I want him to suffer the way he's making me suffer."

After the victims and their families, Patricia Madrid, New Mexico Attorney General, addressed the court. Claire Harwell, from that office, had assisted with the prosecution of this case, but was unable to be there that day.

"I am very pleased to be here," said Madrid. "I thought this was a case that warranted my presence here. The victims, the court and the communities in which these cases have been tried have been subjected to horrors beyond the boundaries of their worst nightmares. As these two trials have demonstrated, David Ray is a criminal sadistic rapist; any speculation that the defendant only fantasized these horrors has been put to rest by the painful testimonies of Cindy Vigil and Kelli Van Cleve. If any doubt remains, the defendant himself has [provided] an illustrated manual [showing] what he is capable of. We know from his demented writings that even his earliest sexual experiences were shaped by his desire to harm and torment women. He does not even seem to view women as human, but refers to them as packages. There is also reason to fear his future actions, as he is different from most other sexual offenders. Not only because he thrives on violence and psychic trauma, but also because he elicits assistance from younger accomplices, thereby prolonging his ability to commit these crimes far beyond the age that most defenders cease to offend. As a community, as a state, we cannot risk any chance of his freedom because his carefully-constructed plan made clear his intent to torture, to torment other human beings as long as the State allows him to do so.

"This offender's crimes are extraordinary for their duration, and for his desire to inflict emotional scars on his victims, which obviously by testimony of his two victims, he succeeded in doing. The audiotape, the written materials introduced at trial showed that the defendant's intent was, at a minimum, to reduce his victims to abject terror through the rhythmic imposition of periods of anticipation of torture, followed by actual torture. To achieve his goal of reducing women to slaves, extended captivity was necessary; they spent days and nights wondering if they would live or die. He intended to reduce Kelli and Cindy to wounded animals who would do anything to survive. I'm happy to see both here today and that they have survived, to some extent. On behalf of the State, Your Honor, we are here to ask that you impose the maximum sentence including aggravation [enhancements]. This defendant's behavior is worse than any animal; this defendant can no longer live among us."

Then Prosecutor Jim Yontz spoke. "First I want to give special thanks to special people in this case. Agent Carrie Parbs and Agent Larry Haulpt have put in not only their regular hours of work-time, but many, many hours beyond that, to bring this case together. Agent Schum and Agent O'Toole have been phenomenal in their support of the District Attorney's office and Attorney General's office. Agent LaQuesta, the State Police, Agent Maxwell, K. C. Rogers and John Briscoe put together the initial case. There are literally hundreds of other names I should mention.

"For almost two-and-a-half years I've thought of what I was going to say about this case. As I thought of the events of last week, I realized—in the reality of what we were dealing with here in our own little microcosm of Truth or Consequences—some of the events of terror. Those accounts [presented in the courts] have only been in scope, not in nature."

Yontz continued, "He picked the wrong victims. He picked Kelli Garrett who has had the guts, the intestinal fortitude, to relate this horror three times in open public forum, to stand up and say, 'I don't remember certain things but I do remember what he did.' To recount a life with Patrick that was destroyed because of what Ray did to her. I've talked to Patrick quite a bit; he feels guilt, anger.

"The defendant not only committed a horrible crime against Kelli, but also against the State because he hid behind his uniform.

"He picked the wrong victim in Cindy. Because, as she said, 'there was no way in hell he was going to let me leave alive from that trailer,' she struggled at the peril of her life to escape, she ran down the street [of Elephant Butte] wearing nothing but an iron collar and a chain, screaming for help. Thank goodness, the Breech family was there to help her. Had Cindy not had the courage and the fortitude to do that, the nightmare would still be going on in Truth or Consequences.

"This court sat through testimony, this court has heard the victims and saw the evidence, and saw more photos than any person should ever have to view.

"I have asked various individuals about Mr. Ray, what their medical and scientific opinion is. They tell me that if he is ever released, he will re-offend before he gets home. These people do not change. These people are not amenable to treatment. This monster, like others, should never be allowed to walk the streets again. Regardless of his age, his life expectancy or where he goes [which state correctional facility], or how good he is there, under no circumstances should he have any light at the end of the tunnel. The only way he should ever leave there is in a box similar to the one he had for his victims."

When it was the defense's turn to speak, McMillian went over the possible sentences. "I figured the maximum penalty is 245 years, is that about right? The minimum you can impose is ten years. Anything over six months is a death sentence in this case." He asked the judge to combine counts and sentences and to run all of the sentences of all the cases together concurrently. "Structure the sentence in the most humane way," he asked. McMillian referenced a New Mexico case wherein a defendant's sentence of more than a hundred years was suspended, and he was ordered to serve only ten years of actual incarceration time. "There is no question the State is dealing with a sick man," he said. "Mr. Ray is a paraphilliac."

McMillian continued, "I agree with Dr. O'Toole, it is a learned behavior. Mr. Ray is sixty-one; he probably learned this behavior in his early teens, most likely around puberty. He has had this disease for almost fifty years. He's made efforts of rehabilitating himself. There is a possibility of redemption on earth and in the world beyond. I ask the court to give him no less than ten years."

Judge Sweazea reviewed the charges and counts of both cases against Ray with defense and prosecution attorneys before he proceeded with sentencing.

Then Ray addressed the court.

"I'm not a good public speaker. I'm not quick-witted and silver-tongued like most of the people in here. My defense was concerned that if I testified, Mr. Yontz would distort everything I said. Nobody but my attorneys ever heard my side of all of this. There have been numerous distortions and lies and exaggerations in this case that nobody will ever know about. Judge Mertz, God rest his soul, was one of the most honest and unbiased men I've ever met. He said there was no way I would ever have a fair trial in New Mexico because of the media. But he gave his best effort to give me one in Tierra Amarilla and I got a hung jury there. Judge Mertz passed away during the second trial and it's been downhill for the defense." Ray claimed there was juror misconduct during one trial, and he said there had been three trials scheduled in Moriarity (Estancia is near Moriarity) on the same change of venue. "Begging your pardon, Judge, but that was really convenient since you lived nearby. I never had a chance with three trials in the same location."

He said he was happy with the part of the agreement that released his daughter.

He continued, "The federal agreement fell apart; that's out the window. I don't remember much about the agreement because Corrections was giving me ten different medications a day. I don't know what the collective effect was ... Right now I don't really know what is going on because the state pen won't allow me sufficient access to my attorney since I've been in Las Lunas, no more than fifteen-minute calls ... Who can get a lawyer in fifteen minutes? I've lost my retirement, home, property, my health, I don't have anything to go back to on the outside, no income."

Ray (who had claimed he practiced Satanism and witchcraft) said his solitary confinement had given him time to reflect and "an opportunity to get back with God." He claimed that he was reading the Bible. "I'm no longer in the wilderness."

And he added, "Can't change the past ... can only be sorry and try to deal with the future."

Ray ended his address to the court with this parting shot: "... I notice Patricia Madrid is here in front of the cameras. It's a shame Ms. Harwell isn't here; she is an excellent attorney. She did all the work and Patricia Madrid is here to take the credit."

Then Judge Sweazea addressed the court before he presented Ray's sentences. "Sentencing in criminal actions serves a number of purposes. Those include incapacitation to remove the offender from the streets to protect citizens of state and country.

"After listening to the extremely compelling evidence provided by the testimonies of Ms. Garrett and Ms. Vigil in their respective cases, one can only imagine the horrors that they were put through by Mr. Ray ... That leads me to the firm conviction that the purpose of incapacitation in this case is the primary purpose to be served, so that other individuals never again have to be subjected to the same horrific treatments that Ms. Garrett and Ms. Vigil were subjected to, and also Ms. Montaño, whose testimony we did not have due to the plea agreement by Mr. Ray.

"Another factor that is very compelling in this case, when considering the appropriate sentence to impose, is the extensive level of preparation that Mr. Ray undertook before he committed his crimes. His level of preparation, as shown by the FBI and the State Police through their investigations, demonstrated the extensive time, effort and money that Mr. Ray devoted before the horrific crimes he would later commit on these ladies."

Sweazea said he listened to the defense's request to suspend part of the sentence, and to combine portions of the sentence, and to order the imposed years served concurrently rather than consecutively, but he was "not inclined to do so." Further, he would impose additional years to the sentence because of the proven prior planning and preparation by Ray before he committed his crimes.

Judge Kevin Sweazea proceeded to sentencing.

He sentenced David Ray to eighteen years for count one, nine years for count two, and nine years for count three; these sentences to run consecutively to those imposed from the guilty verdicts concerning Kelli Van Cleve Garrett. He was sentenced to 132 years on charges pertaining to Kelli, and thirty-six years pertaining to Cindy Vigil. Additionally, Sweazea invoked his right to increase Ray's sentence up to one-third of the base sentence on each count in each case because of the prior planning and preparation factor.

On September 20, 2001, the judge wrapped up the day's proceedings by sentencing Ray to a total of 224 years in the state penitentiary.

Chapter 43– The End

David Parker Ray was sentenced in late September 2001. From April 16 to May 28 of 2002, he was kept at the prison near Las Cruces for questioning by the State Police, who continued to try to resolve their many open cases of missing persons.

Ray was assigned to serve his prison sentence at the New Mexico Corrections facility in Hobbs, in southeastern New Mexico.

Danette Monnét, Crime Analyst Supervisor, Criminal Intelligence Section of the Special Investigations Division (SID) of Department of Public Safety, provided this glimpse of David Ray's last hours.

On May 28, 2002, he was transported from Las Cruces to Hobbs' Lea County Correctional facility. While his paperwork was being processed, he was taken to the cell where he was to live the rest of his life.

The door clanked shut and the key locked behind him.

He sat down on his bunk and slumped over, dead.

He was transported to the Hobbs hospital where he was pronounced dead at 8:40 p.m. May 28, 2002.

A later autopsy revealed cause of death was a massive heart attack.

David Parker Ray died at age sixty-two before officially serving even one full day of his sentence.

He did not suffer.

Postscript

The mind can only believe what it can conceive. For most people, some things—like the extreme cruelty of man towards other men and women—are inconceivable.

The vast scope and ugliness of this case became nearly inconceivable even to its investigators.

To add to the overwhelming frustrations for them, the district attorney's office and the State's judicial system, the case had an unsatisfactory ending. It left far more questions than answers.

It had an unusual amount—thousands—of pieces of evidence, including records written and recorded by the primary perpetrator, detailing crimes. Evidence indicated a huge number of victims and that many of those died in captivity.

Few if any cases across the nation have had as much evidence to prove guilt of the defendants as was available in this one, yet little was presented in court.

Is that typical of cases tried in U.S. courts?

Witnesses called to the stand at the trials were identified in this book so readers could see how few, of the many possible, testified.

Despite the quantity of evidence, David Parker Ray faced convictions only for kidnapping and sexual abuse of three victims, and ultimately stood trial for just two. Then he died in what seemed to be a painless, untraumatic way.

Even if he had lived, it seems unlikely he would have been tried for murder. Where were the bodies?

Readers are given an eye-opening glimpse of the judicial process by following this unusual case from its beginning to its ambiguous end.

The audiotape, in David Ray's own voice, detailing what he did to his multiple victims, was not allowed in the first trial—the one that ended without resolution; and it almost wasn't allowed in the subsequent trial. There were nine similar audiotapes, and only one that was redacted was ultimately allowed. Without it, would a conviction of Ray have resulted?

The tremendous costs of justice determine the extent of trials, and are often causal factors in plea bargains.

Another factor is time. Firm deadlines must be met for the prosecution of criminal cases. A defendant is entitled to a speedy trial unless it is he who delays it. More than her death, it was that time factor that determined that the case of Angelíca Montaño—as important a claimant as Kelli Van Cleve Garrett and Cindy Vigil—was ultimately not presented in the courtroom.

The greatest frustration of this case was that the answers to thousands of questions died with David Parker Ray. Investigators were left with countless loose strings and many unresolved cases of missing persons.

Because of the sophisticated cameras and recording equipment found in the Toy Box, and because of Ray's psychological profile, they believe he must have had a large stash of videos showing his victims in bondage and being tortured. Investigators believe those videos would be invaluable for identifying many victims and perhaps close out some of their backlog of missing person reports. Except for the one video with Kelli Van Cleve Garrett, they found none. Even if he sold copies of the videos to other sexual sadists and as snuff films, Ray's profile indicated that he would have kept the originals to gloat over. Where was his stash? Investigators desperately needed those videos to confirm and identify his other victims. They still need them, years later, for the many probable cases that remain open.

Investigators knew Ray and his publicized cohorts had sexual sadistic associates, some living beyond Sierra County. Some cops said he was a "ringleader" with many followers. His known associates were scrutinized but not charged with felonies.

Local rumor said many were not brought to face charges because they were "higher-ups" within the local communities and some other communities. However, as O'Toole had said, sexual sadism is not unlawful until it crosses over, involves unwilling participants and becomes potentially lethal; only then is it a criminal matter. It had not been proved that those others practiced sexual sadism to the criminal degree. One T or C resident commented, "At least this case and its publicity caused those others to scurry away and hide, like cockroaches caught in the light. And that's a good thing."

A local elected official later commented: "What people do in private is their business; I have no problem with that as long as they don't bother me."

Despite the facts brought to light by this case, public indifference continues.

In late November 2002, the New Mexico State Police tried to renew media attention to the case, hoping that might lead to identifying additional victims and suspects.

The KRQE Channel 13 television station in Albuquerque, in conjunction with NMSP investigators of the David Parker Ray case, aired a special to renew public awareness. Details of the special remained accessible on the Internet for an extended period. With it, the State Police asked the public to help them close cases.

During the special on Channel 13, Dick Knipfing said a tremendous amount of investigation was still being done. "You are about to see evidence that may identify dozens of missing and most likely murdered women," he told his TV audience. "Watching along with you will be investigators from missing persons units from all across the country."

He told his viewers, "Only a handful of investigators had seen much of this evidence we are about to show you. We hope you will pay special attention to dozens of pieces of jewelry, clothing and other items."

Among the two-thousand items seized from Ray's property were disturbing clues that Ray was a prolific killer, he said.

A portion of one of David Ray's audiotapes was played. In his soft voice, Ray said, "… they would probably scream a lot, which is exactly what I'd want them to do, that's what turns me on." And his recorded voice said, "I tortured girls in ways I'm not very proud of. When I'm [pissed]-off, I don't mind having blood all over the place. And sometimes they didn't survive."

The case agent, New Mexico State Police Agent Norman Rhoades, said, "I know he's killed … but it's very frustrating because no bodies have been found." (A probable exception was the body of Billy Ray Bowers.)

The TV special said investigators suspect two known deaths were linked to Ray. One was Billy Ray Bowers of Arizona, whose body was found floating in Elephant Butte Lake in 1989; the other was Marie B. Parker, a young mother of two little girls, whose body had not been found. Dennis Roy Yancy, who serves a twenty-year sentence in State Corrections for that murder, told arresting officers that, after Ray had tortured her for days, he had ordered Yancy to strangle Marie with a rope. Although a suspect, David Ray was never charged with her murder.

Assisted by a computer program that tracked his movements for many years before his arrest, and comparing his locations to reported missing persons cases in those areas that also matched his profile, the police believed they found as many as twenty-five unresolved cases with links to him.

The investigators invited the public to see hundreds of pieces of women's jewelry, several pieces of clothing and other items found in his cargo trailer and home, which they believe were his "trophies" that had belonged to some of his victims. Some of those items were displayed on the televised special in hopes that someone would recognize them and help identify the persons to whom they had once belonged. Those included earrings, necklaces, bracelets, watches, belts, sunglasses, a red leotard, a red leather jacket size 10, a sweater, two empty purses and a phony photo identification, with false information, for a pretty sixteen-year-old girl.

Viewers saw the inside of the Toy Box, three-and-a-half years after it was discovered by law enforcement. It looked cluttered with cardboard boxes, not the way Ray had kept it, and most of its pornographic contents had long before been packed up and removed. The "ob-gyn" chair remained with some of its electrical attachments, as did the stainless steel cabinet, the gurney and shelf for stashing up to two victims at one time inside a cabinet. Also still in the Toy Box were the "coffin box," and the "head box" that Ray used to lock over victims' heads to increase their terror.

The special showed a small portion of pages taken from Ray's "abduction diary," as well as from his "log of tortures."

NMSP Sgt. Rich Libicer said, "The sheer volume of entries [in Ray's journals] was discouraging. The meticulousness of it caught my attention."

He added, "No one ever came forward telling us about being abducted and tortured on those dates and at those places." That caused investigators to reach chilling conclusions.

Viewers were told that the Toy Box and a collection of its contents were now being used as training for officers so they could understand future sex killers.

The special said there was strong indication that Ray had been in the business of buying and selling young women as sex slaves. They found evidence, including on his computer, that he ran ads with details of his dealings. In one of Ray's tapes, he said, "I like really young girls between the age of thirteen and sixteen …"

News 13 said they saw eight handwritten ads that provided in graphic detail how long women were held captive and how they were tortured. Each ad featured the victim's first name, age and race.

The special showed a portion of an anonymous letter—in hopes the handwriting would be recognized—that had been sent to the FBI's Albuquerque office shortly after Ray was arrested and his crimes began to be publicized. It was written on a sheet from a lined yellow legal tablet. The unknown author of the letter claimed to know specific information about instances of Ray's kidnappings, tortures and murders. The FBI believed the letter was credible and asked the writer, by means of the televised special, to contact them.

"Our priorities are closure to families," said one of the officers. "There's no way Ray's behavior could have not resulted in a certain amount of deaths. You can imagine what families have gone through and what officers have had to go through working this case. Help us bring closure for a daughter or sister who never came home."

The special ended with this appeal: "Unless [people] come forward, the case will be closed for good next summer [2003]. The search continues. Investigators were at Elephant Butte just days ago looking for more evidence."

The New Mexico Department of Public Safety, the New Mexico State Police and the Missing Persons Unit of the Albuquerque Police Department asked citizens to contact their offices if they have any helpful information concerning this case.

Since that televised special, the case is still sometimes mentioned in televised specials and published reports.

In February 2003, the State and District Judge Kevin Sweazea reviewed Cynthia Lea Hendy's plea deal to consider revoking it and adding years to her sentence.

In that May 2000 agreement, District Judge Neil Mertz (now deceased) had sentenced her to thirty-six years in prison. For that lesser sentence, she had agreed to plead guilty to reduced charges; but that deal included her agreeing to assist the State with their investigation of the case.

Early into the case, Hendy claimed she knew of fourteen victims Ray had killed, that she could identify some of the murdered victims, and she knew where Ray had buried or dumped some of their bodies.

According to New Mexico State Police's spokesman, Lt. Robert Shilling, investigators had received no valuable information from Hendy and the investigation of the case had not progressed since David Parker Ray's sentencing in September 2001.

"There's genuine concern that there are victims out there," Shilling was quoted in a published AP newspaper article, and "there are families attached to those probable victims."

Investigators continue to believe Ray buried some of the bodies of his victims in the desert terrain of Sierra County and—after taking measures to prevent them from later surfacing—dumped others in Elephant Butte Lake.

The New Mexico State Police Search and Recovery Dive Team searched the depths of Elephant Butte Lake on three occasions since March 22, 1999, but found no remains. According to NMSP Sgt. Mike Waring, who heads the dive team, they searched on November 18 and 19, 2002, and on February 26 and 27, 2003. On February 24, 2003, they borrowed the State Park Service's sonar system to search the bottom of the lake for any anomalies that might indicate bodies. They found nothing pertinent to the case.

When the case began, the lake's water was too deep for divers to safely search its bottom, and the layers of sediment too bottomless and enveloping. When the case was active, said one diver, the water below Kettle Top was 160 feet deep, and only "hard hats" could dive it on a sustained mission, as would have been required. Since then, continued drought in New Mexico considerably lowered the level of the lake—by as much as one hundred feet, and the receding water exposed much more beach.

Because of Hendy's comments about the areas where Ray had disposed of bodies, and the marked map of the lake found in Ray's residence, investigators took particular interest in the area of the lake below Kettle Top. In 2002 and 2003, the lake level had dropped so low that the base of Kettle Top was no longer under water. It was surrounded on all sides by dry land, yet no remains were found.

In addition to the ongoing statewide drought, an old compact to supply Rio Grande water to Texas burdened New Mexico. In April 2003, New Mexico Governor Bill Richardson and the State Engineer announced that additional water would be released from Elephant Butte Lake, dropping lake levels yet another thirty feet by the end of that summer.

Will the lake and the desert ever give up some of their secrets?

One State Police investigator had publicly said they believed Ray had killed at least ninety-seven people, and that number has been repeated in 2007. Did he kill that many? Who were they? Where are their remains?

We will never know all the answers.

The one who does, David Parker Ray, will never tell.

EPILOGUE

Where Are They Now? Were They Affected By The Case?

David Parker Ray died of a heart-attack in his cell as he was to begin serving his sentence. He had leased the land at 513 Bass Road from the Elephant Butte Park, but after the case began, his personally-owned residential property on that lot was listed for sale by a local Coldwell Banker realtor, presumably for back taxes and other debts.

Cynthia Lea Hendy serves her sentence in the women's state penal institution at Grants, New Mexico. She was given thirty-six years in a plea bargain; for lesser charges and that reduced time, she agreed to provide information about Ray's other victims. However, she has not talked. As consequences for her lack of truth, in 2003 the court considered extending her time.

Dennis Roy Yancy serves a twenty-year sentence at the state's penal institution at Los Lunas, New Mexico for the murder of Marie B. Parker. The court also ordered him, when he gets out, to pay restitution to Parker's daughters.

Glenda Jean "Jesse" Ray, while awaiting her trial on kidnapping and criminal sexual penetration charges concerning Kelli, was offered a deal in conjunction with her dad's plea bargain. She pled no contest to kidnapping, and the rest of her charges were dropped. The court applied credit for time already served awaiting her trial, towards that nine years' reduced sentence on the kidnapping charge; the balance of her time was converted to supervised probation until September 2006. She was set free September 17, 2001. Neighbors saw her gathering items from her dad's residence in October 2001.

Kelli Van Cleve Garrett married, had a child and is trying to resume a normal life.

Angelíca Montaño died of pneumonia before Ray's trial pertaining to her began.

Cindy Vigil had a child, and for a while tried to resume a normal life. However, when police searched for her to testify at the trials, they located her again working on the streets. The district court clerk said Cindy must like that way of life, since she continued to choose it. More likely, despite her horrible experiences with Ray, the only way she knew to feed her costly drug addiction was by prostitution. That addiction gripped her even more powerfully than her fears.

Patricia Rust, the FBI Special Agent, after cataloguing the contents of the Toy Box, went home to El Paso for the weekend and committed suicide. Officers believed that was because of a personal matter, not the case she worked.

Judge Neil Mertz of Socorro, presiding state district judge, suddenly died of a heart attack in 2001 after jury selection had begun for David Parker Ray's retrial.

Jeffrey Rein, David Parker Ray's first state-assigned defense attorney, was physically ill after seeing the inside of the Toy Box. His son committed suicide before Ray's first trial had begun, yet he fulfilled well his court-assigned duty by successfully defending his client in Tierra Amarílla. After that trial ended without conviction, Rein resigned from serving on Ray's defense team in subsequent matters and trials. He took a year's sabbatical from practicing law and left the state, perhaps the country. He has since returned and is again a practicing New Mexico defense attorney.

Darren White, Secretary of the Department of Public Safety, New Mexico's "top cop" during the Ray investigations, resigned from that position in 2000 in opposition of then-Governor Gary Johnson's liberal stand on wanting to legalize drugs. White ran for Sheriff of Bernalillo County in 2002 and won.

Keith Clayton "K. C." Rogers, NMSP sergeant in charge of the command post during the David Parker Ray case, later retired from New Mexico State Police. He founded and heads ASPEN, Alternative Sentencing Programs and Educational Network.

John Briscoe, NMSP agent involved with the Ray investigations and trials, was subsequently promoted to lieutenant in the uniform division, and assigned to a different duty station.

Lou Mallion, special agent for the Department of Public Safety, continues to live in Roswell and work on state-level crime investigations, as well as enforcer of drug, alcohol, tobacco and gaming laws for the Fifth Judicial District, which covers three southeastern New Mexico counties. He is also a pilot for New Mexico's Civil Air Patrol, performing air search and rescue missions.

Lee McMillian, who had been assigned to defend David Parker Ray for his second and third trials, totally reversed gears after those trials ended. He became an assistant district attorney in Estancia.

James Yontz, assistant district attorney and head prosecutor of David Parker Ray at all of his trials, relocated to Edgewood near Albuquerque but continued as a prosecuting attorney. His wife, Karen Yontz, was an investigator for the State Attorney General's office. Her office had not realized she was troubled. She had run up serious gambling debts, attempted suicide, and stole the credit card and identity of an attorney associate of her husband's, damaging that woman's credit. On May 2, 2003, while driving her state-issued car, Karen Yontz robbed an Albuquerque bank. Aiming her state-issued gun at responding officers, she dared them to shoot and kill her. They did.

The Blue Waters Saloon, publicly featured as the kidnap setting in two of the cases, closed after the case broke. For a while, the building became a church. More recently, it was torn down; no evidence of it remains. It has vanished without a trace.

About the Author

- This is the author's first, but not last, published book.
- Has been published in a variety of publications, including the *New Mexico Magazine*.
- Publisher and editor of an Internet magazine.
- Editor of a print magazine for a New Mexico historical society.
- Previously a newspaper reporter covering police and court beats.
- Student of multiple community police academies
- Attended multiple law enforcement seminars
- Rides with local police officers on their busy beats
- Member of Southwest Writers, a literary organization
- Member of Toastmasters International
- Magistrate Court Civil Cases Mediator
- Member of the county's Tourism Council
- Active community volunteer

CPSIA information can be obtained
at www.ICGtesting.com
Printed in the USA
BVHW030859120721
611483BV00010B/278

9 780978 773403